# TURNING POINTS IN HISTORY

THE LATE EARL OF BIRKENHEAD

# Turning Points in History

## By The Rt. Hon.
## The Earl of Birkenhead

(Frederick Edwin Smith)

WITH 32 PAGES OF ILLUSTRATIONS

*Essay Index Reprint Series*

BOOKS FOR LIBRARIES PRESS
FREEPORT, NEW YORK

First Published 1930
Reprinted 1969

STANDARD BOOK NUMBER:
8369-1246-2

LIBRARY OF CONGRESS CATALOG CARD NUMBER:
78-86730

PRINTED IN THE UNITED STATES OF AMERICA

# NOTE

THE final proofs of some of the chapters of this book were not corrected by the Author before his death. While every care has been taken to avoid any textual errors, Lady Birkenhead wishes it to be known that passages may be included which Lord Birkenhead might have changed or re-written, for it was his custom to correct and revise his first proofs very considerably.

# CONTENTS

# LIST OF ILLUSTRATIONS

# TURNING POINTS IN HISTORY

## SALAMIS AND PLATÆA

THE subjugation of Greece by the Persians would not have been wholly destructive of the Greek race, or of Greek culture, but the history of the Greek states in Asia Minor after the conquest does lead to the conclusion that a Persian victory would have resulted in an intellectual sterility and thereby deprived us of almost all that ancient Greece means. It is true that the greatest achievement of Greek verse had appeared and that much had been done in the development of art, science and literature. Nevertheless, the greatest age of classical Greece had not yet begun and might never have come to pass. Moreover, behind the Greek states was a small town in Italy known as Rome, holding its position against the Etruscans, and to a great extent guarded against the Carthaginians by the Greeks of Magna Græcia and Sicily. Had the Persians triumphed, and the Carthaginians enlarged their domains by the defeat of the Greeks, then we should never have known the glories that were Rome.

The decisive moments of a long crisis were the sea fight at Salamis in 480 B.C., and the battle at Platæa in the following year.

The Greeks had settled in city states along the coast of Ionia in Asia Minor, and on the islands of the Ægean and nearby seas and in the land we know as Greece. Further west, they had colonised Sicily, Southern Italy and many other parts along the coasts of France and Spain. Their political organisation was in theory aristocratic, the government being vested in the descendants of the original settlers, but in many power was in the hands of a monarch, who was king if his rule was recognised by the constitution, and tyrant if it was not. The numerous plebeian inhabitants of the cities were grasping at power, and if they succeeded their rule was termed democratic. A king or a tyrant might be in conflict with both the other parties in the State, and he or they might easily be led to appeal for aid to other Greeks or even barbarians. The Greeks were great fighters and traders, both on land and sea. Though the Greek leaders were often men of genius, many were vain, avaricious and treacherous, capable of unworthy dissimulation and venal to a degree. In days of great peril they were apt to insure against defeat by maintaining relations with the enemy.

The Persians were a race of frugal and hardy warriors, simple by comparison and less civilised, but, having gained supremacy over Western Asia and Northern Africa, were gradually losing their primitive virtues. Their advance to the shores of the Mediterranean had brought under their dominance Egypt, Phœnicia and the Greeks of Asia Minor. Apart from Carthage and the Greeks of Europe, no civilised races in the West had escaped their rule. That Greece and not Carthage was the object of their advance from Asia was due no doubt to the facts of geography. It was impossible to keep the Greeks of Europe away from the coasts of Asia Minor, to which they could advance under cover of the islands which bridge the interval between the opposing shores.

Suzerainty over the Ionian Greeks involved relations with their kinsmen, and the Persian Court formed a ready, if not the only, refuge to Greeks whose political fortunes had met with disaster. The Persian monarch understood absolute rule, and in his relations with subject nations found a kinglet easier to manage than a mob. A republic was almost beyond his mental grasp and certainly was abhorrent to his ideas. A stream of Greek aristocrats and tyrants found their way across to Asia Minor. The democracies of the Greek states in Asia Minor looked to the sister democracies of Greece itself. Each party on each shore had a counterpart on the other.

The expulsion of the Athenian tyrants had led to a haughty command by the Persian satrap that Athens should kiss the rod and re-admit its rulers. The Ionian democratic parties revolted and were subdued after prolonged fighting, and the Persians extended their rule over the Islands and the Northern coasts of the Ægean Sea. The control of the sea had passed into the hands of the lords of the land. Athens was to be overwhelmed by an invasion across the waters. But when the enemy landed in Attica the Athenians rallied under Miltiades and routed the invaders at Marathon in 490 B.C.

Before another attempt could be made, Darius the Persian died and his successor Xerxes was compelled to spend years in establishing and strengthening his authority. In the meantime Athens went to war with Ægina, a keen trade rival, and realised as a consequence how inadequate her fleet was. Under the driving force of Themistocles this deficiency was remedied, and Athens soon possessed the largest fleet in Greece, thereby gaining power and influence in Greek councils.

By 481 B.C. it was known that the storm was about to break. Xerxes had collected his forces, his magazines had been formed, and an invasion of Greece by the Hellespont and along the coastal regions was realised to be inevitable. He would not be met by universal and wholehearted opposition. Some Greeks from jealousy of the more powerful, more from fear, and others by reason of the ambitions of their rulers, were willing to accept fire and water from the Persians and thus undertake to aid his enterprise. Even in the states that determined to resist there was not complete unanimity, and many a popular leader, like the statesmen under William III and Anne, considered it prudent to maintain friendly, if secret, relations with the enemy. In any case, the only unity of the resisting Greeks was that of race ; their co-operation was affected by mutual jealousies and distrusts and the peculiar interests or hopes and fears of each of the states.

The question where to base the resistance to the Persian advance was not soluble by merely military and naval considerations. With Argos likely to take selfish advantage of any weakening of the Spartans it was difficult to induce the latter to advance beyond the Isthmus, but a stand there would sacrifice most of the Greek states, and Athens, with its fleet, indispensable to any naval resistance, would not stomach such a method of repelling an invader. From the purely military standpoint, the affair was desperate. The accounts which came in, though exaggerating beyond belief the numbers and prowess of the Persians, made it clear that the Greeks must be hopelessly outnumbered. They were very deficient in cavalry, and the fleet was also out-numbered by the ships that Persia had gathered from Egypt, Phœnicia and the Greeks of Asia Minor. In open fighting with adequate leadership defeat for the Greeks was inevitable. Yet, while Xerxes in 481 B.C. was at Sardes putting the finishing touches to his preparations, the Greeks met at the Isthmus and declared for war. The decision was not so wholehearted as it seemed. Not all the states were present, and some who were proved lukewarm. Many would think that if they must endure subjection, the distant Persian was preferable to the Greek close at hand. Appeals to the Greeks of the West yielded little result. It may have been a coincidence, or a part of Xerxes' plan, that, just when Gelo, the tyrant of Syracuse, could have done so much to equalise the naval forces, he had to retain his ships at home to resist an invasion from Carthage. It was a serious matter for the smaller states to send ships to the Greek fleet, as they were all vulnerable from the sea, and might thereby invite attack from enemies, or even neighbours.

The command of the Greek forces was entrusted to Sparta. The Athenians possessed the strongest fleet, but Themistocles was too wise to push their claim, and Sparta led both on land and at sea.

The problem before them was a difficult one. Though not more than half the land armies of Xerxes could have been diverted for this war, and many must have been detached to guard lines of communication and numbers must have been lukewarm and of small military value, it is impossible to ignore the deep impression made on contemporaries by the march of these myriads. Neither could the army of the Greeks join battle in open country nor their fleet fight in open water. They must select a position which could be held notwithstanding the disparity of forces.

Fortunately the mountains of Greece bar the way to an invader. He must advance, if at all, through defiles where a smaller force may defy a greater. If therefore the Greeks could take a stand where they could oppose an equal front to the invader, and use their ships to guard them against the enemy's fleet turning their sea flank, resistance would not be hopeless. The most obvious place was the Isthmus but it would leave Athens and the greater part of Greece open to the Persians and the Peloponnesus would alone be defended. Moreover, even if the Athenians consented, and their refusal would not only have broken up the League but also have left Sparta open to attack everywhere from the sea, defence would be at least as difficult as a position further north.

While Xerxes was crossing the Hellespont, the Greeks moved forward to Tempe supported by the fleet. It was, however, not the only pass through the mountains in that district, and could not have been usefully defended unless the other passes were held. It was found impossible to garrison the whole of the positions. The southern Greeks would not come in force so far north, and the Thessalians, who were essential to this plan, mainly held aloof. The Greek forces withdrew, as the Persians gradually approached without opposition.

Meanwhile the leaders pushed forward their respective schemes. The Athenians naturally wished the resistance to be located at the next suitable position north of Attica, with the army at Thermopylæ, and the fleet at Artemisium sheltered from direct attack by Eubœa. The Athenians decided that their whole fleet should go and that they would resist the enemy with whatever other Greeks would join them. The risk that Athens would make terms and assist the invaders was too great and the League adopted the plan, but only sent an advance force. Leonidas the Spartan led 10,000 troops to Thermopylæ ; of these some 300 were his bodyguard of Spartan hoplites, then the best foot soldiers in the world. They were just in time, and occupied their positions as the Persians approached the district. Meanwhile, the fleet concentrated at Artemisium, prepared to resist the enemy ships if they attempted to sail between Eubœa and the mainland to outflank the line of defence at Thermopylæ. Protected on their left by the coast of Hellas and on their right by the island, they could meet the Persian ships on equal terms. To guard against a rear attack southward along the strait, a squadron was detached to defend the Euripus at Chalcis, where the strait narrowed to 200 feet. When Xerxes at last decided to move, his ships set out towards Eubœa but were caught and scattered by a fierce gale. One enemy detachment

THE CONQUERORS CELEBRATING THE BATTLE OF SALAMIS

sailed into the arms of the Greeks and was captured almost before they discovered their mistake, and the remaining ships were in no plight to overcome the Greeks.

It was therefore without naval assistance that the Persian Army assaulted Thermopylæ, then a narrow pass between the sea and the mountains, though now the sea has retreated some miles. The position was strong but turned by a mountain path watched by the Phocians. On the first day Leonidas easily repulsed the attacking forces. On the second day he easily maintained his defence, but treachery had revealed to the Persians the existence of the path. The Persians detached a force which marched at night. In the early dawn they alarmed the Phocians who sent word to Leonidas, already informed by deserters. A council of war was held and most of the Greeks marched away. Leonidas with the Spartans, the 700 Thespians and 400 Thebans remained. When the Persian detachment was due to reach the rear of the Greeks' position, but before they had actually arrived, Xerxes attacked with overwhelming forces. The Spartans and the Thespians were all slain and the survivors of the Thebans left isolated in the midst of the enemy surrendered.

The main army of the Greeks was too far in the rear to support Leonidas or to advance in time to restore the situation. Attica was left uncovered. The Athenians realised that their city must fall and escaped to the island of Salamis where they were protected by the fleet. Many refused to leave and threw themselves into the Acropolis which Xerxes after a serious resistance stormed and captured.

The destiny of the Greeks was now hanging in the balance. The only position left to defend was the Isthmus with the fleet guarding the sea flank on the right. But on the left was Corinth with its long gulf, across which troops could easily be ferried. Once the Isthmus was stormed or turned, the Greeks were doomed. It is not surprising

B

therefore that a claim arose to transfer the fleet to the Gulf of Corinth, since it was no longer needed for the defence of Athens. Had this plan been adopted the whole Eastern coast of the Peloponnesus would have been open to the sea, and the Persian fleet could have blockaded the Gulf of Corinth with a small squadron. Supplies were running short among the Greeks and many despaired. The Persians had their supply problems too. The season was advanced and supplies were short. If the war were not soon ended, then the troops would have to be sent into winter quarters. Xerxes decided to finish the campaign by blockading the Greek vessels at Salamis while his army stormed the Isthmus.

Meanwhile the Greek leaders continued to dispute. Corinth threatened to withdraw her ships. Sparta was inclined to agree to the transfer of the naval base, but Themistocles was firm. He pointed out that this would uncover the whole coast and render the turning of the Isthmus a mere matter of manœuvre. He threatened to withdraw the Athenian ships, without which the Greek sea forces could not make head against the enemy Their defection would have rendered hopeless the plan to defend the left of the Isthmus by the fleet in the Gulf of Corinth and the ruin of the Greek cause would have been complete. The Athenians would, so Themistocles threatened, desert Attica and attempt to found a new city in the Western Mediterranean, where so many Greek colonies existed to extend them a welcome.

Whether the Corinthians persisted in their intention to sail away, and there was grave danger of the fleet disintegrating, or whether Themistocles adopted the plan while discussion was still proceeding in order to render his solution inevitable, whatever was decided, or whether the Greek leaders joined to delude the enemy, is hotly disputed, and will remain disputed. The fleet at Salamis could not in any event afford to allow itself to be blockaded and starved out. Nor could it come out to meet superior forces, which were expecting reinforcements almost at once. The only salvation was for the Persians to attack them at Salamis where the disparity of forces would not tell against the Greeks. There was no compelling reason why the Persians should thus play into their enemies' hands. The decision of Xerxes to blockade Salamis was right.

Themistocles decided to tempt the Persians. He sent his sons' tutor to Xerxes with momentous news. That monarch called a council of war to revise the decision. The Acropolis had fallen on the 21st September. It was now only the 22nd September and no irrevocable steps had been taken to carry out the plan of campaign. Sinnicus, the messenger, told the council that the Greeks had decided to slip away from Salamis during the night. If they escaped, they would be free-lances scouring the seas. They might even attack the sea coasts of Egypt or Phœnicia, now denuded of defence. It was resolved to sail at once against the Greek fleet so that none should escape.

On the side of Attica, the entrance to the Bay of Salamis is cut in half by the Island of Psyttaleia, which the Persians therefore occupied. Each half of the entrance was barred by a line of Persian ships, while a third squadron sailed to close the further entrance to the strait between Salamis and the mainland.

The news that the Persian ships were at hand was brought by Aristides who was returning from a visit to Ægina, and narrowly escaped capture. He had been the great rival of Themistocles but in this crisis he and his friends had been recalled from exile. His news was confirmed by a Tenian ship that had deserted. The blockade was now a fact, but it still remained to induce the enemy to come into the strait to fight. They may not have required much enticing in their confident belief that the Greeks were abandoning an unequal contest. Accordingly at dawn on the morning of the 23rd September 480 B.C., while the Corinthians sailed to defend the other entrance against the third Persian squadron, the remaining Greek vessels advanced to the attack. They sailed beyond the protection of the outlying cape of Salamis and came in sight of the enemy. There it was necessary to turn to face the enemy, and the ships delayed, formed front and advanced to the rear, backing towards the Attic shore. Xerxes was on that shore to witness the victory of his fleet. The Persian seamen, when they saw the Greeks apparently falter and refuse the attack, which they had obviously intended to deliver, could not resist the impulse to finish the foe in sight of their monarch. They dashed straight at the Greek centre which continued to give way. The Athenians on Salamis were horrified. It seemed as if their ships were determined to run ashore rather than fight. The cry arose, afterwards believed to come from the Gods, " Madmen ! How much further are you going to back ? " By now the Greeks were in two lines with the re-entering angle at the centre. The Persians, strung out in their haste, were in a scattered line between them. The signal was given. The Greek lines advanced on the Persian advanced ships, which thus were attacked on both sides. The clash came in confined waters. There was no time to manœuvre or to avoid even a friendly trireme as it dashed forward. The vessels met in a mighty shock, but the weight of the impetus was with the Greeks who crushed the Persians, caught in their pincers. The Persian centre was broken and opened a gap in their line. The entrance next to Salamis was closed by the Greeks, but the other they could not quite master, and through it many Persian ships escaped. Some indeed sacrificed their comrades. Artemisia, Queen of Halicarnassus, escaped by rowing down her own vessel under the eyes of Xerxes who praised her courage, thinking that she had rammed an Athenian trireme. Aristides crossed to Psyttaleia and massacred the Persian troops who held it. The Persian ships which remained fought stoutly. Quarter was neither asked nor given and night fell before the slaughter ceased. Among the slain was Xerxes' own brother.

Neither side realised, any more than the English when the Spanish Armada sailed north from Calais, how decisive had been the victory and that the sovereignty of the seas had passed to the victors. Xerxes had had enough of the Greeks. It was now impossible to finish the campaign that year. He decided to return to Asia. The fleet was ordered to the Hellespont to guard the passage from Europe, and the troops, placed under Mardonius, were ordered to evacuate Attica and winter further north.

The Persian land army, undefeated for many years, was still at hand, and next year the attack would be renewed. Meanwhile the armies rested, while the Greek fleet recaptured the islands.

Mardonius must have lost the Immortals and many other troops detailed to escort Xerxes on his return, but he would on the other hand be recruiting among the Greek states who had submitted. Part of the Persian army seems to have been under the independent command of Artabazus, but Mardonius' own forces were superior in numbers to the Greeks. His task when he broke up his winter quarters in Thessaly was to pass the Isthmus and subdue the southern states of Greece. Xerxes had failed to accomplish this with greater forces and the command of the sea. The Thebans and his associated general Artabazus advised Mardonius to delay while the Greek leaders were being subjected to the solvent action of bribes. He adopted another plan. He knew that Themistocles had given up office in the ordinary course, and that the Athenian command was now vested in Aristides and Xanthippus. In the hope, based on their political connections, of gaining them over, he sent Alexander of Macedon to negotiate peace on favourable terms. It was a temptation to Athens, which still lay open to the enemy, and her citizens were still forced to endure the discomforts of the island of Salamis. The Athenians rejected the offer, and called on their allies to deliver Attica.

Mardonius then planned a sudden attack, hoping to rouse the Argives so as to embarrass the Spartan forces on the Peloponnesus itself. He marched south from Thessaly but Argos remained quiet, and he changed his plan again. He entered Attica for the second time and sent again to the Athenians. They stoned his emissary, but the citizens in alarm led an embassy to the Spartans to urge them to advance. The envoys arrived during the festival called Hyacinthia and were delayed for ten days. Meanwhile the extra fortification of the wall of the Isthmus was pushed forward. If Sparta decided to take her stand there, she would bring about the risk that Athens would surrender, and the command of the sea would again pass to the enemy. Neither state trusted the other too implicitly but, as the Athenian envoys prepared to depart with reproaches, they were told that the first troops, 5,000 Spartans and 35,000 Helots, were already on the march.

Pausanius, the regent of Lacedæmonia, was in command of the Greeks, and he halted at the Isthmus for the arrival of his allies. In August he advanced to follow up the retreating Mardonius and was joined by Aristides with the Athenians, but not in time to prevent the sacking of Athens. From Attica the Persian forces marched to Bœotia, and took up a position behind the river Asopus, to the north of Platæa. There they fortified the camp. The Greeks, pursuing, reached the northern slopes of Mount Cithæron, some three miles away. To reach the Persians the Greeks would have to cross open country, favourable to cavalry action ; and this was entirely to the advantage of the

Persians. Fortunately for the Greeks, an opportunity for an attack presented itself to the Persian cavalry. They pressed too far and were repulsed with heavy losses. Masistius, their general, was slain. His body was paraded along the line of the Greek forces and his golden armour was taken to the Temple of Athene Polias in the Acropolis.

This success encouraged Pausanias to advance to some ridges in the plain near Asopus. His water supply depended on the left upon the river itself and on the right upon a fountain. It was a position from which to make an attack, not one to hold. What happened then is not clear, but the Persian forces seem to have deprived the Greeks of their water supply, and a retreat towards Platæa was ordered. The retirement was carried out at night in three columns. The Athenians were on the left, the Spartans on the right with the other Greeks in the centre. A gap opened, and the Persians, discovering the Greek retreat, advanced to the attack. They had some distance to go, and imagining that an easy victory was at hand, hurried in pursuit, losing order and touch with one another. The Spartans faced round when they reached the hills, safe from cavalry attack, and with the slope in their favour, counter-charged the Persians, and drove them back on their comrades rushing up behind. In the resulting confusion they were slaughtered by hundreds. Mardonius, conspicuous on a white horse, attempted to make head against the Greeks, but was slain and his men dispersed.

Artabazus, who was approaching the field of battle, promptly retreated to the Hellespont and the Persian invasion was over. The battle, named from the town of Platæa, was fought on the 29th August, 479 B.C.

Thus the united Greeks repelled the invaders and survived to develop a civilisation which will benefit mankind while the world lasts.

# THE CONVERSION OF ST. PAUL

OF all men who may claim to have changed the course of the world's history, St. Paul must surely take the first place. He altered the basic ideas of Western civilisation : the whole of our history bears the marks of that busy career of impassioned teaching which the Jewish tent-maker undertook after his conversion to faith in Jesus Christ. Yet it was not until comparatively late years that he was considered a fit subject for description by lay writers ; only theologians might presume to examine his life and to interpret his writings and the traditions which grew up round his hallowed name.

Gibbon's detestation of everything Christian broke this spell. Every reference he made to St. Paul reminded his readers that the apostle was a tent-maker, as if that were either a satisfactory or a fair description of the man. Since Gibbon, we have learned a great deal about the conditions in which Paul lived and worked. Among other matters, we know that his tent-making was not a sign either of intellectual incapacity or of practical inferiority. Every young Jew in those days—as is still much the case to-day—was obliged by his family to learn a trade ; Paul was apprenticed to a tent-maker. But we know from statements about him, no less than from the high intellectual standard of his writings, that he had received a good education and belonged to a prominent and possibly wealthy family.

" Saul, who is Paul " belonged to the Tribe of Benjamin

His father was a Roman citizen domiciled at Tarsus, in Cilicia ; the son was equally a Roman citizen. His Jewish race and the privilege of Roman citizenship which he enjoyed explain his dual name. Professor Ramsay, who has ingeniously examined the whole question of Paul's name and position, reminds us that " Most of us have no difficulty in understanding that a Jew at the present day may be a thoroughly patriotic English citizen, and yet be equally proud of his ancient and honourable origin.     In the extraordinarily mixed society of the Eastern provinces [of the Roman Empire] it was the usual rule in educated society that each man had at least two nationalities and two sides to his character." Paul, then, was " Paul " when he was regarded as a Roman citizen ; and " Saul " for his Jewish family and friends. The very similarity of the two names made this double usage convenient.

That his family was of local prominence is clear from the statement that he was " of Tarsus, a city in Cilicia, a citizen of no mean city." Thus not only did he hold the rank of Roman citizen, but he was also a member of an old and honoured family in Tarsus itself. This family was Pharisaic, that is to say, it strictly observed the customs and ritual of Judaism. Professor Ramsay conjectures, from the frequency and force with which the apostle urges parents to respect their children's feelings, that, either at some time in his youth, or, more probably, by his conversion, Paul must have participated in a " terrible family scene " with his strict relations. This would partly account for the poverty in which he passed his later years.

We know that Paul sat in Tarsus " at the feet of Gamaliel, and (was) taught according to the perfect manner of the law of the fathers." This Gamaliel was a famous teacher and scribe, and the grandson of Hillel, the most revered of Jewish rabbis, whose maxims have been handed down to the present day as an anthology of patience and neighbourliness.

Like his grandfather, Gamaliel rose to the highest rank among his contemporaries, becoming president of the Sanhedrin.  He was also in high favour with King Agrippa.  It is certain that Paul, as one of his pupils, learned thoroughly the Jewish Law ;  he must also have acquired, with this traditional doctrine, the more humane and broad-minded outlook for which his teacher was renowned.  We may assume that Paul was well grounded in Hebrew, Greek and Latin ;  and spoke all three languages with equal ease.

" His bodily presence is weak," we are told, and an early narrative elaborates this by the statement that he was short, bald-headed, bow-legged, sturdy, gracious in presence, and with strongly marked eyebrows that met across a prominent nose.  It requires little study of his life and works to deduce that he was always a man of great energy and vivacity, able in argument and eager in the presentation of his views.  That he was highly nervous is equally clear from his own account.  He speaks of the " thorn in his flesh, the messenger of Satan to buffet me," and his " infirmity of the flesh," which commentators, also bearing in mind his description of his conversion, have assumed to refer to intermittent epileptic seizures.  Considering how little exact evidence we have about him, the picture which can be drawn from these fragments is surprisingly clear. He is perhaps the most recognisable of all the apostles.

We know nothing of his life from the time when he completed his rabbinical training under Gamaliel in the University of Tarsus, until he enters the New Testament as a participant in the stoning of Stephen :  " The witnesses laid down their clothes at a young man's feet, whose name was Saul."  But it is in this interval that he would have undergone his apprenticeship as a tent-maker.

He was not merely a willing participant in Stephen's death, but a prominent agent in the persecution of the

Christians which accompanied it.   Mr. Bernard Shaw, in the preface to his play, *Androcles and the Lion*, has made a noteworthy attempt to reproduce the atmosphere of that moment in terms applicable to modern life.   " A quite intolerable young speaker named Stephen delivered an oration to the council, in which he first inflicted on them a tedious sketch of the history of Israel, with which they were presumably as well acquainted as he, and then reviled them in the most insulting terms. . . .  Finally, after boring and annoying them to the utmost bearable extremity, he looked up and declared that he saw the heavens open, and Christ standing on the right hand of God.   This was too much ; they threw him out of the city and stoned him to death. It was a severe way of suppressing a tactless and conceited bore."   Mr. Shaw's preface, with its acid attack upon Paul as a " shamebound soul " and a prototype of the soap-box evangelists of to-day :   " Whenever he addresses an audience he dwells with great zest on his misdeeds before his pseudo conversion, with the effect of throwing into stronger relief his present state of blessedness ;  and he tells the story of that conversion over and over again, ending with exhortation to the hearers to come and be saved, and threats of the wrath that will overtake them if they refuse : "   naturally brought down on its author's head the wrath of all those who regard Biblical figures as too sacred to be treated in so unconventional a manner ;  but it did not raise any point which had not previously been made by scholars, albeit in less irritating phrases.   That St. Paul developed the doctrines of Jesus in a manner which carried them far beyond, and away from, the simplicity of their first enunciator, is a commonplace.   Whether he developed them along inevitable lines of progress, or whether, as some say, he deformed and degraded them is not a matter into which I feel qualified to enter.   It is enough to say that his methods of thought were native to a quick Jewish brain, whose natural capacity for synthesis and organisation had been sharpened by contact with Greek culture and Roman civilisation. The cultural side of his teaching is the very element which commended it to the leaders of the Reformation, inspired as they were by the renaissance of Hellenic philosophy and literature, and which made Paul as much the patron of Protestantism as St. Peter has remained that of Roman Catholicism.

The death of Stephen, so well deserved as it must have seemed to Paul, aroused in the latter a zeal for persecution. After he had helped to make havoc of Christian homes in Jerusalem, he went to the High Priest and asked to be sent to Damascus as his representative, in order to take prisoner and bring back in bonds such men and women as there followed the new heresy. The unfortunate impression which Stephen's apparent blasphemies had made on him may have been strengthened by the news that a certain Simon had become a convert to Christianity ; for this Simon was a notorious person who had formerly set himself up as an inspired magician, " giving out that himself was some great one." Paul, as a scholar and rabbi, must have been horrified at the effect which a new religious movement, spread by such fanatics as Stephen and Simon, might have upon the more ignorant and uncouth sections of the people ; it seemed his duty to do all in his power to stamp out the heresy at once.

His conversion is told in some of the noblest words of all literature : " As he journeyed, he came near Damascus ; and suddenly there shined round about him a light from heaven : and he fell to the ground, and heard a voice saying unto him, Saul, Saul, why persecutest thou me ? " He was struck blind for three days by his vision ; led by his companions (who had also heard the voice) to Damascus, he recovered his sight there and was baptised into Christianity by one Ananias.

*After Michael Angelo*

THE CONVERSION OF SAINT PAUL

It is useless to attempt to discover the exact significance of this narrative. On the most rational basis, it may mean any of three things : First, that Paul was overtaken by an epileptic fit, which transformed his overwrought brain from hatred to adoration of the founder of Christianity ; secondly, that the light was an actual occurrence, visible to all, which had this effect on Paul ; or thirdly, that an actual disturbance of the heavens coincided with a physical seizure. The only clue which we can have to this problem, if we care to treat it as such, is that such visions are not unusual in the history of religious psychology. From the great light which shone upon Paul to the heavenly voices which rang in Joan of Arc's ears is no further than from one page of a psychologist's case-book to the next.

What is certain is that Paul's whole mind altered its direction. All the ardour, all the reasoning, and all the certainty with which he had determined to persecute Christianity were now turned towards spreading its tenets. His equipment was far greater than that of any other of the apostles ; and his superiority seems to have been almost immediately recognised. His birth, his education, and his rank as a *civis Romanus* gave him ascendancy over the simple men who hitherto had shared the task of preaching the gospel. They were reluctant at first to accept as a genuine convert one whose record was so notoriously hostile ; but apparently only Barnabas's intervention was needed to convince them of the truth.

Peter had conceived the idea of carrying the gospel to the Gentiles, but it was Paul who gave form to what was otherwise only a dream. His threefold status, as a Jew, a Tarsian and a Roman, made possible a wide vision of the field to be covered, and the haste with which it must be covered before, as Paul like the others supposed, the imminent second coming of Jesus brought their labours to an end.

It is probable that the ease with which he could contemplate the vast *Pax Romana* coloured his vision of a Christian church which should be co-determinate with its frontiers. Nor was there anything revolutionary in this prospect, for the authorities tolerated many religions ; why not the Christian among them ?

The apostles in Jerusalem, however, were not all so farsighted as he. To them Christianity was pre-eminently a Judaic creed, to embrace which a man must first acknowledge himself a Jew, and submit to the rite of circumcision. This narrowness would have hindered Paul's mission enormously ; better than the majority of his enthusiastic colleagues, he knew the opposition that the new faith would arouse among strict Jews, and how much more certain it was to appeal to Gentiles, many of whom would naturally have hesitated to accept Judaism as a preliminary to Christianity. He won his point and carried his mission far and wide through the ancient world.

The second part of the thirteenth chapter of the Acts gives a graphic picture of his manner. He and Barnabas entered the synagogue at Antioch on the sabbath and let it be known that they had a new message to give to the Jews worshipping there. After the customary rites, the chiefs of the synagogue invited Paul to preach. Paul reminded his audience of their ancient history as God's chosen people, and of their tradition that a saviour would be sent to them to lead them to salvation. This promise was now fulfilled in the person of Jesus. The whole centre of the Jewish faith, therefore, was shifted from the Law, which had proclaimed the coming of a saviour, to the message of the Saviour Who had now appeared among men : " And by him all that believe are justified from all things, from which ye could not be justified by the law of Moses."

The non-Jewish inhabitants of Antioch, hearing of this new creed, begged Paul to address them also. On the following sabbath, therefore, he addressed an assembly of the whole city, without respect of race. When Jews objected to their co-religionist turning to the despised Gentiles, he replied : " It was necessary that the word of God should first have been spoken to you ; but, seeing ye put it from you and judge yourselves unworthy of everlasting life, lo, we turn to the Gentiles." He obtained many converts, but the Jews raised " the devout and honorable women and the chief men of the city " against him and Barnabas, and expelled them.

I can see little warrant for Mr. Shaw's opinion that " Paul succeeded in stealing the image of Christ crucified for the figure-head of his Salvationist vessel, with its Adam posing as the natural man, its doctrine of original sin, and its damnation avoidable only by faith in the sacrifice of the cross. In fact, no sooner had Jesus knocked over the dragon of superstition than Paul boldly set it on its legs again in the name of Jesus." It may be true that a similar criticism, though in less provocative terms, has been set out by more competent theologians than either Mr. Shaw or myself ; but I should not myself draw any such conclusion from the record which we have of Paul's teaching. Such, at least, is not the interpretation which any ordinary mind would place on the illuminating account which I have just quoted of his speeches at Antioch, and from his other speeches and writings.

The subtlety and even the sophistry which sometimes ran through his arguments perhaps account to some extent for the criticisms which many have made of his development and enlargement of the Founder's doctrines. But these qualities were natural to a man of Paul's genius and his education ; moreover, they were necessary if he was to spread his faith in the world of his day. Had Christianity been left to the other apostles to preach, it might well have remained a purely Jewish concern, even an insignificant heresy, to be studied as a curiosity by rabbis and their pupils. But Paul made Christianity great ; it was due to his ministry that it rose up and overpowered every other creed in the Roman Empire, and that, to-day, it is the religion of the whole Western world.

We may without great difficulty picture the impression which Paul must have made on the peoples whom he visited. They saw a man of unprepossessing but magnetic appearance, one whose eyes (here I adopt Professor Ramsay's ingenious deduction from certain texts) were of extraordinary penetration. Excitable and gesticulating in moments of emotional stress, he demonstrated his personal dignity when any attempt was made to contemn him as a vulgar freak. Any man of intelligence must have seen, from Paul's bearing, his voice and his vocabulary, that he did not by birth or training belong to the simple peasants and artisans among whom he chose to live. The contradiction between his natural parts and his environment must of necessity have attracted to hear him many who would have passed by a mere vulgar salvationist.

Another feature which must have interested observers was that, although a Jew himself, Paul's teaching appeared to vex the members of that race to a pitch of irritation which drove them to demand his punishment or, at least, expulsion. Again, his ability to turn from addressing the congregation in a synagogue to haranguing the Gentile mob outside showed that his message was one of wide, and therefore interesting, application.

Finally, the knowledge that this itinerant preacher, with his quaint gestures and ceaseless eloquence, consorting with the humblest inhabitants, but ready to dispute with the most learned rabbis, was a Roman citizen must have aroused curiosity to hear him among even the most weary sybarites of the towns he visited.

He was clearly a man of commonsense, for all his idiosyn-

THE CONVERSION OF SAINT PAUL

crasies—so observers must have reasoned. He did not seek persecution for persecution's sake, like so many self-appointed prophets of his day. On the contrary, he was astute enough to anticipate persecution and avoid it, wherever possible. And, if he were arrested and brought before the Roman authorities, we may be sure that he demanded his rights as a Roman citizen, and claimed to be left in peace while he broke no laws.

It has been pointed out how he sought at first, on entering a new field of his missionary work, to catch the ear of the women. Conversely, it was the " devout and honourable women " of Antioch who were first roused against him. His appeal to women shows that he was not the " shame-bound salvationist " of Mr. Shaw's accusation, but one whose desire was to accomplish the greatest possible results in the shortest possible time. Everything that we know of him helps to increase his stature as a propagandist ; and to enlarge our respect for his genius.

His career was interrupted at last by the hostility of the outraged Jews of Jerusalem who demanded his death from the Romans. He was bound and brought to the scourgers to be tortured, or, as it was euphemistically termed, " examined." The official before whom he was carried had become a Roman citizen only by purchase— " With a great sum obtained I this freedom "—but Paul, declaring his free birth, both impressed the official with a due sense of their respective social positions and obtained his release from the scourgers. Led before the Jews for inquiry, he proclaimed his Pharisaic origin, and adroitly caused dissension between the Pharisees and the Sadducees who were sitting to try him. He was removed to the castle for his own safety ; his nephew, who evidently occupied a position of some importance among the Jews of Jerusalem —another proof that Paul's family was one of mark— learned that his fellows had prepared a plot to assassinate

c

him ; and he was sent off with a large escort to Cæsarea, the residence of Felix, the governor.

There he was followed by the rabbis, who accused him to Felix of sedition and of profaning the temple. Paul denied this : " They neither found me in the temple disputing with any man, neither raising up the people, neither in the synagogues, nor in the city." But he admitted that the doctrine which he taught was at variance with their beliefs—in itself no venal offence. Felix ordered him to be kept under supervision until a higher official arrived ; he was not to be incarcerated, or to be refused visits. In the modern term, he was placed under domiciliary arrest. This lasted for two years.

The arrival of Porcius Festus ended this period. Festus, baited by the Jews, examined Paul, but could find no evidence that he had offended Roman law. He invited him to go to Jerusalem, to confront his accusers there ; but Paul, perhaps rashly, exercised his privilege as a Roman citizen, and demanded to be judged by the Emperor at Rome. I suspect, however, that he foresaw the possibility of extending his preaching more quickly by this procedure. He knew also that the Jews of Palestine were determined to assassinate him.

King Agrippa, informed of the affair, sent for him and heard his version of his life and mission. Like Felix and Festus, the King could find no cause for official action against him ; that he had offended the Jews by preaching the resurrection of Jesus did not in itself lay him open to punishment. When Paul was taken out of his presence, Agrippa said—whether in sadness or sarcasm, we cannot know—" This man might have been set at liberty, if he had not appealed to Cæsar."

Paul and some other prisoners were given in charge to a centurion named Julius, who was one of a body founded by Hadrian or Augustus to carry messages to remote parts of the Empire, to convey prisoners and to gather news. They thus combined the duties of a modern King's Messenger and a Secret Service agent. Between Crete and Malta they were shipwrecked ; Paul seems to have shown his usual energy and intelligence, and to have impressed his captor by his commonsense. They stayed in Malta for three months, and then at last, when spring made navigation easier, continued their course to Italy through Syracuse.

On their way from the coast they passed a spot called the Three Fountains where a company of Roman Christians came to meet Paul, " whom when Paul saw, he thanked God, and took courage." Yet it was at the Three Fountains, if tradition may be believed, that he afterwards suffered martyrdom.

The Acts, our principal guide to his life, leave Paul dwelling in Rome, with a soldier to guard him and to bring him, when summoned, into court. He is said to have lived " two whole years in his own hired house . . . preaching the kingdom of God and teaching those things which concern the Lord Jesus Christ, with all confidence, no man forbidding him." His appeal to Cæsar had thus not been in vain, for he was able to carry his message into the city which was ever afterwards to be the centre of his religion. But the hatred of the Jews could not be withstood ; eventually, according again to tradition, Paul was tried and condemned, not presumably for sedition, but for causing a dangerous breach of the peace, likely to rouse disorder among the Jews everywhere, and for such contempt of court as lay in his refusal to abate his teaching.

Yet it is not impossible that he escaped execution. The judges at Rome may have been as fair in their view of his alleged offence as their colleagues in Judæa. It is only a late tradition which declared his execution, and placed it at the Three Fountains. But such speculation is fruitless.

Paul's death has no importance in any estimate of his achievement.

It is enough that we see in him a man beside whose achievement even a colossus like Napoleon seems a pigmy, and Alexander the Great the creature of an instant.

I cannot look out from the windows of my house without my eye resting on the dome of the cathedral which Wren raised above the busy capital of an Empire greater and more powerful than any which Paul could contemplate on this earth ; the cathedral bears the name of that earnest, clumsy, epileptic " tent-maker " of Tarsus—that Roman citizen who, by his teachings, transformed the Roman Empire and altered the whole face of the world.

# THE FALL OF JERUSALEM

" And when ye shall see Jerusalem compassed with armies, then know that the desolation thereof is nigh. Then let them which are in Judæa flee to the mountains ; and let them which are in the midst of it depart out ; and let them that are in the countries enter thereinto. For these be the days of vengeance that all things which are written may be fulfilled. But woe unto them that are with child and to them that give suck in those days, for there shall be great distress in the land and wrath upon this people. And they shall fall by the edge of the sword, and shall be led away captive into all nations ; and Jerusalem shall be trodden down of the Gentiles, until the time of the Gentiles be fulfilled."

St. Luke xxi, 20–24.

IN ancient times the coast route between Egypt and the northern countries of Asia Minor and Mesopotamia was the way by which all invasions from the south or the north came. The empire of the civilised world was disputed between the kingdoms of the North of Egypt, and in Palestine and Syria the first clashes of arms were bound to occur. Whenever one obtained undisputed mastery then the land had peace, but whenever the great nations were at war, the lot of the inhabitants was hard. At most times the rulers in Palestine were mere tributary kinglets, but at intervals when the mighty were both exhausted they blossomed into monarchs. Wars followed wars and in their train came famines and pestilences, leaving only the memory of the happy days when peace reigned.

Jerusalem had a long history before the Israelites entered the promised land. It was a noted stronghold, placed within striking distance of all routes over the plain. Its only defect was that the twin mountains on which it was perched were deficient in water.  The ruler of Jerusalem was a man to be conciliated or overcome if those routes were to be safe and lines of communication secure.  It was always a holy place, exceptionally holy in a land where so many hills and groves and fountains were sacred.

For many years after the coming of the Israelites, Jerusalem held out.  With their knowledge of siege-craft it appeared impregnable to the Jews who overran the neighbouring plains.  They drew the bounds between Benjamin and Judah so as to run through the city, which indicates that to them it was not a possession.  At last in the days of David, the fortress fell and Zion became the city of David, the centre of the religious life of the Jews.  That monarch was moved to build on the summit of Mount Moriah a Temple to the Living God, but the man of blood was denied the fulfilment of the sacred duty.

Solomon succeeded him and wellnigh established Israel as the ruler of the world.  He built the Temple which remained one of the wonders of the world until it was destroyed by the Babylonians.  Rebuilt by Nehemiah, it was the occasion of the rising of the Maccabees, who called the people to arms when Antiochus the King, assuming godship, ordered his image to be set up in the Temple.  God had commanded that there should be none other worshipped than He, and had forbidden the making of graven images. A second time the Temple was destroyed.  The kingdom of the Maccabees fell into anarchy and the dissensions of the Sadducees and Pharisees led to the coming of the Romans who set up Herod as vassal king.  He was a Jew of Edomite origin, Greek in education and sentiment.  With the idea of conciliating his subjects and glorifying his reign, he built the third Temple, so often mentioned in the New Testament.

On his death, fresh revolts broke out and Judæa was placed under a procurator administering as the direct

representative of Rome. Many Jewish patriots remained
defiant and, driven forth, lurked in secret places, hunting
the Romans and being hunted. These were the Zealots
who became mere bandits. Others sought relief from
earthly woes in an ascetic life and remained apart from
town life. Such were the Essenes. In the settled country
and in the towns Pharisees and Sadducees still disputed.

All these Jews believed that the city of Jerusalem was
the indispensable centre of their religious and political life.
There it was that they journeyed to worship God, who had
chosen that place to reveal Himself on solemn days to the
High Priest in the Holy of Holies. Without Jerusalem, they
could not conceive of themselves as having a country;
hardly could they conceive of God. Many had settled in
other countries; perhaps more Jews lived abroad than in
Judæa, but wherever they were dispersed over land and
sea Jerusalem was their spiritual home, the visible symbol
of all their hopes and aspirations.

The Civil Wars of the Romans had not unduly disturbed
the course of life in Judæa. The struggle was between
Romans for the mastery of the world, but there was no
doubt that to Rome belonged that mastery. At last
Augustus gained the Empire and for years Judæa had only
her internal troubles to disturb her peace. It was in the
years following the Civil Wars that Jesus was born. When
He first saw the light, Herod was on the throne. He
died after the administration had been taken over by the
Romans.

Soon after his death, the religious beliefs of the Jews
came into sharp conflict with the political ideas of their
masters. The custom had arisen of deifying the Emperor.
This was a device which had been originally adopted in
Greece in order to reconcile the fact of overlordship with
the existence of constitutions inconsistent with such overlordship. It was in essence a kind of legal fiction, possible

only when religious belief was universal but lukewarm. Most pagans recognised the existence of gods other than their own and were willing to concede to them such recognition as was politic. It meant in their religious life merely the setting up of a statue and paying to it compliments more or less sinceer. A lax idolater with such ideas could have no sympathy with a religion which would deny a cult at once so natural and so convenient. To a devout Jew, the notion was necessarily a vile blasphemy which could only be tolerated at the cost of his own faith.

Caligula became Emperor in A.D. 37. He was a close friend of Herod Agrippa upon whom three years later he bestowed all the realms over which a Herod had ruled. Once again the Kingdom of the Jews was re-established, and all seemed to promise that their future was assured. But Caligula was not only Emperor but also God, and in the year Agrippa became King, the citizens of Alexandria complained to Cæsar of the Jews of their city. They neither acknowledged the Emperor as God nor would they worship him. The dispute was composed rather than settled, and when Caligula died in A.D. 41 Claudius made no change in the government of Judæa.

Agrippa found the two mountains of Jerusalem enclosed in two walls, and the summits crowned by the Temple and the Acra were divided by a ravine. Formerly it was of great depth, but the desire to prevent the Temple from being attacked across the valley had led to the lowering of the other mount, and the materials and the rubbish accumulating for centuries had wellnigh filled the ravine. The lower city had spread beyond the walls and Agrippa set to work to build a third wall. He was, however, only a vassal king, and the Romans, not caring that his stronghold should be too powerful, stopped his works. Three towers only were completed. In A.D. 44 Agrippa died, and the administration reverted to the Romans.

THE DESTRUCTION OF JERUSALEM

The procurators found their task difficult and thankless. Alien in religion and opposed to the political aspirations of the Jews, they found that firmness caused unrest and that conciliation was impossible. The Zealots robbed and harried the countryside, and as Governor followed Governor, things grew worse and worse, so that the land was drifting into anarchy. Claudius died in A.D. 54 and matters were not improved by the accession of Nero. The rule of Rome became feebler and the outlaws bolder and more defiant. The peaceful population gained no material advantage from their political subjection and were outraged in their religion. At last they murdered a band of Roman soldiers. The Greeks of Cæsarea, nominally a Jewish town, massacred their Jewish townsmen. Nero at last roused himself and commissioned his veteran general, Vespasian, to conquer the land and restore law and order. The year was A.D. 67. The curtain rose for the last Act.

Vespasian based his advance upon Antioch. Accompanied by his son Titus and a powerful army officered by experienced generals, he moved slowly forward into the parts of Galilee. Each new advance led to the occupation of a new jumping-off place, but Vespasian took care to consolidate his position after every forward move. Once conquered, there was to be no more rebellion and certainly no attacks from half-subdued enemies in the rear.

The Roman Army had its fill of fighting. The Jews of Galilee were stout and warlike and resisted manfully. Probably they were man for man a match for the soldiers but they lacked their discipline and found no leader. Jotapata the first important fort to be attacked was commanded by Josephus the historian. It resisted might and main but at last fell. Josephus claims that he revealed to Vespasian that he was about to become Emperor. As town after town fell to the Romans they advanced towards the land of Judæa.

Gischalla was the last town of Galilee to fall. Its chief defender John, called John of Gischalla, was leader of a robber band. Before it was too late they deserted the town and fled to Jerusalem, pretending that their only reason was to concentrate upon that vital position rather than dissipate strength by defending weak towns. As the enemy grew near, the Zealots crowded into Jerusalem, quarrelling amongst themselves but united in plundering the citizens. Even the priests were treated with contumely. In a city awaiting an enemy's attack civil discord raged. The Zealots even invited the Idumæans to whom they secretly opened the city gates. These raiders slew the high priests and many others and retired overladen with booty.

Vespasian's staff watched this turmoil and wondered at his inaction. Why not take advantage of all this internal strife and by one stroke end the whole business ? But their general was wiser. He explained that if they advanced, the Jews would oppose a united front, while if they awaited events, the factions would slay one another and waste their munitions and stores. When they were exhausted the victory would be easy.

Vespasian underestimated the endurance of the Jews, but he had this reason for his error. Many of the better class were deserting Jerusalem, but this movement, which might have ended the struggle, did not suit the Zealots, who set guards round Jerusalem to kill all who attempted to flee. Supplies were growing scarce, as all Judæa was infested with robber bands, and the city gained no support or supplies from the surrounding districts.

At last Vespasian decided to move forward and advanced to Jericho. From that advanced base, he sent out forces to seize strong points near Jerusalem. He was then preparing to move against the city, when he was stopped by the news of the revolt in Rome and the death of Nero. It was of the utmost importance for him to keep his forces in hand until he knew the course that events would take. Titus even sailed for Rome, but came back.

During this respite, another partisan leader arose, one Simon, who fought both with Zealots and with the Idumæans. When Vespasian heard that Vitellius had gained the mastery at Rome, he again began to move forward. Simon and his bands, retiring before the Romans, came to Jerusalem and camped beneath the walls, ravaging and destroying, so that the city was as truly besieged as though the Romans were at the gates. To overcome John, the priests admitted Simon to the city. He was received with joy but remained as a master. The priestly faction gained no help. There were now three hostile camps within the walls, and while they fought the Romans waited.

The army, however, proclaimed Vespasian Emperor and he departed to Rome, leaving Titus to carry on the task of subduing Judæa. Titus was in Egypt and marched with an army along the coast past Jerusalem to Cæsarea, where he concentrated his forces for the final advance. Jerusalem had had a breathing space of eighteen months, but gained no advantage thereby, but rather loss. Eleazar revolted from John and so now three leaders strove with one another. But they all agreed in plundering the unfortunate citizens, setting guards to prevent them seeking safety in flight. Within the city men fought and plundered day and night. It seemed that human misery had reached its climax.

But worse was to come. The Romans were at last nearing the city to destroy it. Against this foreign enemy the three factions turned and fought like tigers. Titus in his first reconnoitre was nearly slain. The legions who occupied the Mount of Olives were attacked as they were encamping and only saved after a fierce battle. At last the lines were completed and the investment began.

It would be expected that now some understanding would

unite the defenders, but, whenever the Romans ceased to advance, the civil tumults continued unabated. Eleazar's men held the Temple and at the Feast of Unleavened Bread he opened the Temple for worship. The Zealots mingled with the worshippers and drove out Eleazar and his adherents, polluting the Sanctuary with blood. One faction was destroyed, but the two which remained still continued war to the knife.

They did not neglect the Romans. Once by a clever stratagem, they caused the rank and file to believe that the defenders were panic-stricken and that the city would fall to a cry of triumph. In spite of Titus' commands, hundreds rushed forward and were met by the Jews who stopped their simulated flight and routed their assailants. Thenceforward the Roman soldiers paid heed to their commander.

Titus now resolutely advanced his siege works. Fighting daily, they pushed forward the mounds and fighting-towers. Catapults hurled huge rocks at the walls. The Jews sallied again and again fighting to destroy the siege works and engines. Now at last it was obvious that union was essential if the city was to hold out. John and Simon patched up a working arrangement and for the first time the Romans met the resistance of a united defence. Sallies multiplied and the advance was stayed again and again, but gradually the approach to the north wall gained ground. That wall was taken and rased. A second wall remained to be captured. After fierce fighting the Romans gained a lodgment, were driven off, but at last they secured and destroyed the second wall.

Further resistance was hopeless. Thousands had been slain and famine was claiming its victims. Titus decided that a short respite might make the Jews see reason. For four days, successive legions were assembled in full battle array to receive their pay in the sight of the town. The device failed. Though the Jews knew the worst, they were determined to resist until death. They made no sign. Titus therefore renewed the siege, but twice thereafter he sent Josephus to harangue the defenders but without the least success. Famine was driving many to despair, but the guards slew all who attempted to desert to the besiegers. Some of course succeeded and were received by the Romans. This welcome encouraged many to come out and forage, but the ruse being discovered, the Romans too seized deserters and crucified them before the walls or struck off their right hands and sent them back.

The townsfolk were at their last gasp. The soldiers in the city searched everywhere for food. Destitution threatened all from the highest to the lowest. The High Priest's wife, whose feet were too delicate in happier times to be defiled by contact with the soil, now joined with the women of the people searching in alleyways for filthy crusts. Cannibalism broke out and grew. Even the searchers were horrified on entering to search for hidden food, to find that there was food, but that it was human. Murder and sacrilege continued. Famine was destroying whole families and streets but still the city held out. The operations were proving too expensive and Titus set to work to surround Jerusalem by a wall, behind which his army waited until sheer want had sufficiently weakened the defence. At last Titus ordered his men forward for the final attack.

The Jews were not so exhausted as the Romans thought. The fires of religion, patriotism and hate more than counterbalanced the weakness due to disease, famine and despair. They knew that the fall of the city would not save their lives and they prepared to cause the Romans as much loss as human courage could inflict. Near the Tower of Antonia the wall was breached, but its fall only revealed a new wall built to supply the anticipated loss.

At last a select body of men crept secretly at night into the Tower. The sentry was surprised and first he and then the guard were silently killed.  The forlorn hope then called up their comrades who seized the wall and advanced towards the Temple.  The alarm brought thousands of the defenders hurrying to the rescue, and in the narrow streets the Romans found that the defence was still too powerful. They fell back to the wall and spent some time in demolishing the works and preparing a wide and easy breach for a further assault.

Titus was anxious to end this expensive and prolonged siege.  In the confusion many of the citizens had taken refuge with the besiegers.  Among them were the High Priests.  They were kindly received, but further desertions were stayed by the report that the Romans were giving no quarter.  When the refugees were paraded under the wall alive and well, the occasion was seized to revile and insult them.  If Jerusalem was to fall, it could only be by the power of the sword.

A fresh sally almost reached the Mount of Olives but failed, and fighting continued under the walls and within the city.  When the assault on the Temple was ready, the attack was launched, but the Roman columns were stayed in murderous combat.  Thereupon Titus ordered the Temple gates to be set on fire but strictly commanded his men to spare the Temple, too precious to lose as a trophy. As the flames caught, they spread in the outbuildings and an excited soldier seized a brand and thrust it through the Golden Window.  This lighted the rooms built round the north of the Temple.  They burst into flames and the fire spread to the Temple itself.  While it was blazing the Romans advanced and were met with the fiercest resistance. It was a scene of horror and despair.  The fighting prevented all chance of saving the Temple and the Romans' conquest was a hill of smoking ruins.  Thus the lower city and Mount Moriah were now in the hands of the enemy.

The other mountain was still resisting.  Titus offered

the defenders their lives but they refused to yield on any terms and the Roman soldiers continued their advance through the streets, fighting, burning and plundering. The Idumæans decided to depart but Simon slew their leader. Street by street the Romans increased their hold upon the city and at last all resistance was crushed. Jerusalem had fallen.

Simon and John hid in caves but at last were forced out by hunger and surrendered. Simon was reserved for the triumph when he was led through the streets of Rome and then slain. John was sentenced to perpetual imprisonment. The people were scattered.

Titus had no intention of repeating so arduous a siege. Under his orders Jerusalem was rased to the ground. Three towers and a portion of the west wall alone were left to serve as a fort for a small garrison. The site of the city was thenceforth a solitary desert. It was not until generations afterwards that Jerusalem was again allowed to become inhabited and to be once more a town of living people.

For the Jews the fall of the city was more than a military disaster : it was the end of the Jewish Kingdom. Thenceforward they had no nationality, no country, no common centre of worship. Scattered over the world, it seemed that they would in the course of time disappear and be left as a mere memory of a race that once had made history, like to many nations that have flourished in those parts for a time and then ceased to be. But time reserved for them another destiny.

Tenacious of their rights, united by the ties of race and the bond of common suffering, separated from the heathen by their worship of the One God, the Jews lost none of their vitality. Their destiny was changed, but not their existence. Prophets, priests and kings had ceased to lead them, but they still clung to the worship of the Most High.

Jochanan ben Zakbeai was a learned Jew who had fled on the first approach of the Romans. To him the city offered no hope, held by a band of sacrilegious outlaws and menaced by an alien army. With the invaders' permission he settled at Jabuch, a village on the coast where he established a little house of learning. There such rabbis as survived sought inspiration and a home. A new Sanhedrin was created. The rabbis replaced the Temple priests, as the synagogues perforce were made to supply the function of the destroyed Temple as well as their own. The old sacrifices ceased and were replaced by study and by prayer. Wherever the Jews went, there they set up their places of worship. The fall of Jerusalem had destroyed the Temple, but not their faith ; it had ended their kingdom but not their sense of race and religion. With no political bond and without a country or home, the Jews remained and still remain united in race and religion.

In spite of the immense sufferings inflicted upon the Jews in their exile by their persecuting and reluctant hosts, we may say that both they and the world have gained by the destruction as a unit of the Jewish State. Had it survived they would have been a small Levantine power, unstable and divided by fierce internal disputes. As it is, they have spread throughout the world so that there is no country which has not gained by the achievements of the Jews in commerce and in all the arts and sciences. Rightly received and given proper opportunities for developing their peculiar gifts, they are a source of material and intellectual power. And their faults, which are many, may be forgiven them for their manifold sufferings, tribulations and endurances.

# THE BATTLE OF HASTINGS

THE Battle of Hastings or Senlac—or, more exactly, of the hill " with the hoar apple tree," for the site had then no other name—decided the fate of England, and so of the world for five hundred years. It determined that this island, which must by its position be joined to the culture and traditions of either Scandinavia or Continental Europe, gradually lost its connection with the former and, until the genius of its people created for it a vast Empire in the furthermost parts of the world, became part of that European feudal system of which the Normans were the nearest examples.

True, the Normans possessed qualities which distinguished them from their French and Germanic neighbours. They were themselves descendants of Vikings who had settled on the southern coast of the Channel ; thus, while adopting the habits and religion and, to a large extent, the tongue of the people among whom they had settled, they nevertheless added to these qualities certain fundamental assets of courage and determination, not to say brutality, which combined to make them for a long period the most progressive and the most redoubtable nation of the Middle Ages.

Few portions of Europe do not retain, even to-day, marks of their irresistible career of conquest. From England to the foot of Italy, we still find traces of their churches and their castles, the very architecture of which breathes the lively vigour of their character.

Until recent historians restored a sense of reality to their art, and balanced national sentiment with clear-sighted erudition, Englishmen were brought up to believe that, on the whole, the Normans had been a power for evil in our history ; that they came as alien conquerors to destroy a genuinely English civilization, of which Harold, the " last of the Saxon Kings," was a noble and patriotic representative.  Such prejudices must be set aside if a proper understanding of the importance of the Norman Conquest, consummated at the Battle of Hastings, is to be obtained.  Harold was a patriot perhaps, so far as that term had any meaning in the eleventh century.  But he was not a patriot in our modern sense.  He, like his enemy, William the Bastard who became William the Conqueror, was far more a local chief fighting for his own clan and his own glory than a hero filled with modern notions of nationalism and self-determination.  It is useless to judge such men by modern standards, or to appeal to present-day ideals to explain their conduct, whether in praise or in condemnation.

The story of the Norman Conquest begins properly with the death of Canute.  That extremely able young Emperor had succeeded in welding Norway, Denmark, England and the Hebrides into a single Empire—a feat of statesmanship equal to the achievements of Charlemagne and Napoleon.  With his death his Empire fell to pieces.  The North Sea was in those days a gigantic barrier to communication ; even Canute himself, had he lived to old age, could hardly have hoped to bridge it for long.  His sons, with all his Viking impetuosity but with none of his statecraft—of which the apocryphal story of his rebuke to his courtiers on the sea-shore is a contemporary tribute—dissipated their inheritance.  The separate portions of his Empire began once more a separate existence.  In England the chief power fell into the hands of the Earls, a handful of great territorial chieftains who held sway over the various divisions of the country.  The chief of these was Godwin, and it was he who persuaded his fellows to summon to the English throne Edward, a descendant of the older line of Saxon kings. In 1043, eight years after Canute's death, Edward was crowned at Winchester.

Of all the men whom popular tradition has misunderstood, Edward the Confessor is one of the most misinterpreted. He has been given credit for virtues which were rather weaknesses ; for achievements which he never performed. Maitland has truly said of him that " In after days the holy but imbecile Edward won not only the halo of the saint, to which he may have been entitled, but the fame, to which he was certainly not entitled, of having been a great legislator. In the minster that he reared "—Westminster Abbey—" king after king made oath to observe the laws of the Confessor. So far as we know, he never made a law. Had he made laws, had he even made good use of those that were already made, there might have been no Norman Conquest of England."

Even his piety is somewhat discreditable, for it was founded in the weakness, rather than in the strength, of his character. He had been brought up in Normandy, and his tastes were those of a French monk. He spoke Norman French ; his thoughts were bounded by the narrow limits of a Norman abbey. No more unsuitable candidate for a troubled throne could have been chosen ; it seems certain that Godwin, the only real statesman of the day, selected him as an instrument through whom he could himself wield quasi-royal powers. Physically Edward was an albino, with white hair and pink eyes and long, white, effeminate hands. Godwin married him to his sister, and Edward's incapacity as a husband was transmuted by loyal chroniclers into a remarkable instance of princely chastity, hitherto unknown to our ancestors. Though he professed, or was said, to hate cruelty of every kind, he indulged in the pleasures of bull-baiting, as is shown by an ancient document referring to the city of Norwich. His one active achievement was to erect a great church, two miles outside the city walls of London, on the " thorny island " which to-day is called Westminster. His chief passive achievement was, by his weakness and incapacity, to forward the Norman Conquest.

His only aptitude for ruling was a certain talent for intrigue. Whether by accident or design, he countered Godwin's attempts to become the power behind his throne by attracting numerous Normans to his court. In their sympathetic company he passed his languid days ; and, by appointing them to important positions in his retinue and to the chief ecclesiastical posts in his kingdom, he for some time maintained a balance between himself and his turbulent English father-in-law.

The most noteworthy of his Norman protégés was one Robert, abbot of Jumièges. Such was this man's ascendancy over the King that a chronicler said that " if he said a black crow was white, the King sooner believed him than the evidence of his own eyes." Edward appointed him first Bishop of London, then Archbishop of Canterbury. About Robert's appointments flared up the most serious of the many quarrels between the King and the Earls, headed by Godwin.

Godwin had forced his sons into positions second only to his own. The eldest, Sweyn, disgraced himself, however, by carrying off a consecrated virgin, the Abbess of Leo-minster, a crime which even in those days always stood between him and power. His next brother, Harold, was a far abler man, whose talents mirrored those of his great father. He it was who, after Godwin's death, became the banner-bearer of the English party at court and in the country, and who, as we know, ascended the throne for a short and disastrous reign.

Shortly after Robert's appointment to Canterbury, with

THE BATTLE OF HASTINGS

*After De Loutherbourg*

its implied triumph of Norman civilisation over the despised Saxon tradition, a band of Norman knights ravaged Dover, meeting with considerable opposition from the inhabitants. Edward called upon Godwin to punish the town for its alleged unruliness.  Godwin, less, we must suppose, from any true sympathy with the outraged burghers than from fury at Robert's challenge to his own authority at court, rose in rebellion against the King.  But his followers deserted him, and he fled to Flanders, which then was always ready to receive refugees from England.  His cause was soon taken up by the other Saxon dignitaries, and he and Harold sailed up the Thames to London ;  confronted the King's forces with their own ;  and compelled Edward to restore them to their old positions, while the frightened Normans fled the country.  Robert of Jumièges had to fight his way through the streets of London before he could find a vessel to carry him back to his native land, whence he never came again to England, though he carried his complaints to William of Normandy and to the Pope at Rome, both of whom were, or professed to be, deeply incensed at the apparent outrage offered to so high an officer of the Church.  It was due in no small degree to Robert's pleading that William's expedition to England, when it came, was regarded by contemporary opinion on the continent as a salutary visitation upon impiety and lawlessness.

In place of Robert, a certain Stigand, a partisan of the Godwin faction, was made Archbishop of Canterbury. This appointment, though it later received the hesitant blessing of a pretender to the Papacy, was frowned upon by devout Churchmen overseas as a direct challenge to the Holy See.  All those who were principally concerned in it, especially Harold, were therefore regarded as schismatics. Englishmen may be proud perhaps that, even in those early days, the claims of Rome could be set aside—a clear presage of that national obstinacy which caused us several centuries later to embrace the philosophy and the revolutionary politics of the Reformation—but it cannot be doubted that, at the time, Stigand's appointment was rash and improper.

Godwin's return was in 1052 ; in the following year he was fatally seized with an apoplectic fit at dinner, an incident which was duly magnified by his enemies into a divine vengeance on him for his truculence towards the King. Harold took his place, and asserted an almost complete ascendancy over the half-imbecile monarch. When Edward died in the first week of 1066, the only persons present were Harold and Stigand ; Harold's sister, the King's wife ; and a Norman valet. Edward first prophesied in his agony, declaring that monkish friends of his youth were appearing to him in a vision and foretelling that " They who hold the highest place in thy realm of England, the Earls, the Bishops, the Abbots, the men in holy orders of every rank are not what they seem to be in the eyes of men. In the eye of God they are but ministers of the Fiend. Therefore hath God put a curse upon thy land ; therefore hath he given thy land over into the hand of the enemy. Within a year and a day from thy death, shall fiends stalk through thy whole land, and shall harry it from one end to another with fire and sword and the hand of plunder." After this mournful discourse, with unconscious irony, Edward, so it is declared, named Harold as his successor : " To thee, Harold my brother, I commit my kingdom." He was buried in the new Minster which he had built on the thorny island.

It must be remembered that Edward's naming of Harold as his successor, if it ever occurred—and neither Harold nor Stigand was a disinterested witness—was only one factor in the succession. It was for the Witan of England, that embryonic House of Lords, to make the final choice.

Its members, however, freed as they were from Norman pressure, instantly chose Harold as King, and he was solmenly crowned, probably at Winchester, almost certainly by Stigand, with whom his fortunes were allied.

On the continent his claim to rule in Edward's place was received with horror and contempt. It is difficult for the modern reader to understand the resentment which was felt at the coronation of Harold, and the overwhelming support given to William the Bastard of Normandy in his decision to contest this by force of arms. Yet to the mediæval mind, William's right was indubitable.

Many causes went to produce this feeling. William, with a cunning in advance of his age, had spent years in tireless propaganda of his own claims. And there were circumstances, as yet unknown to Harold's countrymen, which immensely strengthened the Norman's position.

In the first place, it was said that Edward had promised William the succession. Whether or not this is true, and while all probability seems against it, the hint was sufficient to undo much which Harold had won by his declaration of Edward's alleged dying bequest. Certainly Edward. alive or dying, had no right to hand on his throne to anyone ; the Witan alone had the right to choose. But clearly Edward's wish might be invested with both worldly and perhaps divine insight ; it was worth while for his competing heirs to claim the support which he could no longer confirm or deny. In any case, the story spread by William's party balanced Harold's, and weakened to that extent the latter's position.

Secondly, Harold's support of Stigand and opposition to Robert of Jumièges had done him incalculable harm. If the Pope's writ did not run in England, it at least nullified any attempt by Harold to oppose William's intrigues abroad, and also made the Norman's claims almost those of a crusader. William appeared to foreign Churchmen as a prince resolute to uphold divine authority against greedy and schismatical usurpers. Robert's plaints had been heard at many foreign courts, and at Rome. All clerical sympathy was with William and against Harold.

Thirdly, to pass over all minor points, it now appeared that Harold had probably perjured himself. Two years before—or at some such period—he had sojourned with William in Normandy, during which time, if the Normans may be believed, he had sworn to uphold William's claims to the English throne on the holiest relics of Normandy. William, it should be remembered, was by blood no more remote from the English succession, once his bastardy was overlooked—as was easily done then—than Harold.

Much controversy has reigned over the incident of Harold's oath, and it has never been determined when, where, or what Harold swore.

Some suppose that Harold deliberately travelled to William's court to promise the latter his aid. Improbable as this seems, it is not wholly out of keeping with Harold's character ; he may well have thought fit temporarily to buy off Norman opposition to his own domination of Edward's court by an oath which he had no intention of keeping. A more reasonable conjecture, however, is that his presence in Normandy was accidental. He had set out from Bosham, that favourite harbour of the eleventh century, either on a hunting expedition abroad or on a diplomatic mission to Flanders. Stress of weather drove his vessel ashore on the coast of Ponthieu, where he was seized and held to ransom by the local Count, Guy of Ponthieu.

Rescued by William, he found himself compelled, either by gratitude or by compulsion, to swear assistance to his benefactor. William is alleged to have made the oath more solemn by concealing in the casket, on which Harold swore, a number of holy relics which he had prudently gathered

THE DEATH OF HAROLD AT THE BATTLE OF HASTINGS

together from various churches in his kingdom.  It will be seen that, whatever William's motive, he can hardly be accused of perfidy in this matter.  After all, if Harold swore an oath, it can hardly have mattered, in respect of his conscience, how sacred were the relics on which he swore.  But for William's propagandist designs, it was of considerable importance that these should be especially holy.  The more remarkable they were, the more disgraceful in the eyes and ears of the continental princes and abbots was Harold's perjury which William seems shrewdly to have foreseen.

Freeman makes the interesting point that the truth of this story of the oath is most attested by the very silence of Harold's Saxon advocates.  As he points out, they were quick to answer every other claim which William made, wherever answer was possible.  But on this matter of an oath they are silent.  He argues, and it is difficult to disagree with him, that they were silent because they dared not speak.  In short, they as well as the Pope and the generality of William's supporters believed that Harold had indeed sworn his hopes away ; and was a perjurer.

William at once consolidated his position.  His emissaries preached the coming crusade with becoming fervour to all who were likely to be impressed by religious arguments ; to fortune-seeking adventurers and mercenaries they set out vivid accounts of the rewards which would fall to men who joined forces with the Norman king in his effort to possess himself of the English throne.  The two motives, piety and greed, combined to persuade a sufficient number of men that they might well embark with William on this joint-stock crusade.  The lure of double profit—in this world and the next—is very strong.  The Pope, still outraged by Stigand's rise and Robert's fall, sent his blessing and a holy banner, as well as a ring containing a hair of the Saviour.

William gathered his host together.  The numbers of our Norman conquerors—only a third of whom, perhaps, were Normans—have been absurdly exaggerated by tradition. There were probably not more than eight or nine thousand men in William's army.  But these were enough to conquer England.

Harold's debut as King had not been propitious.  He was at once faced with disaffection in the North.  Tostig, his younger brother, who inherited the wilder without the wiser strain of the Godwin blood, joined forces with Harold Hadrada, King of Norway, to stir up the North-East of England.   In September, 1066, Hadrada entered the Humber with a large fleet, while his English allies marched southward from Northumbria with their levies.   They captured York and wasted the whole county.

Harold had been watching the Channel for some time in expectation of William's coming, but contrary winds, despite the Pope's blessing and the eloquent exhortations of the Norman bishops, had prevented the armada from sailing. The news of the rising in the North sent the English King headlong in that direction.  His principal force consisted of his House-carles, a guild of warriors of whom he, like Canute, was an initiated member.  The House-carles may be described, in distinction from the Norman cavalry, as mounted infantry.  That is to say, they travelled from place to place on horseback, often at surprising speed, but on the battlefield they dismounted and, leaving their horses behind them, fought as infantry with the old Viking battle-axe.

With these trusted supporters, Harold spurred North. He came upon the Norwegian invaders and his rebellious brother at Stamford Bridge, a few miles outside York.  It is pleasant to know, on the authority of a contemporary legend, that Edward the Confessor appeared in a vision to one of Harold's abbots, promising him supernatural aid. Thanks to this comforting news and to the prowess of the House-carles Harold won at Stamford Bridge, in Freeman's

quaint words, " the last victory of pure and unmixed
Teutonic England." Tostig and Harold Hadrada were
both slain, and the invaders were driven back to their ships.

But at the banquet which Harold held to celebrate his
triumph a messenger arrived from Sussex with the long-
awaited news that William's armada had sailed. The
Normans landed at Pevensey three days after the victory
of Stamford Bridge.

Harold's courage was the chief of his virtues. He
instantly called his House-carles together, and rode South.
They reached London in four days, an amazing feat for men
who had just endured a tiring and sanguinary campaign.
On October 13th, Harold and his army stood face to face
with the Normans, who, in the fortnight which had elapsed
since their landing, had ravaged the Sussex coastlands.

The site which Harold chose for this decisive battle was
some seven miles from Hastings. Freeman, who has a
liking for odd names and spellings—does not he compare
William, though favourably, with " the Nabuchodonosors,
the Swegens, and the Buonapartes, whom God has sent
from time to time as simple scourges of a guilty world " ?
—calls the place Senlac, on the dubious authority of a
later chronicler. In any event, it is now marked by the
church and village of Battle, named after this engagement.

What precisely happened during the fight will never be
known. There is a great difference of opinion between
learned historians as to the exact tactics followed by either
side. But some things are certain. One is that the English
stood on the defensive. They could not hope, since they
fought dismounted, to attack and put to flight the well-
armed Norman and French knights. Also it is sure that
the Norman archers were better armed and could out-
shoot their English adversaries. The battle resolved itself,
from the military side, into a contest between old and new
methods. The English used the tactics with which their

Viking forebears had overcome all enemies. The Normans had superseded these by new weapons. The result was inevitable.

It would seem, however, that the House-carles, Harold among them, fought with desperate bravery. They must have beaten off many attacks upon their hill-top position, attacks led by such picturesque creatures as Taillefer, the minstrel, who threw his sword in the air and caught it again, thus juggling until he was killed ; and by Bishop Odo, William's half-brother, who, because the Church forbade him to shed blood with the sword, ingeniously outwitted this prohibition by using a heavily studded mace. There is every reason to suppose that the Normans, not for the first time in William's wars, made a feigned retreat in order to draw out the English in pursuit, and then turned upon the foremost of these. Meanwhile their archers, taking advantage of their long range, rained missiles on the kernel of the English force on the hilltop beside the hoar apple tree, until at last Harold was left with only a small ring of devoted adherents.

By evening all resistance ended, and William knew that England was his. He refused to give up Harold's corpse to his relatives ; nor was there any means apparently by which the body could be traced, so mangled were all those who had died on the hilltop. But in the darkness Edith Swan-neck, Harold's mistress, was led to the field and searched among the dead. She recognised the body of her lord, not by his features, which were mutilated beyond all knowing, but by certain secret marks which she alone could tell.

Thus ended England's short-lived independence alike of Scandinavian and Norman Europe. With William, our history becomes linked to the great feudal tradition of Latin Christendom.

# MAGNA CARTA

**B**ESIDE the London road there lies a green eyot between Staines and Windsor known as Runnymede. Upon this island King John set his seal to a document unique in English history, which has been claimed by historians up to the nineteenth century as the foundation of English liberty. It will be the object of this article to make plain the intrinsic (if somewhat exaggerated) importance of the great Charter, and the circumstances in which it was forced upon the King.

Ever since the Conquest of 1066, it had become evident that beneath the feudal machine, the seeds of anarchy were deeply inherent in the Norman State. Against it the Conqueror had struggled, pruning judiciously the powers of his great feudatories ; it had been subdued by the iron hand of William Rufus, crippled a little further by the subtle perseverance of the first Henry, but had recaptured in the disastrous reign of Stephen all the vigour of which three Kings had laboriously deprived it.

By that curious and incalculable equipoise of succession, of which there are many examples in mediæval English history, there came to the salvation of England at this dark moment the greatest of her early Kings, Henry of Anjou, who laid the foundation of the Common Law, and created order and prosperity out of the chaos of the England to which he succeeded. Before his death he had perfected a machine of excellence : for taxation, for justice and for general administration. Great as its power for good might be in the hand of a strong King, it could become just as

potent an instrument of evil in the hands of an arrogant and
worthless successor.  All the opponents of the Crown had
been subdued, local government had been systematised,
and the Church, whose brightest prizes fell to officials
trained in the Exchequer, was the unestrangeable ally of
the Crown.  It must be remembered also that Henry II
was the ruler of a large empire.

An indulgent and even foolishly devoted father, he died
pathetically cursing his sons.  Powers which he exploited,
on the whole moderately and for general good, were abused
for selfish ends by Richard and John.  Richard, who has
acquired an almost legendary fame as the Crusader, the
Cœur de Lion of the East, was an impossible son, and a
King so insolently indifferent to English interests, that in
a reign of ten years he only twice visited her.  But he,
pursuing abroad war and tournament, was safeguarded
from the odium of the heavy taxation which fell upon his
Ministers.

His death in 1199 at least brought the end of absentee
government, and with it the end of an embryo ministerial
responsibility, for John endeavoured to isolate himself
from powerful advisers.  The result was to deflect unpopularity from justiciars to King.  The Throne became the
focus of general discontent, and it became evident that
grievances could no longer be redressed by a change of
Minister.

The first period of John's reign, 1199–1206, was spent
in a dilatory and losing war against France.  During the
years 1206–1213 he quarrelled with the Pope ; the years
1213–1216 were occupied with his great struggle against the
barons.  The initial period emphasised the disgust which
England had grown to feel for the King.  After an indifferent
reign a new King always inspires a pathetic hope of better
things, just as a reader will turn with expectant relief to a
new chapter in a tedious book.  Hopes of lighter taxation

were swiftly disillusioned. John's needs were as great, but less excusable than those of his brother and his growing demands of money form the background of the reign. His foreign activities were not more successful than his home policy. The loss of Normandy was the prelude to the forfeiture of all his continental possessions (1214) consolidated by his father, by a prudent marriage and by timely conquest. The loss of Normandy is a significant incident. The indifference of the barons shows that the descendants of William I had lost vital interest in their land of origin ; many of them had developed into purely English magnates. By his arbitrary conduct, John had definitively shaken their allegiance ; the whole machinery of feudal land-tenure and military service degenerated into an excuse for extortion. Feudal obligations had been increased ; feudal jurisdiction infringed ; while demanding the uttermost of services, John curtailed the counter-balancing privileges, and thus disturbed the whole equili-brium of the system.

By the death of Hubert Walter (1205), his Archbishop of Canterbury, the King lost a valuable adviser ; a breach was made between the Crown and the Church, and the filling of the vacant See of Canterbury led to the quarrel with Rome. To John, the death of Hubert meant the removal of a restraining influence, and an occasion for con-venient patronage. He had his own ideas about the desirable successor to the See, and made every effort towards the appointment of John de Gray, whom the royal favour had already raised to the Bishopric of Norwich. The Canons of the Cathedral Church had, however, secretly elected their sub-prior Reginald ; John intervened to secure his favour-ite's appointment in a second election, and both parties sent their representatives to Rome for confirmation. Both suggestions were repudiated by the Papal Curia in favour of Stephen Langton, the nominee of Innocent III.

John refused this compromise, and showed his true judgment by a gesture of defiance to Rome, which he was incapable of supporting. The Pope in 1208 placed the whole Kingdom under an interdict. We read how on the appointed day the Churches were closed, the bells were still; administration of the sacrament was refused to all but to children and the dying; the bodies of the dead were placed silently in unconsecrated sepulchres. This abrupt extinction of the outward forms of religion impressed the people with horror; John improvident of the future, wore an air of serene cheerfulness. In 1211 Innocent, in a moment of indulgence, released the English people from their allegiance to the Sovereign.

It was a minute of ephemeral success for the King. In the face of Papal interference, he considered himself entitled to confiscate the property of the clergy. He was thus able to refresh a jaded Exchequer, and attempt to ingratiate himself with his powerful opponents, the northern barons, for whose benefit the tax of Scutage was temporarily remitted. This action was insufficient to gain the goodwill of men whose antagonism was too deep-seated to be appeased by so transparent a concession. Indeed it succeeded only in bringing his enemies into line, for without winning over the barons, he had confiscated the property of the clergy and shifted his oppression to the humble. Magna Carta, as will be shown, was brought about by the barons, but it could hardly have succeeded without the sympathy of the lower orders.

In January 1213 John was formally excommunicated and the King of France was appointed as the executor of the sentence. There was no course for him, being an ignoble man without resource, except to agree unconditionally to the demands, the refusal of which had excommunicated him; Langton was to become Archbishop, and Church property was to be restored. Afterwards he

*After Rippingille*

KING JOHN SIGNING THE MAGNA CARTA

suffered the further humiliation of resigning the Crown, and receiving it back as the vassal of the Pope. John swore to defend the Church, and to observe the laws of Edward. Thus the conditions which the great William I had refused were sanctioned by the degenerate John.

## 1213-15.

For the time the danger seemed to be spent ; the King of France was forced to abandon his invasion owing to the removal of the ban, and the barons and people were compelled to renew their allegiance. Had the King followed an unagressive policy he might have postponed the final humiliation, but he considered it a favourable moment for the recovery of Normandy and Anjou. He required large numbers of levies for these campaigns ; and the barons on one pretext or another refused Knight service. John marched to Nottingham to punish the northern barons, but was compelled by muttered threats of excommunication to promise defaulters trial before the Curia Regis.

In 1214 he suffered the crushing defeat of Bouvines, which cost him all his continental dominions. The enemies of his misrule had been awaiting anxiously the issue of the campaign, deferring action until they should hear the news of failure. His military exactions had given birth to an organised and angry confederacy, and the news of the defeat of Bouvines banished the last fears of the malcontents.

On his return John was confronted with an unique situation, but humiliated as he must have been by his defeat, which was justly ascribed to his own incompetence, he was in no mood for conciliation. From those barons who had denied their liability to service, he again demanded Scutage to defray the expense of the war. Again they refused, and the leaders of the opposition met together at Bury St. Edmunds, and bound themselves by oath never to leave John Lackland in peace until he had confirmed

E

the Charter of Henry I. Meanwhile John strained all the resources of a crooked ingenuity to alienate the Church and the lower orders from the cause of the baronage, promising the Church the right of free election, exacting oaths of fealty from freemen ; raising and as quickly disbanding troops. His own supporters were now a mere handful of favourites, while the barons had collected a force of several thousand Knights. From the grey town of Brackley they sent their ultimatum to the King, which he rejected in fury, swearing that he would never consent to become the serf of his own subjects. The army then entered London and made it their headquarters ; magistrates joined the Constitutionalists. Government came to a standstill ; the sessions of the Kings Court ceased and the King's officers, the sheriffs, lost every vestige of authority. John at last realised the futility of resistance, and instructed Langton to come to the most favourable agreement that he could with the barons. The Charter was hurriedly drafted, and John set his seal to it upon the island of Runnymede.

Magna Carta made no novel assertion of liberty ; introduced few abiding principles ; the framers had no intention of disturbing the national jurisprudence. Their object was rather to trim the abuses which had arisen out of feudalism, and their remedies were contained in the Charter now granted by the King to his subjects and based upon the Coronation Charter of Henry I. The barons appealed to the laws of John's father, they made no proposals for change in legislative or executive, but they acted in a very honest unanimity. There were reactionaries among them, who hoped to procure from John in his eclipse a return to their old independence, and invidious class-privilege. The progressives were men recently elevated to the baronage by Henry, the class who had crushed the rebellion of 1173, men trained in his administration, who desired the continuance of his administrative system ; and indeed many of his innovations had become plaited into the structure of the nation, and found a permanent place in the clauses of the Charter.

The barons appear indifferent to the claims of the Church, and Langton in his moderation asked nothing further than a confirmation of its old liberties. We find the barons reacting against the centralisation of Henry II ; the writ præcipe is not to be granted in such a way that any free man shall lose his court by it. They were to impose on their tenants no taxes beyond the recognised feudal aids.

We are impressed by the poverty of the Concessions to the liberties of towns, mesne tenants, serfs, and the trading classes. No steps were taken to protect towns, other than London from the taxation of the King, or to intervene in the feudal relation between baron and serf.

In its constitutional clauses the Charter is conservative ; its authors desired no drastic constitutional changes. They attempt to restore the great Council to its original character of a meeting of tenants, and the subject of taxation is reserved for it. John is instructed to delegate powers of local government only to those who know and respect the law. Yet the Charter, clearly as it resented local abuses, made few changes. The King was subjected to a Committee of twenty-five lay feudatories to adjudicate upon complaints against the Crown, but to respect the persons of the King, the Queen, and the barons themselves. We read of the arrogance of this tribunal, and how, when John was sick and unable to appear before them, they decided that if he could not walk into their presence he should be carried.

We have referred to the light in which the great Charter appeared to the historians of the last century. Having attempted a rough analysis of the events which preceded its compilation, we should examine this claim. Was the Charter, as Green, Stubbs and Hallam and others maintain, the composite and successful protest of a united nation against the Crown ? Has England been for seven hundred years the herald of liberty ? Or was it the victory of a class, the barons in arms, exacted from an oppressive prince at the point of the sword ?

The barons did not combine and succeed as the champions of liberty, or as convinced theorists. Such a role did not present itself to them. Practical grievances prompted their action. They were incapable of understanding a contract between the King and the free classes. As a symbol of English Constitutional genius the Charter, four centuries later, was extolled only as an anti-monarchical necessity in the Civil Wars, and as an excuse for combating the exactions of the Stuarts it can be disregarded.

Contemporary chronicles reveal the Charter as a feudal bargain in which the King was forced to make certain promises, rights of relief, forest laws, feudal justice and so forth, but make no mention of the alliance between Church, baronage and people. Roger of Wendover, Ralph of Coggleshall, represent the revolt as entirely feudal, as a desire to restore the liberties of the Coronation Charter of Henry I, to shield Church and baronage from royal encroachment.

King John himself recognises that he was only patching up a peace with the barons, and refers to " discordia inter nos et barones nostros."

We conclude therefore that the Charter was prepared for the baronage and not for all classes ; further proofs of this vital fact will be found in its actual clauses. But it is obvious that although the remainder of the people played no active part in the exactions of the Charter, it was their sympathetic neutrality which made that exaction possible.

Great men have attached importance altogether excessive to the Great Charter. Chatham placed it beside the Petition of Rights, and the Bill of Rights, " in what I call the Bible of the English Constitution."

J. R. Green says : " The Rights which the barons

claimed for themselves they claimed for the rest of the nation." This is palpably false, for the villeins who formed three-quarters of the population only obtained protection as being the valuable property of their lord; they obtained no political or civil rights whatever; it follows that for the great bulk Magna Carta might never have been framed. Preference is throughout given to the barons and clergy, and only freemen and important land-owners derived substantial benefit. No immunity from arbitrary arrest, no popular right to control taxation, were secured by the Charter.

An examination of its clauses will indeed disprove the surprising claims of Green and Stubbs. Of the forty-nine important clauses, twenty-four secure the barons against the feudal encroachments of the Crown; they in fact restore ancient custom, and are reactionary rather than progressive. The clause relating to the Church is a formal guarantee of freedom. It is followed by a series of measures to remove from the King the arbitrary methods of raising money, which he had used in the past. It is only for the tenants-in-chief of the Crown that these Chapters make provision. From their position in the Charter the authors regarded them as of the first importance. Ten other clauses relate to royal justice, and all, if not exclusively favourable to the barons, were of advantage to them direct or financial. For Example, No. XVII declares that common pleas must be heard in a fixed place, and suitors in this court need no longer pursue the King over the country. This had as great an interest for the greater as for the minor litigants.

The concessions to towns and villages are most nebulous. London alone obtained a vague grant " of its ancient liberties and free customs." The free customs of the other towns escaped the attention of the barons completely, were later included in the Charter, and were of little value to them.

As to the alleged exemption from fines of the villeins wainage, it has already been said that they were protected only as the property of the lord  They are still liable to the impositions of the Manor Courts.  Villeins were protected from the amercements of the King, not of their manorial lords.  The original phrase is, " si inciderent in misericordiam nostram."  The purpose of this cannot have been one of consideration to the villein, for John was entitled to use as he pleased the villeins in royal Manors. (Ed. of 1217.)  The villein was the lord's chattel, and his usefulness must not be impaired by the King.

The " palladium of liberty " dealt with the rural population, by removing it from one control, so as to leave a clear field for the arbitrary action of another.

In the clause relating to taxation, it is stated that no feudal aid or Scutage except the three conventional aids was to be levied without the consent of the Commune Concilium, of the Nation, and those only at a suitable rate. The barons had also indeed vaguely stipulated that aids and tallages must not be taken from London and other places without the consent of the Council, but the Chapter gave the people no control of taxation ; it merely gives those concerned control over one form of taxation, and protects one class, the most wealthy, from irregular exactions There is no enunciation in the Charter of a general consent to taxation ; its framers only concern themselves with one aspect of taxation, the feudal aspect.  It was an incredibly limited document.

# THE FALL OF CONSTANTINOPLE

THE fall of Constantinople to the Turk in 1453 represents the collapse of Eastern Christendom and the triumph of Islam ; the extinction of a great Christian Empire and the rise of a sinister, alien, reactionary power in Europe. This collapse was primarily due to the apathy of European nations, who hesitated to send aid to the Byzantine Emperor in his hour of bitterest need—a neglect which they have never ceased to regret. Competent historians assure us that the arrival of a Venetian fleet or a detachment of Hungarian soldiers outside the walls of Constantinople in the spring of 1453 would have changed the course of history. There is no doubt that, but for the entrenchment of the Turkish power in Constantinople, European diplomacy during the past five centuries would have been infinitely less complicated by Balkan alarms, which have so often spread tragedy beyond their own borders.

To all ardent Mahomedans, of course, the idea of a Mahomedan Constantinople had always been the ultimate goal ; to hear the praises of Allah supplant those of Christ in the great church of St. Sophia the ultimate bliss. Mahomet is said to have declared that the best prince would be he who should capture Constantinople. For this and other reasons, the Arabs, before 1453, had made numerous attempts to conquer it, and generation after generation of Turks had hoped that theirs would be the favoured moment. Even the amiable, supine Sultan Amurath, who cared in later life only for seclusion amidst his houris at Magnesia, made an unsuccessful attempt upon the city in 1422. In spite of his cannon, then appearing in the East for the first time, and his regiment of Janissaries, who were to become the best troops in Europe, he failed. It was left for his son, the crafty, intelligent, cruel Mahomet II to bear off the coveted prize and win glory in this and the next Mahomedan world.

It has long been the custom of the Western nations to underrate the Turk as a fighting man. He was called slow, sensual, effeminate and backward. All of this was more or less true ; but, when called upon, he fought admirably, as he does now. Every Turk was required to serve as a soldier ; and the Janissaries, to whom I have referred, made a place for themselves in military history.

Their rise is curious. It was the right of every Sultan to exact one-fifth of all captured property for his personal use ; this tally included captives. The Sultan Orchan hit upon the idea of taking one in every five Christian boys whose parents were his captives, and of training them up as a personal guard. Subsequent Sultans followed this practice, until the regiment of Janissaries became an established force. The boys were chosen for their beauty, their strength and their intelligence ; they were separated entirely from their Christian parents and forcibly converted to Mahometanism. Their natural impulses were stifled —in the early days of the regiments, they were not even allowed to marry—in order that they might devote themselves more fully to the science of war. The training which they were forced to undergo was most rigorous ; but the reputation of their corps became so high, and they were given such unprecedented opportunities for advancement, that many young Christians voluntarily forswore their faith in order to join them. The Sultan Amurath had found them an admirable weapon against the Hungarian adventurer, John Hunyadi, at the battle of Varna ; his son was to find them invaluable.

Mahomet II was one of the most baffling personalities who ever ascended a throne. He was only twenty-one years of age when he succeeded his father in 1451 ; and he inherited all the father's natural intelligence. But, where Amurath had smiled and retreated from the cares of State, Mahomet leaped into the arena, full of high ambitions. He distinguished himself on his accession by causing his infant half-brother, Ahmed, to be put to death. Then, in assumed indignation, he himself slew Ahmed's murderer. In spite of this hideous cruelty, which disfigured his entire life, he was a man of great openness of mind and of enormous vitality. He was a skilled linguist, and showed extraordinary interest in, and aptitude for, military affairs, encouraging all who could give him new inspiration. He even dared to run counter to the Mussulman belief that all pictorial art is idolatry, by inviting the Venetian painter, Gentile Bellini, to his court, and by rewarding him lavishly for his work.

His private life seems to have been disfigured by lusts as unpleasant as his desire for blood ; on all sides he is accused of unnatural vice on a large scale. There is the tale of the Grand Duke Notaras, the second man in importance after the Emperor in Constantinople, who chose rather to follow his sons to the headsman's block than to deliver them over to the Sultan. There is also the story of the son of Phrantzes, the historian, who was killed by the Sultan for spurning his advances. Gibbon is only too pleased to affirm that " the noblest of the captive youth were often dishonoured by his unnatural lust." While we must remember that most of the available testimony comes from sources bitterly inimical to the Sultan, it seems likely that he, like most Turks, would step aside to avoid treading upon an ant, and the next moment would order his best friend to be disembowelled.

He was sufficiently shrewd to make good use of Urban, a Wallachian cannon-founder, who came to him from the Greek service in the confident expectation of higher wages. Encouraged by Mahomet, he was able to produce a cannon which was, to all who saw it, one of the wonders of the world. Gibbon tells us that the stone bullet which this mighty weapon projected, weighed more than six hundred pounds ; but military authorities declare that this, and the dimensions of the cannon itself, must be grossly exaggerated. But other chroniclers tell us that sixty oxen were needed to draw it, and that a hundred men marched beside it to keep it in position.

In the city of Constantinople, all was inertia and quarrelling. The Emperor, John Palæologus, had come to some kind of compromise with the reigning pontiff at Rome, Eugenius IV, regarding the union of the Latin and Greek Churches, which had long been one of the Emperor's cherished plans. Surrounded by a powerful and growing infidel power, he realised that his only chance of withstanding it, and of preserving the Byzantine throne for his descendants, was to ally himself with the Papacy. He made his first offer of union in 1429 ; differences within the Latin church postponed matters, and it was not till 1438 that the Emperor and his suite arrived in Venice, to be dumbstruck by the magnificence of the city and its inhabitants. More than a year later, the union between the two churches was signed, with due pomp, in the Duomo in Florence, and a Te Deum was sung in Greek. In return for this complacency on the part of the Emperor, the Pope paid the expenses of the Greek mission, promised all the aid at his disposal and sent ships of war for the Imperial service.

John Palæologus died in 1448, and was succeeded by his brother Constantine, the last Emperor of Christian Byzantium. Constantine was upright, generous, and loyal according to the standard of his time ; but he utterly lacked tact. Two blunders cost him dear.

First, he dismayed the powerful Doge of Venice, Foscari, by opening negotiations with him for the hand of his daughter and, when his Byzantine subjects plainly declared the unpopularity of a close alliance with the hated Latins, by abandoning the proposal of marriage. Thus he bitterly offended the wealthy city-state of Venice.

Still worse, he made a formal assent to the union of churches which his brother had negotiated, and received a legation from the Pope to celebrate this union in Constantinople itself. He may or may not have been genuinely convinced that this union was for the good of the Empire ; but his bigoted subjects were not concerned with reasons of statecraft. The Grand Duke Notaras declared openly, " Better the turban of the Turk in Constantinople than the Pope's tiara." Nevertheless, on December 12th, 1452, the formal union of the Greek and Latin churches was celebrated in St. Sophia, with a mass in which both Greek and Latin priests took part. The Emperor and the more important clergy accepted it, outwardly at least ; but the nuns, the monks and the common people looked upon it as an act of sacrilege. Inflamed by the monk Gennadius against the union, they ran through the streets, crying aloud against those who celebrated the Communion with unleavened bread. They began to shun St. Sophia as though the Black Death, which had swept through the Levant a century earlier, raged once again within its sacred doors. Thus Constantine lost the affection of his subjects, and the friendship of those who might, and should, have been his allies.

The designs of Mahomet upon the city were so open that a pretext was hardly necessary for attack. But the tactlessness of Constantine provided one. A certain Orchan, a pensioner of the Sultan, who had some pretensions to the Sultanate, dwelt in Constantinople ; the Emperor received a considerable sum yearly in return for keeping him there out of mischief. As soon as Mahomet succeeded his father Amurath in 1451—three years after Constantine had succeeded his brother—the Sultan received an impertinently worded message from the Emperor, demanding an increase in this subsidy and hinting that, if it were not granted, such pretensions as Orchan might make to the Sultanate would not be hindered at Constantinople.

A friendly vizier told the Greek envoys that they were mad, warning them that if they persisted in their rash demands, they would lose even the small fragment of the Empire which still remained to them. Mahomet, more subtly if less amiably, remarked that he would give the matter his most urgent consideration, and immediately began to collect masons and materials to build a fort at Asomaton, about five miles from the city. This was a definite threat of war, since the fort would be on the European side of the Bosphorus.

The Greeks, seeing the Turkish masons beginning to destroy their beloved church of the Asomatoi, drove them away. Blood was spilled, and Constantine demanded redress. This Mahomet naturally refused.

Constantine was no coward. He was resolved to fight. He implored assistance from the Pope—no longer the Eugenius IV who had arranged the union of the two churches with John Palæologus, but Nicholas V—but little came. A Papal Legate, however, who had come to Constantinople to celebrate the formal union, had brought with him a small body of papal troops ; who took part in the city's defence. Both the Venetians and Genoese had important trading stations at Galata and in Constantinople itself ; they furnished contingents to aid the city, while some Spanish residents took a share in the defences. Most important of all, however, was a Genoese soldier of fortune,

Giovanni Giustiniani, who brought his own men, two ships of war, and a small force of mercenaries to the aid of the Emperor ; in return for his services, he asked as a reward, in the event of victory, one of the islands of the Greek Archipelago.

He was given command, and disposed the defenders upon the walls of the city. The Christians made a pitiful showing, despite these foreign aids. Estimates of the number of the defenders vary considerably ; but it seems likely that there were not more than ten thousand, including the half-hearted levies from the city, to defend the great length of wall ; while Mahomet commanded, in addition to at least twelve thousand Janissaries, faultlessly trained and equipped, some fifty thousand troops of all descriptions and a considerable fleet.

Both sides made their final preparations during the winter of 1452-53. Early in April, Mahomet gathered together his troops and marched upon the city, planting his standard before the gate of St. Romanus. His fleet, numbering perhaps three hundred vessels, stretched across the Bosphorus in the shape of a crescent.

A successful naval encounter almost at the beginning heartened the Christians. Four large ships, laden with supplies were striving to make their way into Constantinople ; one was Greek, the other three sailed under the Genoese flag. They had lain weatherbound at Chios, and were anxiously expected at Constantinople. They found all the strength of the Turkish fleet opposed to them, three hundred vessels against four. However, they were larger than any of the Turkish boats ; they were better navigated ; and the wind was in their favour. They sailed against the press of Turkish ships, attacking them boldly enough under the eye of the Sultan, who had ridden down to the shore to watch this beginning to his campaign ; they were able to crush some of the tiny vessels which came against them and to beat off the attack of the Turks. They poured liquid fire from their tall bows into the smaller ships and, according to one chronicler, dropped huge blocks of stone, which formed part of their cargo, on board the Turkish vessels.

Two determined Turkish attacks failed. Mahomet, in a frenzy, spurred his horse into the sea, and screamed abuse at his captains. Even when the wind dropped and the vessels were becalmed, the four lashed themselves together, and stood like a strong rock in the middle of a seething sea, which did not harm them. Towards evening, the wind rose again, and they sailed triumphantly through the Turkish fleet to the boom of the harbour, which was opened to them in the darkness. They were then towed into the port, to the delight of the besieged and the fury of the Turks. These four vessels had boldly challenged the entire Turkish fleet, and had emerged victorious. Mahomet degraded his admiral and ordered him to be bastinadoed. The defenders of Constantinople hailed this amazing victory as a glorious omen, and believed that these four triumphant vessels were the forerunners of a fleet of deliverance.

They needed all the encouragement they could draw from this success ; for, within the city, signs and omens augured ill to the Christians. A statue of the Virgin, which was being carried in procession, fell from the shoulders of her bearers, and could be raised only with the utmost difficulty. Late in the spring, a dense fog enveloped the city, and it was believed that God had abandoned Constantinople and was passing away in a cloud. It was not easy to explain a miraculous light which shone over St. Sophia ; both Greeks and Turks shook their heads over it, and felt that evil was brewing for the city.

His ignominious naval defeat stirred Mahomet to greater cruelties and activity. It is impossible to give a detailed account of the progress of the siege, which is both complicated and tedious.   A double wall and a ditch encircled the city ; the latter is said to have been a hundred feet deep.   Upon the walls, sparsely manned by the force of mercenaries and untrained men, Constantine looked down upon Mahomet's admirable modern cannon, his well-trained troops, and all the siege implements of antiquity—scaling ladders, battering rams and wheeled towers.   Unless reinforcements arrived —and he could expect none—the siege could only have one result.

The Turks were tireless in their attempts to fill up the great ditch round the city, while their batteries did not cease, night and day, from pounding at the walls, and opening some effective breaches.   The citizens, unfortunately, were not nerved to feats of valour by these intimations of Turkish superiority ;   they merely redoubled their imprecations against Allah, and prayed a little more fervently for succour.   It was easier to do this than to aid an unorthodox Emperor by force of arms.   Mahomet offered the city immunity on the payment of an enormous ransom, or on condition that everyone should leave the city and allow it to fall, deserted, into his hands.   These offers were refused—Constantine had never, at any time during the siege, shown signs of weakness or terror—and Mahomet, after a council of war, proceeded to a grand attack.

Throughout the night torches flamed through the Turkish camp, as the followers of the Sultan fasted and prayed in readiness for the great day.   Mahomet, after a final survey of the walls of the city and of his own forces, summoned his leaders and delivered a discourse which has become famous.   He whetted their appetites by telling them of the glories of the city—the gold and the silver, the palaces and the gardens, the lovely women and boys of the noble families.   He told them that the enemy were weak and weary ; that there were dissensions among the foreigners who were defending the walls.   According to

Gibbon, he promised his troops double pay for a successful assault ; while his dervishes visited the tents to attend to the spiritual aspirations of the troops, assuring them an eternal youth amongst the houris of Paradise if they fell in so righteous a cause. " The city and buildings," Mahomet said, " are mine ; but I resign to your valour the captives and the spoil, the treasures of gold and beauty ; be rich and be happy. Many are the provinces of my empire ; the intrepid soldier who first ascends the walls of Constantinople, shall be rewarded with the government of the fairest and the most wealthy ; and my gratitude shall accumulate his honours and fortunes above the measure of his own hopes."

Within the city walls, a very different scene was being enacted. There had been no doubt, from the bustle in the enemy's camp, that the greatest attack of all was being launched ; now the Turks' silence and fasting seemed even more ominous to those listening from the city walls. A last religious procession was held through the streets of Constantinople, where all who could be spared from the defences collected, watching the passage of the ikons and the sacred emblems and praying God to deliver His city from the hands of the Turks. The Emperor, following the example of all heroes of antiquity, called his captains together, and told them that he was prepared to die in the defence of his religion and his Empire. The Turk, he said, had provoked the war, and wished to enslave the citizens ; he urged them to fight bravely, to remember that they were the offspring of the heroes of antiquity, and to try to emulate their feats of valour. He then gave a separate address to the Venetians and the Genoese, who had supported him throughout the siege ; thanked them for the help ; and assured them that he and they together were still more than a match for the besiegers.

In the evening, the Church of St. Sophia was thronged

THE TAKING OF CONSTANTINOPLE IN 1453 BY THE TURKS

*After the painting by J. H. Valda*

for its last Christian service. The townsfolk who had avoided it because of its defilement by Latin rites now crowded into it in their extremity. Emperor and nobles, Venetians, Genoese and Spaniards, all sent representatives to this tragic ceremony. The last mass was celebrated, and the defenders went out to their posts. Constantine returned to his palace to rest; then took solemn leave of his household, asking their pardon for any hurt he might have done them. He, and they, knew that he was leaving them for ever.

The attack began, long before daybreak, on every side of the city. Giustiniani was wounded severely enough to make him retire from the ramparts; his loss at such a moment of crisis was irreparable. His followers lost heart, and the cry arose "The City is lost." He has been accused of cowardice, of sacrificing the city to a slight inconvenience; but his wound was so severe that he died, some days later, on the island of Chios, whither he withdrew in his vessel. In view of his stout courage throughout the siege, it seems impossible to suspect him of cowardice at the last moment; yet some contemporary historians insist that he deserted his gate, and left it open to the Turks. No such charge can be laid against Constantine. He immediately took command of the gate which Giustiniani had left, and rallied his men.

But the Janissaries were already swarming up the walls to a breach that had been made, and, led by the gigantic Hassan of Ulubad, they gained the summit. Hassan, who has become a national hero, was killed immediately; but the sight of his success nerved on the others who, inflamed by Mahomet's promises of reward, crowded after him. They were able to hoist the Turkish flag, and the cry rang out once more, "The City is taken." Constantine flung himself into the middle of the fight, and checked the onslaught of the Turks for a few moments. He prudently

F

threw away his imperial insignia, realising the exquisite indignities which would await him if he were captured alive ; and went down beneath the triumphant Turks. When his body was recovered, it was so terribly disfigured that it could only be identified by the golden eagles on the sandals.

St. Sophia had remained full all through this dreadful night ; when morning broke, and the news ran through the city that the Turks were entering the city, every Christian sought sanctuary there. The citizens still hoped for the miracle which would save them and their city ; it needed, indeed, the sound of Turkish axes upon the barred doors of the church to make them realise that all was lost. Within an hour, the fugitives were dead or roped together, the spoil of the conquerors ; the holy ornaments and vessels of the great church were being carried off in triumph by revelling Janissaries ; the streets ran with blood. The Turks took the precaution to put all aged people to death, saving only the flower of the city for their own uses.

The morning was given over to pillage and murder. In the afternoon the Sultan made a triumphant entry into the city, through the ruined gate of St. Romanus, and entered St. Sophia. He immediately ordered this to be converted into a mosque, and the remains of the sacred pictures, vessels and vestments were removed ; priceless frescoes and mosaics were painted out and, as soon as the church presented the bareness and simplicity which Islam demands in its places of worship, an *imam* ascended the pulpit and a *muezzin* cried from the roof that there was no God but Allah, and that Mahomet was his prophet.

In the meantime, such Venetians and Genoese as were able to escape from the city sought their vessels, at the entrance to the outer harbour. While the Turks were occupied in pillaging the city, the foreigners managed to embark their families and belongings.  But the Venetian and Spanish baileys, or consuls, were captured and beheaded —a fate which they shared with the Grand Duke Notaras. The Papal Legate managed to escape in disguise.

It is estimated that more than fifty thousand Christians were killed or enslaved after the fall of the city.  So great, indeed, was the loss of population that Mahomet subsequently forced Turkish families to take up their residence there, and even released some of his Christian captives, in order that they might repopulate the city.

Such was the fall of Constantinople, the news of which caused a thrill of horror throughout the Western world. During the previous half-century and more, a trickle of learned men, not only Greeks, from Constantinople had found their way into Italy, Germany and France, teaching Greek and spreading a knowledge of classic Greek literature, the foundation of true culture.  It is frequently said that the spread of Greek learning dates from the fall of Constantinople ; but it had begun almost a hundred years earlier and the stream of exiles which flowed from this catastrophe served only to supply an already existing, and constantly increasing, demand for Greek learning and Greek manuscripts.  The flowers of Renaissance culture in Italy were already deeply in love with Greek.  Boccaccio, a hundred years before, had given shelter and assistance to Leontius, the first Greek lecturer in Italy, and had helped to popularise his lectures in Florence.  Many ardent Italian scholars had already found their way to Constantinople, returning laden with manuscripts ; the Levantine agents of the Medici had standing instructions to purchase manuscripts whenever possible.

Now both manuscripts and teachers might be had for the asking ; not many years had elapsed before this Greek culture had spread even to England, where Sir Thomas More and Henry VIII imbibed great draughts of it ; and it became the glory and the inspiration of the age of Elizabeth.

Mahomet II was too far-seeing a statesman to ruin the city which he had conquered. He crowned St. Sophia with minarets, and made her only less sacred than Mecca to the Mahomedan mind. He repaired the damage that he had done to the city, and even, for a time, permitted the surviving Greeks peacefully to practise their religion.

Soon this privilege was removed. Constantinople became the capital of the Turkish Empire, and a standing challenge to European Christendom. Such she has ever since remained. There was a short period, barely a dozen years ago, when it seemed that at last the work of Mahomet II would be undone and the last Constantine avenged. But revolution destroyed the Russian hopes of capturing the City ; Islam still triumphed.

As if contemptuous of this respite, the Turks themselves have now degraded Constantinople. Removing his capital to the huts and hovels of Angora, in the Anatolian plain, Turkey's present ruler has struck heavily at the prosperity, the importance and the population of the City. Hitherto no disaster has been great enough permanently to ruin it. I do not believe that Mustapha Kemal will succeed in an endeavour which even Mahomet II dared not consummate.

# THE NAVIGATIONS OF COLUMBUS

TO appreciate Columbus it is necessary to understand the fifteenth century. Nowadays it is an axiom that the world is round, and its surface has been almost completely explored. If one sails to the West naturally one reaches America. What would be simpler ?

In the fifteenth century no one knew. Men were sailing along the coast of Africa towards what was thought to be a boiling sea, and had ventured past the Equator. Some had been driven westward and talked of strange birds and trees found floating in the waters. There were stories too in the Fortunate Islands of alien corpses being floated ashore, belonging to a race of which no one had ever heard. It was believed there also lay in the Western Seas certain blessed islands which no one had ever visited. There may too have been stories, based on the Vikings' visits to the Vineland, which also supported the notion that strange lands lay to the West. The wiser and more learned must have known that some of the Ancients had asserted that the Earth must be round, but it was dangerous to be too assertive, since the general view of the Church was that the world was flat and in the Centre of the Universe. It is true that many of the higher and erudite clergy were aware that this current idea might well be wrong, but it is dangerous to combat the instinctive beliefs of the multitude who would be certain to consider that a departure from the accepted view was a dangerous heresy.

For Europe, the Atlantic was the boundary of the globe.

Did not everybody know that the world was surrounded by a broad river ? Despite sailors' yarns no one had ever found that there was anything beyond the Ocean. Besides, it was dangerous. Apart from storms and the other perils of the sea, there was the risk of falling off at the extreme edge, and in any case what was the use of going there to see how far it was ?

No one but an exceptional man favoured by exceptional fortune would dream of going to find out.

The times were exceptional. For more than a millennium the Byzantine Empire had held the key to the East, from which Europe derived necessaries for the people as well as luxuries for the great and the rich. At last that Empire had succumbed to the repeated onslaughts of the Turks, and for many years the land route to the Orient was closed. The problem of reaching the East by another route was engaging the attention of statesmen, tradesmen and mariners. The idea that Africa could be circumnavigated was widespread and the Portuguese were well on the way which shortly was to bring them to India. Another notion held then, and which survived for many years, was that sea routes could belong to individual kings. If there was a sea voyage round Africa to India, then it belonged to the King of Portugal. It was not long before Vasco de Gama found the way, but in the days of Columbus' obscurity the task remained as yet incomplete.

Columbus was an exceptional man. Many incidents in his career can only be explained by assuming that he was not sane in the normal sense. The ordinary sober common-sense man indeed would never have wasted time on this man's pet project. He claimed to be an Italian of Genoa and this is probably true, though some have denied it for reasons which are not altogether without weight. He said he was of noble birth, and that is almost certainly untrue. He claimed an experience in sea affairs which is contradicted by his conduct in his known voyages. His powers of persuasion, undoubtedly great, seem to have influenced only those in high places ; he had little control over subordinates. Gifted as he was with the power of enlisting the support of those who favoured his projects, he was almost devoid of that judgment of men which is the secret of command.

Columbus was undoubtedly a product of the Middle Ages. He had read widely but without selection and he was imbued with the mediæval notion that the speculations of the learned must be true, even if not tested by experience. Moreover, once he had conceived the notion that the world was round, he accepted all that he read and heard in a sense that would support his favourite theory. The ideas of philosophers, the observations of the scientists and the stories of mariners were all gathered together as of equal value, if only they seem to confirm his fixed idea. If the World was indeed round, then it followed that to reach the East you need only sail West.

How he spent his early life cannot be stated with any certainty, but in 1477 in early middle life he is found in Portugal, the leading maritime State, urging on the King the practicability of reaching the East by sailing West past the legendary Islands to China and Japan. Of a Continent lying between Europe and Asia neither he nor anyone else had the slightest conception : he died still believing that he had discovered the sea route to China. At this time he must have been about forty. He made no progress with his suit, but did get into communication with the aged Toscanelli who had calculated the circumference of the Globe and had drawn the deduction that from Europe to India by Western seas was merely a distance of 130 degrees. He had indeed sent a map to the King of Portugal in 1474 showing distances to China and Japan and also to the legendary Island of Antilia, some 1500 miles, as he thought, nearer than Japan. Columbus by some means obtained access to this neglected map and wrote to Toscanelli, who sent him another with a letter of encouragement. This map, though he never spoke of it, was the chart by which he sailed.

By 1481 Columbus was suing the new King, John. He procured an audience and mightily swayed the King, who was dissuaded by his sceptical advisors. Columbus was refused and in some way came into conflict with the law. In a state of extreme poverty he fled to Spain in 1484 with his son Diego. Exhausted with hunger and thirst he sought alms at the Monastery of La Rabida, and there met the Prior, who had been the Confessor of Queen Isabella, and a monk who was an accomplished cosmographer. In the Monastery, he regained strength, increased his knowledge and gained a friend who could influence the highest lady in Spain. He took heart and approached the King and Queen. They listened to a man so favourably commended, but did nothing. The offer of an undiscovered Empire weighed little with Castile and Aragon, then engaged in a desperate war to expel the Moors from their last strong holding in Spain. Every penny and every man was needed for that great enterprise. Until Spain was united under the Cross, no other venture could be undertaken. Spain cannot be reproached for rejecting the plan. It was carefully considered. Statesmen, warriors and ecclesiastics all examined the scheme from their respective points of view. Columbus was designedly nebulous. He was not even perfectly open. His brother was at work on the same proposals placed before the King of England and the King of France.

Columbus came to Granada in 1491 and witnessed the fall of that stronghold. The Royal advisors took up his suit. They were not impressed, but their goodwill was forfeited by his great demands. He was finally refused and

COLUMBUS IN SIGHT OF LAND

started on the journey to France to renew there for the third time his search for the means to effect his discoveries.

But he had convinced some of the officials. The Queen's lady companion urged her to comply even if Ferdinand would not. Isabella was after all Queen of Castile in her own right, if Ferdinand were King of Aragon. She granted an audience to Sant Angel, the Treasurer of Aragon, who was determined to make one last effort.

It was a tremendous moment. Portugal might at any time send her sailors across the Atlantic. Columbus was about to make an offer to France. Either might have gained the prize for which Spain was declining to strive. If Sant Angel had failed, the whole history of the world would have been altered.

Isabella proved worthy of the occasion. She saw Sant Angel and was convinced. The cost was not excessive, and if Columbus' demands were extreme, they were the reward of success alone. Who could say that such claims were excessive, if he did prove to be right ? She consented. Columbus was recalled, and at Santa Fé on August 17th, 1492, he signed the agreement under which he was to sail to Antilia and the East across the Atlantic.

All that remained was to equip the expedition. By one of the freaks of fortune the town of Palos in Andalusia, as a punishment for some delinquency in the war with the Moors, gained the distinction of furnishing the Squadron. For twelve months, the sentence had run, she was to maintain two caravels in the royal service. The Queen therefore had only to provide one. For crews, there was need for more extreme measures. On April 30th, 1492, a royal decree promised exemption from criminal process to all who should enlist with Columbus. A few months passed by in recruiting and equipping, but at last on August 3rd, 1492, the three vessels weighed anchor and left Palos for the Canaries. They reached their first port without undue mishap, and after a final refit they sailed for the Canaries on September 6th, 1492, bound Westward to the unknown.

Columbus commanded a curious company—sailors and soldiers, criminals and priests. Nearly all were Spaniards, hating the command of a Genoese ; most of them were ignorant, few believed in Columbus or his adventure, but all, including the Admiral, believed the voyage would not be long. Some were scared ; others half persuaded that the journey was an impiety ; most chafed at a foreigner's domination. The state that the Admiral maintained, the naval routine and the military discipline, concealed the spirit of mutiny. Day after day passed by. Nothing happened. Nothing could be seen but sea and sky, and men grew weary, especially as the presence of priests restrained their freedom. Sometimes, indeed, there were signs. A land bird was seen but it departed, and the sea and sky again remained the only things that met the eye. Then floating vegetation raised hopes and expectations, but again the flotsam, left behind, did not fulfil the promise of land. Again day followed day. Murmurs arose. The faint-hearted despaired, the cowardly took fright and the spirit of mutiny stirred. Still no land. More and more became downhearted, and it became manifest that soon Columbus would be unable to control the desire to return. At last matters came to a crisis. A request was made that he should order the ships to shape their course for Spain. It was a request, but one to which blunt refusal was impossible. Should he yield ; should he refuse ? In either case, the grand adventure was over ; his choice was merely whether to return as the discredited leader or as the superseded Admiral. It was a tremendous moment. Columbus knew that he could not refuse, but he temporised. The wily Italian believed that land was near at hand. So he agreed to their demand. If no land were found within

*From a painting by R. Balaca*

COLUMBUS RECEIVED IN AUDIENCE BY FERDINAND AND ISABELLA ON HIS RETURN FROM HIS FIRST VISIT TO AMERICA

three days, then the course would be shaped for home.  It was October 9th, 1492.

They were then nearly three thousand miles from the Canaries and thirty-four days had passed.  Even making allowance for contrary winds and currents, their progress must have been wearily slow, and as time went by and the ships' bottoms, unprotected by sheathing, grew fouler, and the provisions became rank and water and bilges began to stink, the ignorant and fearful must have found this voyage into the unknown too much for their faint hearts.  They had plucked up courage to demand retreat, and if the next three days proved as uneventful as the others, the decisive moment would have passed and the report would have come back : " Nothing but an empty waste of waters." Later, no doubt, the mystery would have been solved, but by others.  Spain had this chance.  If the moment passed, her opportunity would be lost.

Again two days passed without incident, but on the night of October 11th a light was seen.  There could be no doubt about its being of human origin, and Columbus and his officers felt assured that land would be sighted.  Next morning the look-out announced that the long-expected goal was reached.  It was a small island inhabited by a peaceful brown-skinned race and is known to be one of the Bahama Islands.  Columbus had set forth to discover a new route to Asia.  His calculations had underestimated the circumference of the earth and he never realised that he had not discovered the way to the Indies.  To him during his life the lands he discovered were the Indies and that is why to-day they are known as the West Indies.  On that voyage he did not touch the mainland, nor was he the first to do so, and it was left to Magellan to pass the new Continent and make the voyage which by its success showed that Columbus' idea was right and that by the West one could reach the East.

The fame of Columbus and his achievement which has so profoundly affected the world's history rests therefore on two decisive moments. When all was over and the years of effort had been fruitless, he was wearily journeying to France to begin again a twice-told tale ; at that moment Isabella was convinced by the sincere eloquence of Sant Angel, and the discovery of America was assured to Spain. But another moment came when yielding to the fears of cowards would have defeated the plans of Columbus and the faith of Isabella. By temporising, the opportunity was retained. The decisive moment passed. Columbus discovered America.

# THE REFORMATION

ADEQUATELY to describe the Reformation, or even to outline its main features, within the limits of a short essay would be a task as ambitious as that of attempting to carve the Thirty-nine Articles on a sixpence. I am not so presumptuous as to undertake it. I shall be well satisfied if, in this paper, I suggest a few lines of thought which will indicate a modern outlook on this most debated of all historical events.

We must add to the ordinary disputatiousness of historians over past events, incompletely vouched, an emotional bias imported into so many studies of the Reformation by the added complication of sectarian rivalry. No writer on the Reformation can hope to please both Protestant and Roman Catholic readers. He will certainly end by pleasing nobody. I shall, however, endeavour to save myself from the more violent elements of criticism by stating at the outset that I do not propose to discuss the Reformation, in its origin or in its development, from the point of view of religious doctrine. Its religious factors mean little to us to-day, even if some of them still survive in new forms. Its political interest, however, remains. I hope, therefore, that I shall be suspected neither of bigoted anti-Romanism, nor, on the other hand, of anæmic Protestant sympathies if I abstain from any prolonged discussion, or expressions of personal opinion, upon the doctrinal differences bound up with the Reformation ; and if I treat its most respected (or detested) protagonists rather as figures in a political tapestry than as the appointed agents of Heavenly (or Hellish) powers.

The most outstanding fact about the Reformation, to my modern view, was its inevitability. The Renaissance, with its quickening of learning, its broadening of mind, and its development of individual thought among scholars throughout Europe, made necessary some sort of change in the Roman Church. No religious body could regard with equanimity, in a period of introspection and self-criticism, its defilement by such men as the Borgia Pope, Alexander VI, whose record of simony, unchastity, incest and murder had, at the beginning of the sixteenth century, brought the Papacy into contempt among pious Catholics of authority. Had Alexander concealed his crimes until he was seated on the papal throne, they might have brought themselves to regard him as an isolated example of decadence ; but his character was well known at the time when he bribed the cardinals to elect him ; consequently his shame was shared by them, and, in lesser degree, by all who conceded respect to them and him.

Certainly, the extent of Alexander's private failings was known to few ; but his public crimes were hardly less flagrant. Nepotism may in some spheres of activity be defended as a means of ensuring fidelity and competence among one's subordinates ; but nepotism in the Church, carried to shaming lengths at the expense of pious and competent Catholics who had not the worldly advantage and spiritual disadvantage of being Alexander's intimates, was evidently flagitious. Men might have overlooked the Holy Father's private sins as his own affair, for which he would eventually have to account ; they could not pass over his crimes against the Church.

Moreover, the Renaissance made necessary a restatement of Christianity for a world which had now become aware that other civilisations had existed before the Roman

Catholic, and that the voice of God had been heard of old by devout peoples through other lips preaching other doctrines. Both on religious and ethical grounds men demanded a new spirit. At last a few greatly daring called in question the complete intellectual authority of the Church. It does not follow that they were bound then to rebel against it ; but at least some reasoned proof of the Church's right to supreme spiritual authority was demanded.

The Roman Church, then as now conservative, was slow to move ; but motion none the less, if almost imperceptible, began. The Pope, Julius II, began his term by driving out of Italy the Borgias, to whom he owed his election ; he published a bull against simony ; and in other directions set reforms in motion. It is true that his successor, Leo X (Giovanni de' Medici), reverted to the worst traditions of simony, but at least he was a learned and enlightened man vigilant to note the cultural advances of the Renaissance. By the middle of the sixteenth century the internal reform of the Church was in full march. Protestant writers have often been too much inclined to pass over the great change which took place in the Church in these years, and culminated in the counter-Reformation. The Council of Trent, which was held between 1545 and 1563, restated the Catholic attitude towards all the most important questions of the day. It cut away most of the rotten wood from the tree, and directed the progress of the new growths. It strengthened discipline ; above all, it put new life into a body which had fallen behind contemporary movement. The foundation of the Society of Jesus by Loyola in 1539 provided the Church with a body of devoted, energetic and intelligent servants who fought valiantly to suppress the rising tide of scepticism and to counterbalance the Protestant heresies. It is true that, in so far as large portions of the old Church were concerned, these efforts came too late ; but it would be a grave error to overlook their significance. They demonstrate, in relation to the religious decadence of the Church in the previous century, that it was capable, under pressure, of restoring its intellectual supremacy. We are thrown back, therefore, more and more upon the political features of the Reformation to explain why the power of the Church was so seriously compromised at this period.

That sooner or later the Pope would have lost his power over the Protestant countries, I cannot doubt. It is a curious feature of the Reformation that its influence was greatest in the Teutonic countries, smallest in the others. Germany, Scandinavia and England became predominantly Protestant ; Spain, Italy and France remained fundament-ally Catholic. It would seem that the Teutonic races have some deep stamp of Protestantism upon their blood. Modern scientists have discovered that the liability of individuals to certain diseases can be known from blood tests. I do not regard it as impossible that some day this process may be carried a stage further, and the type of a man's beliefs—no matter what his profession—may be determined by his physical composition, so that it will be possible to say, " This man is really a Roman Catholic—or a Low Churchman—or a Freethinker, etc."

A school of historians, led or at least most popularly expressed by the robust writings of Mr. Hilaire Belloc, declares that the character of a people depends upon its religion. I take the opposite view : I believe that the beliefs of a nation are conditioned by its cultural characteristics. Thus, I hold that whether or not Henry VIII had fallen foul of the Pope over the matter of his divorce, whether or not Elizabeth had been faced by her Spanish struggles, it would have been as impossible to keep England Catholic as it would have been, or would be to-day, to transform Spain into a Protestant country. I call to mind the example of Bohemia, nowadays clumsily called, for political reasons,

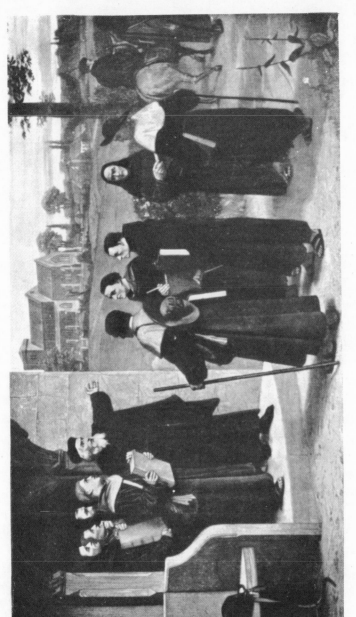

THE DAWN OF THE REFORMATION
Tyndale sending out his preachers.

Czecho-Slovakia. John Hus was as typical a Bohemian as ever lived ; centuries of Catholicism imposed and reimposed by the Austrians upon his countrymen have not changed their nature in the slightest degree. No matter how much they were persecuted ; no matter to what extent Protestantism was officially stamped out ; no matter how Catholic they were pronounced by authority ; the Bohemians remained, and remain to-day, one of the most evidently Protestant peoples of Europe. No one acquainted with their national characteristics can doubt that Catholicism is alien to their minds. You can no more compel such a people to remain Catholic at heart, than you can force a genuinely Catholic nation to relinquish its deep-seated formularies.

These reflections emphasise the social and political significance of the Reformation. It is not even true, as has often been supposed, that this mighty movement represented the affirmation of the rights of the individual conscience against the intellectual claims of Rome. Neither the Renaissance nor the Reformation stood for " individualism " in this sense. A powerful prince might certainly allow himself the luxury of private scepticism ; he might permit his favourite scholars the same pleasure. But he would have been shocked into corrective action by the notion that the humbler of his subjects were entitled to decide religious and philosophic questions for themselves. Nor did such a prince require the stimulus of the Renaissance or the Reformation for this privilege ; the mere possession of power had conferred it even in the darkest days of the Middle Ages. The theory that an individual conscience has inviolable rights is a fruit of later days. Some of its seeds may indeed have been sown in the fifteenth and sixteenth centuries, but they survived only by chance. A good Lutheran would have been scarcely less vehement in his distrust of this heresy than the most obscurantist Roman abbot.

G

Nor is it correct to suppose that the most educated and enlightened men of the age were necessarily Reformers. While it is certain that the revival of learning in the Renaissance had cleared such men's minds of many inhibitions and superstitions, that writer exaggerates who suggests that they led the revolt against the theocracy of Rome. Their new knowledge of the Pagan civilisations was unlikely to fill them with a profound veneration for the literal inspiration of the Bible, which was one of the corner-stones of Reformist teachings ; still less to make them oppose the authority of Rome, the product of centuries of leadership and experience, over the common people. They might smile at the more extreme claims of the Church, but the smile faded when they heard the not less violent, though certainly less mature, claims of the Reformers to be the inspired revealers of divine will. Of the two rivals for autocracy, these sceptics were bound rather to favour the older ; they could not suppose that a world in which a Luther or a Calvin reigned over men's minds was likely to provide a more congenial atmosphere for the propagation of classical studies than the Papacy.

It is rather to the growing sense of nationality that we must ascribe the success of the Reformation in those Teutonic countries which were intellectually predisposed towards its teachings. Society in those countries was growing a new skin ; the old withered and perished. The power of the Church represented a state within a state ; or, more exactly, new national borders had grown up round the various portions of the Church's domains. Even an especially powerful prince could hardly override the demands of Rome ; or by intrigue or compromise make these subserve his own interests. And, if his strength decayed, or if he became overweening in his resistance to the Church, he found himself menaced by an organisation which claimed that he was a rebellious vassal, and could

TYNDALE TRANSLATING THE BIBLE

summon his neighbours and his enemies (who in those days were usually the same) to teach him reason at the point of the sword. The moment then that various obscure individuals throughout Europe lifted their voices against the abuses of the Church, and even challenged the omnipotence of the Pope, ambitious princes readily accepted as much of this new movement of protest as served their own interests. For the most part, they regarded the Reformers with little real sympathy. One may picture their attitude as very similar to that of the German junkers in the Great War, who sent Bolshevists from Switzerland to Russia, backing them with money and equipment, but took care that Lenin and his colleagues should be incarcerated in a sealed train while they were passing through the domains of the exporting country. The German princelings most closely associated with the Reformers may, in some cases, have been moved by genuine feelings of intellectual agreement with them ; but it cannot be seriously doubted that, in general, they were much more moved by the prospect of autonomy. The Emperor was weaker than in previous generations ; the Hapsburg emergence had not yet overshadowed Central Europe. There was, therefore, an opportunity for ambitious princes to become undisputed masters of their own realms, and, what touched them very closely, of drawing the whole of the revenues available for pious purposes so large a portion of which had heretofore been deflected Romewards.

It is impossible to calculate the gigantic drain of wealth which, until then, had flowed from Central and Northern Europe to Rome. The clergy are estimated by some authorities to have owned a quarter of the land on which they paid no taxes. The amount may have been less but it sufficed. Half their income went to Rome ; indulgences and benefices were sold without concealment ; and, though this is more shocking to modern ears than to contemporary, verdicts were bought and sold in the Ecclesiastical courts. Moreover, Mother Church, reinforced by threats of punishment in the next as in this world, wielded powers as revenue collectors more potent than those of the temporal authorities. Naturally the princes' revenues suffered; the richest peasant, like the beautiful girl of the fairy tale, could give no more than he possessed. And having tasted relief he was disinclined to give again.

For centuries the Church had added field to field, treasure to treasure, imagining thereby that she secured herself against every eventuality, that her riches provided insurance against the ingenious perversity of the heretic or the arms of the infidel. A full treasury could finance a campaign of suppression against any internal revolt; it could equally induce princes to lend their armaments, and mercenary captains to equip forces, against any dangers which threatened the Church from outside.

By the irony of events these great possessions of hers ensured the permanent success of the Reformation. The most perfect proof of this may be seen by a glance at the process of the English Reformation.

Henry VIII's decision to suppress the monasteries, and to share their possessions with the newly created Tudor aristocracy finally decided the end of Roman Catholic supremacy as an English religion. When Mary succeeded her brother Edward VI, she strove with all the intensity of her fanatical nature to restore the Roman establishment in England to the precise situation it enjoyed before her father destroyed it. But even she, prepared to restore the Faith by the headsman's axe and the stake, could not persuade the lords to surrender the monastic property which they had obtained under the terms of so happy a development.

They might have abandoned the Lutheran faith which in Edward's short reign had been imposed upon the

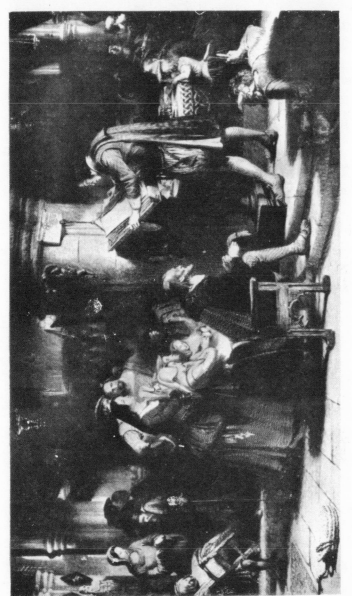

READING THE BIBLE IN OLD ST. PAUL'S

country ; they might have returned to the Mass ; they might have bowed once more to Cardinal and Nuncio. But they would not return their new property to the Church.

This process, so perfectly exemplified in England, obtained in a less complete degree in every country where the Reformation was successful. It is, indeed, the commonest reason for the success of all permanent revolutions. The root-cause of the success of the first French Revolution was that the peasants of France had seized the estates of their former lords and set themselves up as peasant proprietors. Afterwards they might support an emperor, who gave concrete embodiment to the French desire for glory ; they might support a republic which expressed their feelings for politics as a recreation ; but on no account would they tolerate a return of the Bourbons, even though the reform of every abuse which caused the Revolution was assured. For such a return implied the threat that once again their hold on the land would be loosed.

It is perhaps not idle to speculate what course the Reformation might have taken had the Church maintained her apostolic poverty. Since the days of primitive penury she had fashioned from her own ranks one shining example of the political value of complete poverty. St. Francis of Assisi triumphed because he insisted that his followers should literally own nothing but the meagre garments in which they stood. This Saint proved that the man who has no possessions is the most powerful of adversaries. He has nothing to lose except his life, and, since most fanatics are indifferent to this ultimate possession, he cannot be punished for any action except at the risk of conferring on him the martyrdom which he seeks.

An indigent Pope, supported by a penniless church, might have been strong enough to withstand the Reformation. Rome would have feared no dispossessions or evictions ; it would have been supported by the awful and unearthly glory which deliberate poverty confers. The ordinary man is so concerned with amassing wealth, that the spectacle of fellow-creatures choosing the austerities of a vagrant and penniless life, the better to serve ideals which he himself can understand, is peculiarly moving. He sentimentally believes that whatever is undertaken without thought of personal gain—by which, of course, he means only material wealth, forgetting the no less insistent desire for fame and notoriety—must be a noble óbject.

The sale of indulgences was undoubtedly the weakest point in the Church's demands on the people. It is not surprising, therefore, that Martin Luther found in his denunciation of this practice the greatest measure of support from all classes. When he nailed his ninety-five theses on the door of the Wittenberg church in November 1517—an incident which has come to be accepted as the turning point of the Reformation—the items which aroused most enthusiasm among their readers were those challenging the sale of indulgences. Luther argued that God alone could remit the penalty of sins ; the Church could not do so. Nor had the Church power over souls in Purgatory ; its dominion was only over the living. A sinner who felt and showed repentance was secure of God's pardon ; while the Church might exact penalties for offences against its authority, it could not—by penalties or their remission for money payments—give pardons for sins against God.

It is clear that the Church did not lack answers to this argument ; though I do not propose to enter into a discussion of them here. But, once Luther had enunciated his theory, he had made himself, almost unconsciously, the mouthpiece of the new movement in Christendom.

There had been many reformist movements before him. One might say that each of the great heretical movements inside the Church in preceding centuries had been, to some extent, attempts at a Reformation. In our own country,

Wycliffe, in the fourteenth century, had anticipated some of the main features of the Reformation teachings by challenging the temporal power of the Pope and denouncing transubstantiation ; Hus, Marsillius and others had set themselves up at various times in opposition to Rome's claims. But the Church had been strong enough to suppress these symptoms of rebellion. Luther was more fortunate. Not only had he set himself at the head of a widespread movement, but he found himself supported by the secular powers, to the extent at least of protecting him from the worst anger of Rome and permitting him to pursue, somewhat erratically, his enquiries into his own beliefs and the rightful powers of the Church.

Luther is the touchstone of histories of the Reformation. According to the sympathies of the writers, he is displayed as either an inspired saint or a fanatical lunatic. For my part, I see no reason to accept either of these views. That Luther was physically abnormal is certain. Dr. MacLaurin, in an entertaining volume of historical psychopathy, asserts on reasonable authority that Luther's devil—who shouted and roared in his ears—was the produce of a distressing complaint known as " Menière's disease of the labyrinth," which was also accountable for his later deafness. It would also seem that he suffered from an excess of uric acid and a phenomenally high blood pressure. " If there be any worse devil," says Dr. MacLaurin, " than frightful noises in the head, neurasthenia and uric acid in the blood, it would be interesting to learn what it is. Many a man has been driven to suicide by nothing worse."

Luther's physical troubles undoubtedly contributed to a mental condition which sometimes approximated to madness. But all genius approximates to madness ; his violent fervour and determination are as much its attributes as his more extravagant outbursts of superstition.

He was undoubtedly a very great man. There is no

warrant for belittling him as a mere figurehead, whom the Reformed churches afterwards set up as a hero. His prominence and his success were indeed largely due to the favourable circumstances of the moment in which he acted ; but they would have been equally favourable for any other man of his calibre who had acted in the same manner. That he stood alone proved his merit.

The only other figure who, to my mind, emerges on a scale comparable with Luther was Calvin. Though he, like his predecessor, was racked with disease, his brain was cooler and more analytic. Luther blazed a trail, but Calvin, with the practical vision of the Swiss among whom he made his home, paved it with sentiments and formulæ which made it agreeable both to the Protestant peoples who wished to tread it, and to the secular rulers who founded upon it their new independence. Luther was a fighter, a rebel, a visionary. Calvin was a builder, a reconciler, a man of judgment. And for this reason his creed has outdone Lutheranism. Luther set out to serve God ; Calvin to reconcile Luther's God with man.

# THE GLORIOUS REVOLUTION

THE death of Charles II was neither dramatic nor unexpected. He had long lain ill, tormented by the measures his regiment of medical attendants devised to cure him. He had been bled, cupped, poulticed and bled again. The brains of an executed felon, fresh from the scaffold, had been hurriedly distilled into a potion for his consumption. He drank it obediently ; and when he grew too weak to enjoy the clinical wrangles which daily disturbed his bedroom, he still submitted with complete resignation to the remarkable measures his advisers adopted to prolong his life.

This prodigious medical ado seems to have been hopeless from the beginning of the King's illness. Although but fifty years old, Charles's life had not been passed in circumstances which commonly prelude longevity. A youth distracted by the Civil Wars and blighted by his father's execution ; an early manhood debauched by the tedium of exile ; a disposition which combined extreme indolence with extreme appetite—all these had worn out a physique tough but never robust, nor adapted to withstand the demands which the King so carelessly made on it.

The last years of Charles's life had certainly been his most contented, if not his happiest. Ever since he had dished them so consummately at the Oxford Parliament, the Whigs had ceased to trouble him. Anthony Ashley Cooper, first Earl of Shaftesbury, that rash intriguer, half demagogue, half philosophic speculator, who had created the Whigs and then allowed Charles to destroy them, fled to

Holland and exile, to pine and die of the combined ravages of dropsy and a broken heart. The rest of the Whigs, broken by the stupidity of the Rye House Plot, either trembled in hiding or died on the scaffold. Among those whom the Tory proscription thus removed were Russell and Sidney; it was perhaps a form of revenge after the King's own heart that their lives were sworn away by false witnesses who, as the King well knew, had previously perjured themselves to bring Catholics to the gallows.

Through the last four years of his reign Charles ruled without a parliament, and so he died happy; for it had been the political ambition of this strange dark creature to realise his father's desire and tame the stubborn Commons. His father, noble and dignified, whatever his faults, would never have considered the simple method by which his son achieved this end. When Parliament refused Charles I supplies to carry on his government, high words and warlike preparations ensued. When Parliament thwarted Charles II he dissolved it with a smile and subsisted on the gold of Louis XIV.

Yet, even though the Court during Charles's last years was a parasite on France, the King's advisers were sharply divided in their attitude towards this source of income. Halifax, cautious and foreboding, headed a group which set its face against " French Counsels." The great Trimmer could already gauge the danger which Louis' ever advancing territorial sovereignty spelt to England. With uncanny prescience he understood that the gradual French domination of the Spanish Netherlands menaced England's existence as a free power. He feared the advancing armies of Turenne in the low countries far more than the French gold in Whitehall.

It is worth remarking in passing how justified Halifax was in his anxieties. Consciously or unconsciously English foreign policy has concentrated primarily on seeing that the sandy dunes of the Dutch and Flemish coasts, together with the mouths of the Scheldt, shall remain in the hands of a power unable to threaten our command of the sea. Thrice England has gone to war to ensure the maintenance of this state of affairs, and each time she has not contemplated peace until her end was achieved. Twenty years of bitter warfare were necessary under William of Orange and Anne before the French domination of the low countries was broken. A hundred years later Pitt financed the civilised world against Napoleon to attain the same object. To-day we are recovering from a war, precipitated, so far as England was concerned, by German invasion of Belgian territory.

Opposed to Halifax and his adherents in Charles's Whitehall palace stood the heir to the throne, James, Duke of York, and his parasites. On the day when Charles finally expired—after whispering his last pleasantry : " Gentlemen : I am afraid that I am an unconscionable time in dying "—James appeared to inherit all the power and prestige which his elder brother had amassed during these last despotic years. Not even the most sanguine of their adherents dared to hope for the Whigs' revival. James's Roman Catholic religion was a secret so open that it had long ceased to provide even the most bankrupt comedian with the substance of a jest. His stony animosity against the Whigs was notorious and natural. Had they not been broken in an attempt to exclude him from the succession in favour of that handsome, weak bastard, the Duke of Monmouth, the day of English politics would indeed have been different.

In fact, as G. M. Trevelyan has justly observed, " Few political philosophers would have prophesied well of the party system or of Parliamentary government in the year 1685. The two parties, in their first wild boyhood, had set fire to their own house. But the severity of the immediate chastisement that fell on the Whigs and in the new reign of the Tories, taught them lessons of wisdom that enabled them in a few years to save Britain and to save Europe."

Feeling secure in his inherited power, James, almost as soon as he had buried his brother in Westminster Abbey and assumed the panoply of his new state, summoned a Parliament, chiefly composed of his own Tory adherents, and with nearly all the troublesome Whigs removed.

No sooner had this carefully selected body met than a stroke of luck established James more securely on his throne. The Duke of Monmouth landed in the West at Lyme Regis and launched his pathetic attempt to wrest the crown from his natural uncle.

The history of that insurrection does not concern us here, though perhaps we may take notice of one man who played the chief part in turning Sedgemoor into so crushing a rout for all Monmouth's hopes. This was a Major-General Churchill, not long since ennobled as Lord Churchill of Eyemouth in the peerage of Scotland, and lately advanced to the state of Baron Churchill of Sand-ridge in Hertfordshire. James dispatched this thirty-five-year-old soldier as second in command of the forces sent against Monmouth.

Churchill was born at Ash, near Axminster, the son of Winston Churchill. He was educated at St. Paul's School in London, and at fifteen his handsome bearing, charm of address and precocious talents won him a place as a page of honour to James, then Duke of York. From the day of this appointment he rapidly advanced his own career. A commission in the Guards took him on the Tangier expedition, the progress of which so disturbed Samuel Pepys ; the foundations of his pecuniary fortune were laid by a gift of £5000 from the Duchess of Cleveland, with which, as historians have observed as an example of his dominant trait, he was prompt to purchase an annuity ; his military talents were developed by service under Turenne against the Dutch. In 1678 he assured his future by marrying Sarah Jennings, an attendant on the Princess Anne, youngest daughter of James, and a companion on whom the Princess lavished all the abundant affection of her heart.

It was an age conspicuous for accomplished courtiers. A bland countenance, ready wit and urbane address distinguished many of the politicians and placehunters who thronged Whitehall. But Churchill shone among them in every courtly art and artifice, like a sun among stars. The individual he addressed became aware that this brilliant young soldier was not only his friend, but his special friend. He was cordial without being hearty ; intriguing as a gossip without ever rashly betraying a confidence ; adroit without appearing unpleasantly sharp-witted.

Behind this perfect manner, however, Churchill remained indifferent. Except for his wife Sarah, to whom he gave a full and absolute measure of devotion, this peculiar man cared for no human being. If we may judge of two soldiers so widely separated by time and ideas, his temper of mind probably resembled that of Julius Cæsar. Both were without apparent passion or feeling. Both trusted no one, were guided by reason always and by prejudice never, and both inspired the love of the soldiers whom they led to certain victory, and the envy and displeasure of all whom they dealt with as equals. Both perfectly exhibited " the featureless calm of Olympian power."

Having crushed Monmouth and handed him over to the cold fury of his master, Churchill retired temporarily from the direction of public affairs, though with his wife he retained the closest confidence of the Princess Anne. Yet the Sedgemoor expedition formed an important crisis in his destiny, and in that of his King. Because he had

crushed Monmouth, James trusted him, though he knew
well that Churchill entertained small sympathy with Roman
Catholics either in England or on the Continent. This
faith in a soldier's loyalty was one day to lose James his
crown and to inaugurate modern English history.

Confirmed in his prejudices by the happy issue of the
Monmouth episode, James quickly embarked on a policy
of political foolishness seldom paralleled in the catastrophic annals of absolutism. His vindictive revenge on all
who had taken Monmouth's part alienated from him the
sympathy of moderate men. He was strong enough to
afford mercy : Monmouth's and half a dozen heads would
have satisfied all the demands of contemporary political
convention and the vengeance of any reasonable monarch.
But such a modest blood-letting did not suit James. He
chose to unleash first Kirke with a soldiery debased in
their natures and their methods by their campaigning in
Tangier, and then Jeffreys who rounded off the work,
which they had so thoroughly begun, at his " bloody
assize."

The easy victory over his rebellious nephew misled
James into supposing himself able to accomplish all his
ambitions, regardless of the prejudices and determination
of his subjects. At his accession he was already secretly
resolved to devote his life to bringing back his realm and
subjects to their lost allegiance to the Roman faith. Now,
inflamed by Jesuit and French Councillors, he decided on
a drastic and rapid conversion of England to Catholicism.
He imagined that the High Tories and Churchmen would
not dare to oppose his design. The then fashionable doctrine of non-resistance to the royal prerogative misled him
to believe that Parliament and the Anglican Establishment
would allow him to conduct them back to Rome without
more than a murmur of protest.

As a first step to this end, and to prepare against possible resistance from the sulky Whigs or the " dissenting interest," he made excuse to maintain a force of 30,000 men on Hounslow Heath, hoping thereby to render London and Westminster docile. This army, moreover, he officered in the face of all law by Roman Catholics, who, aided in their congenial labour by a squad of priests, attempted to bribe, cajole or threaten the rank and file to profess Roman Catholicism.

The proselytising campaign, however, proceeded too slowly to satisfy James's impatient temper ; he imported a horde of raw Irish peasants and incorporated them in his army. This action finally destroyed all chances that might once have existed of transforming the Royal forces into an instrument which he could trust to extirpate Protestantism from the English shires.

These Irish recruits were mainly Erse-speaking rustics ; piously Roman, it is true, in their reverence to the priesthood, but regarded by their new comrades as wild barbarians, almost as savages from beyond the pale of civilisation. It is important to recognise how James, despite the thought, hard work and treasure he expended, signally failed in adapting the army to his purpose. Had he succeeded, he would not have lost his throne.

Nor did James manage to arouse much enthusiasm for his policy among the Roman Catholic gentry, who ought, of course, to have formed the backbone of his support. This body, large and not unmoneyed, was excluded by law from holding any public office ; but it lived on good terms with its Tory equals, unpersecuted and innocuous. The Catholic gentry realised instinctively what the King's bigoted folly prevented him from appreciating—that the old faith could not be re-established with the help of French gold ; French arms and invasion would be necessary for its accomplishment. And from such a military conversion even the most devoted Catholics shrank.

The next step towards James's downfall was taken not by himself but by his most " Christian Majesty " Louis XIV, who elected, in a mood of exalted piety, to revoke the Edict of Nantes, which tolerated Protestants in France. The revocation was promptly followed by a persecution of the Huguenots, who were pursued with such acute fanaticism that, in Trevelyan's considered words, " the sum of human misery thus wantonly brought about is horrible to contemplate."

This French persecution at once profoundly reacted in England. Fugitive Huguenots arrived here in thousands, with tales of torture, rape and murder. It needed no intelligence to draw the obvious moral ; the ancient cry, " No Popery," rang out even from the most absolute of Tory and Anglican strongholds. Yet James, blindly believing the priestly counsellors who sat nearest to him, stopped his ears against the warning. Secretly he envied Louis for boldly accomplishing the very act he itched to emulate.

The prestige and popularity of the Tories suddenly wilted. Country parsons, who a year before were expounding the sublime follies of non-resistance, and justifying from Scripture the King's claim to dispense with the laws of England whenever they thwarted his design, now confined their eloquence to exhortations to good works and industry. In dissenting conventicles, met in fear of the savage laws of the Clarendon Code, ministers waxed bold in their denunciations of another Nero, another Anti-Christ.

Their prayer and psalms, however, were interrupted, and in the most astonishing manner. From the position of despised and persecuted sectaries, the Nonconformists were suddenly raised to a brief but warm popularity. The King needed their aid to crush the Anglican Church, which the example of France had turned against him. The Church too, alarmed and furious, was prepared to go to

TITUS OATES

the extreme length of conciliating dissent, if the sects could aid it to discipline the King.

James's bait consisted of a promise of civil equality and toleration for all Christians, secured by illegal Declarations of Indulgences. The Church pledged itself to secure, for all Christians, excepting Roman Catholics, toleration which would be established by the statute of the first free Parliament gathered at Westminster. The Nonconformists looked back always to the brave days of Cromwell, when men were allowed to worship how they chose. They remembered that their only full measure of religious freedom was derived not from the Crown, but from one who, whatever he was in effect, was at least in theory a staunch Parliament man. They did not hesitate : they threw in their lot with the Anglican Tories against James.

Despairing of any longer covering his activities by even a pretence of constitutional practice, James now turned openly upon the property, rights and sometimes the persons of his opponents. Catholic priests were unashamedly presented to vacant livings. Magdalen College, Oxford, was turned into an avowed seminary for priests. Every parish parson was required to read from his pulpit a royal declaration suspending all statutes against Catholics and Dissenters.

Seven bishops, resolutely led by Sancroft, the Archbishop of Canterbury, approached the King with a petition that he should withdraw the command to read this profound illegal document. Without consideration or advice, James at once prosecuted them for seditious libel.

They stood their trial in London. Every precaution then known to legal ingenuity was exercised on the King's behalf to ensure their conviction. They were acquitted. London went mad with joy. On the same night, June 30th, 1688, a messenger left the capital for Holland. He was Admiral Herbert who, disguised as an ordinary seaman, carried a letter signed by seven great leaders of political opinion,

H

both Whig and Tory. It was addressed to William, Prince of Orange and Stadtholder of Holland, and invited him in unequivocal terms to bring an army to England and maintain its outraged liberties.

That this letter was despatched on the day of the Bishops' acquittal is merely a coincidence. The immediate reason why the invitation was extended to William was that, twenty days earlier, one of James's dearest ambitions had been realised. His second wife, Mary of Modena, was on that day confined and gave birth to a son, who lived to be known in history as " The Old Pretender." This event killed all hope that James's system was no more than a temporary affliction which would die with him. The news of this child's birth finally converted Thomas Osborne, Earl of Danby, to the necessity of sending for William. And, with Danby's conversion, the men who were powerful and skilful enough to engineer a revolution against James stood united.

During the next weeks the fate of England, and of all Europe, trembled on a knife-edge. It was not until November 2nd, that William sailed from Holland at the head of a respectable armament. Three days later he landed at Torbay, when the country he had come to save was commemorating the frustration of Guy Fawkes' plot to assassinate James II's grandfather and his Parliament.

What manner of saviour had England summoned to her rescue ? Those who first encountered him in Devonshire saw a spare man of middle size, whose long upper lip and acidulated look conveyed a first impression of steady egotism. His countenance had been fixed in youth into a mask of " Immobile, almost repulsive, coldness." Careless in dress, harshly brusque or preoccupied in his ordinary manner, he revealed none of the gracious condescension which so became a monarch in the eyes of the seventeenth century. Yet in that baleful glance, that thin straight mouth and pinched face, lay something compelling to even the most indifferent beholder. The man fascinated while he repelled. His personality possessed as little obvious attraction as a searching east wind, but, similarly, contact with it possessed tonic if not agreeable properties.

Let us glance at the events and heritage which had reduced the Prince of Orange during the thirty-eight years of his life to so unexpansive a creature. He was born at the Hague a few days after his father's death, his mother being Mary, daughter of King Charles of England. His father had planned and carried to success a *coup d'état* which promised him the enjoyment of supreme power in the Netherlands ; but before he could savour the first taste of his dominion, he contracted smallpox and quickly died. With no one to consolidate the fruits of this adventurous policy, they melted ; and his son, from babyhood, lived among men who abhorred his father's memory, and treated himself as an enemy. The control of the Netherlands passed into the hands of John de Witt, leader of the oligarchy of trading and moneyed interests, traditionally hostile to the House of Orange. So placed, William grew up suspicious, cautious and tight-lipped. Circumstances forced on his development to manhood ; his youth was spent in taking statesmen's decisions on questions affecting the policy of all Western Europe.

In 1672 Louis XIV suddenly flung an army into Dutch territory. The preparations made by De Witt for its defeat proved utterly inefficient. The French advanced from success to victory. The people grew terrified at a tale of reverses, and threw over the De Witt régime ; the States General proclaimed William, Stadtholder, Captain General and Admiral until the day of his death.

Equipped with his authority, and cheered by the welcome news that the Hague mob had murdered De Witt and his brother in the course of an *émeute*, the new Stadtholder addressed himself to ridding Dutch soil of living French soldiers.

Immediately his obstinate courage and ability appeared. Determined " to die in the last ditch "—he coined this phrase—he opened the sluices and flooded huge tracts of the country. Frigidly brisk, he so campaigned that by the spring of 1674 the last French regiment had crossed the Dutch frontier.

Three years later he married Mary, eldest daughter of James II of England by Anne Hyde, daughter of the Earl of Clarendon. Thus he acquired a second claim, besides his maternal relationship, to put him some-where in the line of possible pretenders to the throne of England.

From his wedding-day onwards, William kept a beady eye on the development of English domestic affairs. For some years he apparently believed that his father-in-law would join the League of Augsburg—a confederacy he had formed against the aggressive rapacity of Louis XIV. But before Christmas Day, 1687, he realised that such a hope could never materialise. Therefore, practical before all things, he began to ingratiate himself with the parties in the State who detested James.

As a first public step towards this end he caused his Prime Minister to write a letter denouncing James's religious policy. This the English received with remark-able enthusiasm ; Orange flags began to appear on cere-monial occasions, and men whispered of William as the monarch who would be brought over to dispossess James of his wasted heritage.

Learning of William's disembarkation, James dispatched Churchill at the head of an army of 5000 against the in-vader. Soon afterwards the King left London and joined the troops at Salisbury. Although his closest friends had persistently warned him that the man was untrustworthy, it seems certain that James never doubted his Commander's loyalty. The warnings he had received were, however, well founded.

For years Churchill had maintained a close and, in the circumstances, treasonable correspondence with William. In fact, one reason why William had decided to risk all his fortunes on so perilous an adventure as the armed invasion of England was the reiterated assurance of Churchill that, through their commander's influence, James's troops could be relied on to desert his cause.

The betrayal of James took place exactly as Churchill had planned. The Royal Army advanced from Salisbury to the Wiltshire Downs. William, his forces somewhat augmented by enthusiastic Whig adherents, was known to be not far distant. A general engagement seemed imminent. James was full of ardour ; whatever his faults may have been, he was the most martial of men, an experienced and skilful admiral, and a general not without insight into the mistakes by which battles can be lost.

The King retired to sleep, confident or, at least, sanguine that the morrow would see William's departure. Churchill had assured him of the preparedness and spirit of the troops. Next morning he woke to find that his commander had deserted to the invader ; that many of the senior officers had accompanied him ; and that the camp seethed with confusion and disaffection.

For once in his little life James took the measure of a situation justly. He realised that he would risk all if he risked a pitched battle. He prudently retired on London, and attempted to negotiate. William did not pursue the retreating King. He had everything to lose by shedding English blood on English soil ; everything to gain by as mild and pacific a demeanour as could be combined with the fulfilment of his clear purpose. Every day new towns and powerful men declared for him against James. The common people, rising to his bait of a freely elected Parliament to which all grievances should be referred, acclaimed him a deliverer of an enslaved nation.   Therefore, when James sent commissioners to treat with him, William received them politely and spent many hours listening to their arguments with a coldly cynical smile.

Meanwhile James hurried his wife and son to France, and himself essayed to follow them.   Even in this comparatively simple endeavour, a cruel fate frustrated him. Some fishermen at Faversham, near Rochester, detected his identity, and stopped his flight ; the miserable King returned to London.   When William learned of this farcical escapade, he at once circulated the news that James had been caught in undignified flight from his realm.

This news provided the final blow to James's reputation. Those who had remained loyal were now disgusted ; those who, like Churchill, had already joined the winning side, laughed.   James, his kingdom lost by treachery and a joke, was then allowed quietly to " escape " to Versailles, where the sympathy of Louis and a congenial atmosphere of loose living, mingled with piety, did something to restore his self-esteem.

So was effected what to this day is called " The Glorious Revolution."   " Glorious," however, is pathetically inept as a description of this *coup d'état.*   Useful, necessary, inevitable, salutary—all these adjectives might describe one or another of its aspects.   But neither the men nor the events concerned in its accomplishment have anything glorious about them.   As Trevelyan aptly remarks, " The men of 1689 were not heroes ; few of them were even honest men."

From the English point of view, it would be more true to name it the " Inglorious Revolution," for it must seem a shameful thing that a foreign prince, heading a force of alien mercenaries, should be the only means, if indeed the last resort, whereby Englishmen could save themselves and their country from an intolerable and fanatic despot.

It is true, however, that most of the broad constitutional decisions established as a result of the settlement which ended in the coronation of William and Mary as joint sovereigns, still hold good to-day. England governed her governors, not for the first time.

The Revolution decided that parliamentary government should survive ; that the Whig-Tory system should be the machinery by which such government was conducted— an arrangement which seems, even to-day, to be breaking through the Socialist façade of the " Labour " Party ; that the Royal prerogative should never set aside or obscure the will of the two Houses of Parliament ; that England joined the coalition of powers which opposed and finally destroyed the supremacy of Louis XIV of France, and so restored a balance of power.

Whom should we thank for these most definite and valuable heritages ? Is our gratitude due to the Prince of Orange who came to reign as perhaps the most efficient but certainly the least attractive monarch who ever occupied the English throne ? Should we applaud the calculating foresight of John Churchill, who cared little for the means by which he attained the end he most desired ?

While both these men were responsible for the settlement after the Revolution, I believe that the man who forced the issue was James. Had he not been so peculiarly obtuse, so utterly single in his devotion to the ideal for a Catholic England, it is inconceivable that any revolution would have occurred. Many men remained alive who well remembered the Civil Wars and their concomitant horrors. The country as a whole was weary of domestic upheavals and threats of intestinal confusion. It would have tolerated anything from James, except " Popery," rather than risk the dangers of yet another experiment in government.

But James forced the issue by his own gigantic incapacity to understand his subjects. Having done so, he ran away in the hour of danger.

Many writers, conspicuously Mr. Hilaire Belloc, have indulged in extravagant special pleading on James's behalf, professing to believe him a misunderstood monarch and a hardly used man. Here advocates of the last Stuart King of England can hardly be judged either wholly sincere or wholly ingenious. James was a failure both as a monarch and man. No worse than the men who displaced him, he was assuredly no better. His private morals were scandalous ; like every Stuart who reigned in England, he did not hesitate to break his solemnly plighted word to suit his least exigency ; his only virtues were the not remarkably uncommon ones which adorn every soldier who is not shot for neglecting his duty on the field of battle.

Unfortunately neither Churchill nor William can shine as a hero compared with this villain of the piece. Churchill, dignified as Duke of Marlborough, certainly did his country services as remarkable as James did her injuries, but as a man of weak quality he shone no more in his old age than in his youth. Avaricious to the end, he amassed a prodigious fortune ; yet for every shilling he received he gave England a marvellous shillingsworth of service. He established the reputation of English soldiers and commanders on the Continent higher than that of any other nation ; he bequeathed to the English Army the nucleus of those regimental traditions which remain its invaluable and cherished possession ; he brilliantly defeated the first captains of his age, and acquired for England a prestige which was to benefit her continuously until the Napoleonic wars.

# QUEEN ANNE IS DEAD

THIS phrase to-day means that the news is stale, but the circumstance that it has passed into correct speech and is still employed after more than 200 years makes clear how momentous the news was when that monarch died in 1714.

The public were in a ferment, not knowing whether her death would give them a King from Hanover or restore the Stuarts, or in either event bring about a Civil War. It was true that the Act of Succession pointed to George the Elector of Hanover, but they knew that persons in high places, nay, it was even whispered the Queen herself, favoured the exiles. In the welter of rumours and counter-rumours, the fall of Oxford and the rise of Bolingbroke to the chief place in the State made it clear, at least, that the Legitimists might with hope endeavour to frustrate the Revolution settlement when the Queen died. At that stage the news spread that Anne had once more been stricken with illness, and the knowing ones said that this time recovery was impossible. Any day might see a complete reversal in the order of government. They waited with anxiety, knowing that, while the Queen lived, they were safe, but that the last moment of her life might, indeed most believed that it would, be the signal for Civil War between rival claimants, and in that war the lives and liberties of all would be at stake. It is small wonder therefore that, when the dreaded moment had passed, in all places where men and women met, the piece of news that alone was mentioned was Queen Anne's death. The repetition, caused by intense anxiety, brought about satiety, and thus a new cant phrase came into being.  Yet, in retrospect, there seems little to justify such absorbing interest.  We know that Queen Anne died and was succeeded peacefully by King George I, that attempts were made, first by the Old Pretender in 1715 and again thirty years later by his son the Young Pretender, but that neither succeeded, or indeed attracted much support South of the Tweed.  The Hanoverian monarchs naturally relied upon the Whigs, and this confidence began a period of Whig domination in politics which lasted until the reign of George III.  The fact that the risk did not come to pass does not disprove its existence.  It did exist, and might in more resolute hands have turned into an accomplished fact.

The Stuarts had never before been able to produce two consecutive monarchs without a revolution.  The second of his line, Charles I, had been executed during the Civil War.  The fourth, James II, had been ejected in 1688 after a revolution which was to all intents bloodless and complete.  In his place were set up William and Mary who could in no sense claim to be Kings by divine right.  They relied perforce upon a purely statutory title, and Anne had herself reigned by virtue of that title.  In 1714 she was fifty-eight and childless.  She had indeed given birth to numerous sons and daughters, but none had survived early childhood.  Upon her death, the Throne must pass to a new monarch who did not claim descent through her.

The people of England had not received the nomination of Sophia of Hanover and her descendants with acclamation.  The succession of George I meant, as they knew, that England would be inevitably involved in continental politics, of vital interest to George as Elector but of none to him as King.  They were not desirous of being subjected again to the rule of a foreign sovereign.  Nor did his personal character invite love or confidence.  The fact was that the Hanoverian succession was inevitable if this country were to call upon the nearest Protestant member of the reigning family. The leading political principles were the maintenance of parliamentary government and the Church of England. It was because James II had attacked both at once that the loyalty of Englishmen to their sovereign had not prevented his deposition. George could only succeed as inheritor of the principles of the Revolution. If James Stuart, a Catholic, were to ascend his father's throne, it would be in reliance upon the claims antecedent to and incompatible with those principles.

Much depended on the will of the Queen. It was well known that Anne had always been dependent upon others whose force of character enabled them to exert decisive influence over her. She was upright and sincere, but her intellect was not keen nor was her grasp of affairs remarkable. Though her reign marks a series of events which is one of the glories of our history, she herself had no influence in those events as Queen Elizabeth before her, and Queen Victoria in our days exercised. Under the influence of John Churchill, but more of Sarah Churchill, she had deserted her father and joined in the Revolution. Under the same influence she had accepted the throne. As a loyal convinced member of the Church of England, she acquiesced in a position which at times her conscience suggested was not really hers. She disliked her cousin Sophia and the gloomy George. Nothing would induce her to do anything to suggest that she would welcome their succession. But she feared her half-brother, and the disasters in which her beloved Church would be involved if she yielded to the suggestion that he really ought to be King. She was not willing to make any acknowledgment that would involve the admission that she was herself a usurper. But powerful influences were at work to bring about a Restoration.

The predominance of John Churchill and his wife had ceased. It was true that he had risen to the highest ranks in the State, but Anne had gradually become tired of his wife's moods and tempers. After all, she was Anne and Queen. In 1710 the end had come. Sarah, Duchess of Marlborough, was in disgrace and in her stead reigned Abigail Hill, Lady Masham. The new favourite was devoted to the cause of the Old Pretender.

The change of personal influence had been accompanied by a change in the royal counsels. Though it is true that the principles of responsible parliamentary government had not been fully developed, and it was not yet the rule, nor was it generally desired, that the monarch's advisers should depend upon a majority in either House, yet it was felt that the administration should be in general harmony with Parliament. In 1710 the Ministry was reformed and became Tory in character. The Commons had a Tory majority and the Lords were brought into line by the creation of twelve new peers. The Tories were led by Harley, the Lord High Treasurer, and by St. John, the principal Secretary of State. Harley was the older man, who had begun political life as a Whig and relied mainly upon his undoubted gifts of management and persuasion. His love of secrecy and his habits of procrastination gradually lost him his predominant influence. Even then we got tired of being continually told to " wait and see." Soon he transferred to the Upper House as Earl of Oxford. Bolingbroke was left to manage the Commons. He was the only other Tory leader who held a commanding position. Brilliant of intellect, but unsteady of purpose, he outshone his leader. Apart from them, the great intellects of the realm were in the Whig interest. It was in the Lords that the political struggle was keenest. Bolingbroke desired to join his leader there and at last succeeded, but only as a Viscount, much to his chagrin. The election of 1713 confirmed the Tory

QUEEN ANNE'S ROYAL PROCESSION IN THE STRAND, JULY 7TH, 1713, FOR THE THANKSGIVING SERVICE
AT ST. PAUL'S TO COMMEMORATE THE PEACE OF UTRECHT

majority. What was needed was a firm and common policy and consistent leadership.

The Tories were divided in opinion. Many regretted the Revolution. Probably all would have been content with a Restoration if adequate security could be obtained. The Queen was ageing, and her successive illnesses were a warning that, if any change were to be made, it must be done at once. Both leaders maintained relations with Hanover and the Stuarts in exile, though Harley was believed to be lukewarm and Bolingbroke earnest in his support of the latter.

Whenever the Queen fell ill plans were discussed, but the topic was not conducive to harmony, and, whenever she recovered, discussions ceased as though Anne were immortal. The Whigs, on the other hand, were ceaseless in their advocacy of the Protestant Succession. They embarrassed the Ministers in public, and this did not render their private negotiations with one another more harmonious. But changes were made in office and it was noticed that all new appointments were Jacobite in colour. The Jacobites grew confident and the Whigs more suspicious. Queen Anne would do nothing to encourage the Hanoverians, and Lady Masham used all her influence to oust them. Harley and Bolingbroke became rivals for mastery. In the midst of their internal conflict the Parliamentary Session came to an end on July 9th, 1714. Nothing had been done, and, unless and until Parliament met again, the Act of Settlement must remain the law. If the Queen died before then, that law said that George would be King, since Sophia was now dead. The Old Pretender must claim, if at all, openly and in form contrary to the clear terms of the statute. This fact would cost him the support of all those who only desired his recall under and by virtue of the law.

While time passed the vital moments were consumed in

the struggle for power between the two Tory leaders. Harley seemed to regain much of his former vigour, but in his anxiety he forgot the respect which was due to his Sovereign and ought to have been manifested to Lady Masham. His fall was determined upon, but the ladies fixed upon his manners as an excuse for his dismissal. On July 27th, 1714, he resigned the White Staff of the Treasurer into the Queen's hands, and Bolingbroke was now the head of the administration.

That day he made a bid for the support of the younger Whigs, but they demanded as the price of their support that he should require the Old Pretender to remove from Lorraine and restore Marlborough to the command of the Army. He would thereby have declared himself for Hanover. Probably he was not able to comply even if he would, but he went to the Council Meeting that night without the support for which he had bidden.

It may be that Bolingbroke had not yet decided upon his attitude towards the succession. His foreign policy strongly suggests that he favoured the Old Pretender, but it by no means follows that he was prepared to risk power, and even his head, unless a Jacobite succession was assured. It was a vice of statesmen in those days that they desired to keep a foot in either camp. But he should have filled up Harley's vacant office. He had decided to lead the administration as Secretary of State and to put the Treasurership into commission. Time was wasted in discussing who should be the Commissioners, and when the Council, held in the Queen's presence on the evening of that day, broke up in the early hours of the next day, nothing had been settled. It is true the position was difficult. If the Ministry were to rely openly on the Jacobite section of the Tory party, it was doubtful if it could command a majority in the Commons, and certain that it would be in a minority in the Lords. But if the Queen were to appoint as her Lord High

*After Huck*

THE ARTICLES OF UNION BEING PRESENTED TO QUEEN ANNE IN 1706 BY THE COMMISSIONERS

Treasurer a man of position and experience, he might easily succeed to all the power that Harley had enjoyed, and Bolingbroke's pre-eminence would be destroyed.

The delay was fatal. The Queen was suffering from gout, and early on the morning of the 28th she had a seizure. It was certain that she was dying, and the Tories were without a policy. During the 29th the seizures continued. Every rally was followed by a relapse.

On the 30th another Council was held. This time the Queen was absent. It may have been a Cabinet meeting but was more probably a session of the Privy Council. Hardly had they met than the Duke of Argyle and the Duke of Somerset were announced. Though uninvited, they were welcomed, and proposed that the Duke of Shrewsbury should succeed to Harley's place. Why Bolingbroke had accepted the suggestion it is impossible to say. Shrewsbury had held high office and was known to be in favour with the Queen. Harley had anticipated that Shrewsbury would have supported him. The Whigs had counted him as one of their number. It may be that Bolingbroke remembered that Shrewsbury had come to his aid in the discussions on the Spanish Treaty, and thought that his support would again be forthcoming.

Whatever the motive, the proposal was carried. The Queen understood enough to agree, and Shrewsbury received the staff of office from the hands of his dying mistress.

In form, the affair was simply filling up a vacancy in the Ministry. In fact, the appearance of Argyle and Somerset was decisive of events. Shrewsbury at once assumed control and Bolingbroke subsided into acquiescence. There was no doubt about the character of the new administration. All the Privy Councillors, without distinction of party, were summoned to the meetings. Nothing could be done without their knowledge. They took immediate steps to secure the succession as declared by statute. Ten battalions were ordered home from Flanders, and the Heralds were warned to be ready to proclaim George as King. The Elector's ambassador got ready to declare the names of the lords who were to act as Regents until the Elector could come to England. All danger of a *coup d'état* was now over. The Queen lingered during the last day of July, but at seven o'clock on August 1st, 1714, she departed this life. George I was proclaimed King of Great Britain, France and Ireland, and the populace knew that the crisis was over. They had not known what had happened in the last few days, or that the Jacobites, caught unawares, had made no plans or preparations. To them the death of Anne still might have meant the outbreak of Civil War, and their relief was commensurate with their previous anxiety.

It is idle to speculate what would have been the course of our national history if the two unbidden Dukes had failed in their dramatic intervention. What has happened is known, but it is at least certain that if Bolingbroke had been as astute and ready as common opinion had thought he was, he would have decided the destinies of our nation and no man can say now what his decision would have been. It was noticed that the illuminations at his house to celebrate the accession of George I outshone all others, but the gesture deceived no one.

# CLIVE AND DUPLEIX

IN one respect the political history of the Indian peninsula never changes : it is a land of mobs. It does not possess, and has never possessed, racial or social cohesion ; more than in any other country of the world single individuals of outstanding personality have been able temporarily to impose their will upon its destiny, either by leading or scattering spineless or headless mobs. Only a superficial reader of events would say that conquest in India has been due solely to force of arms, whether by Moghuls, Mahrattas, Portuguese, French or English ; in every case it will be found that rulership over a large portion of Indian territory has been mainly due to the force of character with which one man or another has imposed his will upon millions of the native population.

The Moghul Empire began with such a man, Babar, who with 12,000 men swept down from the North and defeated forces of first 100,000 and then 210,000 men arrayed against him ; it rose to its greatest height under a still greater man, Akbar ; it fell into decay when their unworthy descendants no longer stood above the common level of statecraft and courage. Without Sivaji there would, and could, have been no such resurgence of the Mahratta race as raised this people for a short period to a commanding position in the centre and South of India, the fragments of which glory still remain to-day in several of the Native States. The early progress of European power in the Peninsula equally reflected the great personalities which led it. Albuquerque raised the Portuguese to

great power in India ; spinelessness destroyed them.
Dupleix, the Frenchman and the first European to dream
of an Indian Empire in the modern form, was able with a
handful of men to shatter the prestige of the Indian princes
who surrounded him, and made European rule in India
inevitable. And he met his master in Clive, the Englishman,
who fought the French for supremacy in India and defeated
them far less because of any superiority in arms or numbers
than by the exercise of a personality unmatched in the
history of the Peninsula. The clash of wills between these
two men, Clive and Dupleix, and the final overthrow of
the latter in a struggle which had alternated between
advantages to either side, possesses not merely the importance of a turning point in history but also throws a piercing
sidelight upon the psychological conditions with which all
must still reckon who would hope to understand present-
day circumstances in India and their certain outcome.

The history of India has always been a conflict of personality against numbers, of individuals against mobs ; the
mobs have always been beaten.

Dupleix's first sight of India came in 1715, when he was
not yet twenty. It was five years later before his father's
influence and his own promise made him a member of the
French governing body at Pondicherry. It was the rule in
those days—a rule which must be taken into account by
anyone who to-day presumes to pass in judgment some of
the most disputed actions of the founders, both French
and English, of European supremacy in India—that
officials of the chartered companies administering the
concessions in India were expected, and encouraged, to
seek their chief remuneration by private trade. The
conscientious fulfilment of their official duties represented,
as it were, the price of their licence to share in the companies' monopolies : rarely was any man so patriotic or
exalted as to set his company's interest above his own.

Dupleix to some extent, and Clive certainly, were exceptions. But whereas Clive accepted vast sums from native allies and dependents as the reward of services rendered, Dupleix more simply acquired a vast private fortune by trading.

In 1730, at the age of thirty-three, he was promoted to the intendancy of Chandernagore, the French settlement on the Hooghly, twenty miles above Calcutta. In the twelve years during which he held this office, Dupleix transformed the settlement from a stagnant, overgrown village to a thriving town. From half a dozen leaking native barges he created a fleet of seventy stout vessels, which carried their freights throughout the East. He opened up trade throughout the interior, and even to the frontiers of Tibet. The chief instrument in this development was his increasing private fortune, which he employed, both as merchant and as banker, to stimulate his compatriots to extend their activities and to persuade native merchants to settle at Chandernagore. When, in 1742, he was appointed Governor-General of all the French establishments in India, he took with him to Pondicherry an unparalleled reputation as an administrator, considerable riches, and, not least important for his later plans, a wife whose understanding of Indian affairs and of the native character was second only to his own.

He at once initiated in Pondicherry measures similar to those which he had employed so successfully in the north. He overhauled the administration, removed abuses, rooted out corruption, stimulated his subordinates to larger trading efforts and, with prudent foresight, began to set in order the defences of the town. Eighty-five miles away the British settlement of Madras was a constant reminder to him that France was not the only European nation interested in the development of Indian trade. The ancient hostility of the two countries made it certain that sooner or later a new war would break out between them : indeed

Dupleix's directors in Paris made this their reason for reducing their commitments and urging economy upon him.  They even ordered him to spend no more money in strengthening his defences, an order which he contemptuously disobeyed, for it was not in his character to allow his plans to be dictated from Europe ; he had the genius's contempt for tremulous authority.  Meanwhile he hoped to withstand any British threat to French interests in India. As has since become the traditional policy of France in her colonial empire, he intrigued for the sympathy and support of native potentates both as allies and, sometimes, even as nominal superiors.

Thus, only a few months after his transference to Pondicherry, he returned to Chandernagore to be ceremoniously installed as a high vassal of the Emperor of Delhi, who still claimed authority over Bengal.  By thus pretending to subordinate himself to the Moghuls, he automatically acquired authority over their lesser vassals, as well as a definite standing in the Emperor's hierarchy which was invaluable to him in the south.  There too he pursued a policy of assimilating French and native interests.  By treating with the princes of the interior, partly as a French official and trader, partly as a Moghul grandee, he laid the foundations of a prosperity which, but for Clive, would have made France the controlling force for many years in the centre and South of the Peninsula.

It need not be assumed, of course, that such a triumph would have wholly altered the fate of India.  Even without Clive, British sea-power must in the end have won India from the French.  But two important consequences at least would have followed.  Napoleon's campaign would have found a different focus—for the Empire of the East which he sought through Egypt would have lain ready to his hand in India ; and France would have established a tradition in interest in Indian affairs, as she has done in

ROBERT, FIRST LORD CLIVE

Egypt, which would have enormously complicated our task of conquest during the last century and a half.

But Dupleix had to build too quickly. Disaster came upon him before he had properly consolidated the foundation of his political ambitions. In March, 1744, the War of the Austrian Succession broke out in Europe ; an English fleet was despatched to India to harass Pondicherry and the other French settlements. Dupleix, however, took advantage of his relations with the local princes ; the Nawab of the Carnatic informed the British at Madras, who like the French were nominally subordinate to him as vassals of the King of Delhi, that he forbade any attack upon Pondicherry. And when, a few months later, a French fleet arrived and Madras lay at its mercy, the Nawab refused to interfere on behalf of the English ; the town surrendered to Dupleix.

So far his policy triumphed. He had promised to transfer Madras, after capture, to the Nawab, but refused to carry out this undertaking. Backed by his fleet, he thought himself strong enough to defy his nominal overlord ; and determined on defiance. The Nawab sent ten thousand native troops against the five hundred Frenchmen who garrisoned Madras. A sally by four hundred of these, with two pieces of quick-firing artillery, threw the Indians into a panic withdrawal ; their commander turned instead upon a relieving force of two hundred and thirty Frenchmen and seven hundred natives drilled by French officers, and sought to prevent them from crossing the river Adyar. The French, outnumbered as they were by ten to one and unprovided with artillery, were led with consummate bravery by an engineer officer named Paradis. Disregarding the odds against him, he crossed the river with his little force and charged the astonished Indians, who broke and fled.

This small but decisive engagement revolutionised the

history of India. A handful of white men had put to flight a host of Indians. It was a triumph of audacity, which forever established the superiority of the European over the Indian in battle. From that moment there was no more question in fact, though it was sometimes convenient to pretend a diplomatic compliance, of either French or English being the vassals of Indian princes. Dupleix's victory raised the status of the European from the subordinate to the rival of the native sovereign ; it was left to Clive to make that European his master.

It was this very campaign round Madras which set the young Englishman on the path to military fame. Twenty-two years younger than Dupleix, he had reached Madras in the autumn of 1744, near his nineteenth birthday, a penniless clerk in the service of the East India Company. So low were his fortunes, so greatly did he loathe his work and his prospects, that, as a well-known story tells, he attempted to commit suicide ; but the pistol missed fire, in which he saw the hand of destiny. It is likely enough that other young men have had similar experiences and claimed for them a similar providence, which has proved unjustified by events ; of these we never hear, but Clive's story is immortal.

Escaping from Madras in disguise after its occupation, he made his way to the smaller English settlement of Fort St. David, which lay sixteen miles south of Pondicherry. Dupleix despatched a French force to capture this settlement also ; Clive volunteered to serve in the defence and had the satisfaction of helping to keep the enemy at bay. Had Fort St. George fallen, English domination in India might have been postponed for generations. But Dupleix was no soldier.

Brilliant diplomat and administrator though he proved himself to be, bravely though he could fight when his back was to the wall, well though he planned campaigns, he never sought to lead an army in the field, relying instead on subordinates who served him ill. Only Paradis, who died too soon, and Bussy, whom for reasons of policy he sent to maintain French prestige in the interior, ever displayed qualities of leadership ; otherwise, Dupleix suffered from a succession of incompetent or cowardly commanders, whose failure destroyed all his projects. The very qualities of audacity and shock which had demonstrated, on the banks of the Adyar, the superiority of European troops over Indians, now gave the English an almost equal advantage over the French. The successful defence of Fort St. David against the French attack foretold the outcome of the rivalry of the two European nations in India.

For a time the French exercised a superiority in strength, but the arrival of another British fleet altered the balance, and this time Pondicherry was besieged, Clive serving with distinction as an ensign in the attacking forces. The siege failed, a fact due in no small part to Dupleix who, forced to fight, displayed considerable ability. The peace of Aix-la-Chapelle put an end to direct hostilities between the English and French in India ; but actually fighting continued, the only difference being that, instead of openly conducting campaigns against one another, each side aligned itself with rival native princes and, under cover of this arrangement, continued to struggle for supremacy. Thus they took sides in the war waged for Viceroyalty of the Deccan.

The last Viceroy had died while French and English were at war ; his nominee as successor was Muzafar Jang, a grandson ; but his second son, a prince of degraded character named Nasir Jang, usurped the honour. The succession also as Nawab of the Carnatic was disputed between a certain Chanda Sahib and Mohamed Ali. Dupleix allied himself with Muzafar and Chanda ; the British with Nasir and Mohamed Ali. Whichever pair of

claimants was successful, would be bound to give their
European allies a predominant position in the Deccan.
At first the French party carried all before them ; only the
hill-fortress of Trichinopoly held out against them.  In
vain Dupleix sent urgent commands to his subordinates
and his allies to storm the city ; they hesitated and disobeyed.  He was successful, nevertheless, in every other
direction, and in 1751 the French cause appeared supreme
in India and the English desperate.

It was at this dark moment that Clive's military genius
emerged.

He suggested to the British authorities at Madras, who
waited with apprehension for Trichinopoly to fall—and
after it Madras—that the best, indeed the only, means of
saving the situation was to make a counter-attack upon
Arcot the capital of one of the chiefs besieging Trichinopoly.  Saunders, the governor of Madras, disposed of only
three hundred and fifty European troops ; but with extraordinary daring he agreed that Clive, a young man without
military training, should lead half of these against Arcot.

Clive left Madras on August 26th with two hundred
white soldiers, three hundred sepoys and three small pieces of
artillery.  Marching through a thunderstorm, a feat which
impressed the inhabitants of Arcot with superstitious
wonder, he appeared before its walls on August 31st ;
though the garrison was at least double his strength it
abandoned the city without firing a shot.  This victory had
the result which Clive desired : the native armies besieging
Trichinopoly began to waver.  Dupleix despatched a
large force, including one hundred and fifty Frenchmen,
to recapture Arcot, and for two months Clive was besieged
in the fortress.  He was assailed by numbers so overwhelming that their repulse seemed impossible : by the
end of the siege he disposed of no more than eighty European
and one hundred and twenty Sepoys, while the enemy

DUPLEIX

numbered at least twenty times as many. Yet he succeeded
in beating back every attack. At last, at the end of November, the discouraged enemy withdrew.

Clive sallied out of Arcot and, largely through the awe
with which the Indians now regarded him, won two important victories at Arni and Kaveripak. The latter engagement
showed him at his worst and his best. By neglecting
precautions which a more experienced commander would
have exercised, he fell into an ambush ; and his little force
was in imminent danger of destruction. Gauging the
situation with the remarkable coolness that always distinguished him, he resorted to the desperate expedient of
attacking what had been the enemy's strongest point, on
the chance that it had been left insufficiently guarded. His
calculation was right : this daring manœuvre turned
disaster into victory, and still further increased the awe
with which the natives regarded him. These victories
sufficed : the besieging forces outside Trichinopoly became
discouraged and, disregarding Dupleix's frenzied orders
to increase their efforts, became listless and were finally
overwhelmed. Law, the French commander, surrendered ;
and Chanda was captured and killed.

The French never recovered from this blow. Even though
Dupleix was able, especially after Clive was invalided with
fever to England, to compensate himself to some extent
for the disaster at Trichinopoly, his own position at Pondicherry had been undermined. In the autumn of 1754,
orders came from France for his supercession as Governor-
General, and his successor arrived. The directors of the
French company can hardly be blamed for their decision
to remove Dupleix. Though he had come within an ace
of making France supreme in the South of India, he had
failed ; incidentally he had ruined the resources of the
trading company whose representative he was. The
company was nearly bankrupt : Dupleix had been too

intent upon increasing the glory of his country, and his own, to treat his directors with the respectful subordination which they thought their due. Had Trichinopoly fallen ; had Clive never marched against Arcot and held it ; had the French accomplished the political success that Dupleix sought ; it is still probable that he would have been replaced by someone more attentive to the company's interests.

His fate when he returned to France has become a legend of ill-requited genius, of a giant brought to ruin by malignant dwarfs. Modern research has exploded this sentimental theory. The notion cannot any longer be sustained that Dupleix was cheated out of his rightful wealth by the selfishness and cupidity of the directors of the French company, and that his death in poverty was directly due to their unkindess.

What happened was that, on his return to Paris, he risked what money he still possessed in a fantastic venture called " Savons sans feu," which was to manufacture soap by a new process in France, Spain and the Netherlands. No factory was ever built, and Dupleix lost all his money. He now put forward claims for vast sums against the company whose servant he had been. Had he displayed a politer spirit in his demands, he might have been to some extent successful ; but his abrupt methods increased the doubts of the directors.

They pointed out with every show of justice, that he had never made these claims on them while he was in India. On the contrary, he had assured them that the various wars in which he engaged his forces were costing them nothing. Moreover, they knew very well that, when matters had gone well for France in India, Dupleix had taken the cream of the profits ; and it was this very wealth, thus obtained, which he had unsuccessfully risked in the later failures. To them it seemed that Dupleix was arguing, " What I make, I keep ; what I lose, you must pay." And pay they would not. Nor could they well afford to pay, in the sad state of their finances.

They fought his claims until he died, owing money on every side, from large sums to bill-brokers to trifles to his washerwoman.

Clive, now thirty-one years old, returned to India in 1756 with the rank of colonel and the post of Governor of Fort St. David. At the moment at which he took up his governorship Suraj-ud-Dowlah, the new Nawab of Bengal, a degenerate and vicious youth, captured Calcutta. Certain of his subordinates perpetrated the horror of the Black Hole, when a hundred and forty-six English prisoners, including a woman, were thrust into the punishment cell of the fortress of Calcutta, a room only eighteen by fifteen feet in size, with two small barred windows. It was one of the hottest nights of the year, and a hundred and twenty-three of the prisoners perished. Clive was at once sent to recapture the city and avenge the massacre. With two hundred and fifty white soldiers, twelve hundred sepoys and two field guns he marched on Calcutta.

The incidents of this campaign again demonstrated his curious lack of military skill, due no doubt chiefly to his lack of training ; but also his capacity for cool decision and courage in disaster. One night he fell into an ambush similar to that which nearly destroyed him at Kaveripack. With no sentries posted, his sleeping army was surprised by over three thousand enemy troops. Clive, exhausted and ill with fever, rallied his men, charged the astonished Indians and put them to flight. Once again by sheer force of personality, and despite an almost wilful disregard of elementary military tactics, he had transformed apparent disaster into success. With his command reinforced to muster thirteen hundred white soldiers and sailors, eight hundred sepoys and six guns he laid siege to Calcutta. His plan was ill designed, and at one point in the fighting he was in danger of being overwhelmed ; yet once again he so intimidated the Indians by his courage that they sued for peace.

A few months later came the famous Battle of Plassey, outside Murshidabad, the Nawab's capital.  Clive, with eleven hundred white soldiers, twenty-one hundred sepoys and nine field pieces put to flight a native army of sixty-eight thousand men and fifty-three guns.  This battle destroyed all but the semblance of native power in those parts of India where European troops had penetrated. Clive reached England again in 1760, enormously wealthy chiefly as a result of gifts from the Nawab whom he had set in Suraj-ud-Dowlah's place, and with the reputation of the foremost general of his time.

He was granted an Irish peerage—which he thought an insufficient reward for his service—entered the House of Commons and secured the return of a body of supporters. He engaged also in recriminations with the directors of the East India Company, particularly offending them by the far-sighted suggestion that the Crown should assume the administration of the conquered provinces.  At first the directors were too powerful for him and nearly succeeded in depriving him of the main sources of his income ; but the critical situation in Bengal forced them to set aside their animosity and to send him back there in 1765 as Governor-General and Commander-in-Chief, to consolidate the British power and to reorganize the company's administration.

It is unnecessary to set out his further achievements in detail.  He carried out reforms similar to those which Dupleix had initiated in the French service, cleansed the company of much of the corruption and inefficiency which had honeycombed it, and thus rendered it more efficient to undertake the vast administrative duties which he now secured from the feeble Emperor of Delhi.  In doing so, he offended both his civil and military subordinates ; when, in 1767, he returned to England for the last time he found himself bitterly attacked by enemies at home.

The main ground of their indictment was that he had improperly accepted vast presents from native princes with whom he had negotiated treaties ; the most piquant accusation was the admitted fact that, in order to circumvent the treachery of a native agent, he had forged the signature of Admiral Watson to a false document. At attempt was made to have him impeached. After a long controversy, in which he ably defended himself, the House compromised. It set out the main facts of the accusation without extenuation and also without censure, but declared that Clive " did at the same time render great and meritorious services to his country."

Priggish historians have held up horrified hands at Clive's alleged transgressions. I shall not seem to condone peculation and forgery if I say that their strictures appear to me to be exaggerated and even, in the main, unjustified. In those days the servants of the East India Company (like those of the French Company) were expected to carve out their personal fortunes to the full extent compatible with the interest of their employers. There was nothing improper in Clive's receiving gifts from native potentates, provided that he did not in any way prejudice the Company's or the nation's interests. This is answered by his record, for, thanks to Clive, the East India Company achieved a degree of wealth and power which its most optimistic directors can never have foreseen.

On the main issue, therefore, Clive must be acquitted. The matter of the forgery is different. Forgery must always be condemned ; but there are occasions when a man of the highest personal integrity may seriously bring himself to consider whether such an act may not be venial. In Clive's case he considered—and he appears to have been right—that the only means of defeating a vindictive and bloodthirsty enemy, the man responsible for the horrors of the Black Hole, was by closing the mouth of a treacherous agent. Had he not done this by drawing up a false agreement, and forging Watson's signature to it, the consequences might have been disastrous to British interests. Whoever would judge Clive's actions in this affair, should first endeavour to place himself in Clive's position. " He that is without sin among you, let him first cast a stone."

The essence of Clive's greatness, the secret of that personal force which made him great, may be simply defined : imagination and enthusiasm  He belonged to that strange counterstream of English eighteenth-century life which produced Wolfe, Moore and Nelson. They lacked many of the fundamental personal qualities which we habitually associate with that century ; instead, they assumed, and followed up, a heroic pose which sometimes bordered on the theatrical. Dupleix, for all his brains and his vast, logical conceptions of European power in the East was no match for a man who held himself divinely favoured to accomplish mighty ends. Had Clive ever for a moment doubted his mission, he must have perished in one of those crises of battle which he provoked by his own carelessness ; he could never have borne himself and his country to the pinnacle of authority which he attained for them in India, which we have never lost and are unlikely to dissipate.

# NAPOLEON IN EGYPT

ONE of the hardest problems which confronts the historian is to rid his mind of his knowledge of after-events and to see the circumstances of any incident which he is describing against the background which alone was visible to its contemporaries. Looking back to-day, for example, with our knowledge of what happened, we find a difficulty in understanding how Napoleon could have risked the vast hazard of his Egyptian enterprise which began when he set sail from Toulon with nearly 40,000 men on May 19th, 1798. We know its calamitous ending; we recall how he escaped almost alone from that wholesale marooning of his army in the East; but, at the same time, admiration for the amazing qualities of his generalship must warn us that, when he took the risk to which his army succumbed, it must have seemed to him a far more favourable chance than it eventually proved. To us it appears almost a gesture of madness; to Napoleon and the men of his day it must have appeared an intelligent, if admittedly daring, manœuvre.

Was it then as desperate and rash as it now appears to have been? The answer is that, on the contrary, it seemed to Napoleon to possess every hope of success. A grave error often made in considering this campaign has been to underrate the capacity of the French fleet. Shaken though it was by the battle of Cape St. Vincent, it nevertheless remained a very formidable instrument. The first symptoms of technical and disciplinary decay, due to the Revolution, had been overcome; the old French tradition of good seamanship and bravery had been revived. On the other hand, the English fleet had for a year and a half almost completely abandoned the Mediterranean to the French ; Napoleon cannot be blamed for his view that the Mediter-ranean had become a " French lake." Still more important, he had no reason to suppose that Nelson was destined to show himself as great a genius on sea as himself on land. Historians have done Nelson an ill service by decrying the capacity of the French fleets which he defeated, one after another, during his amazing career. By minimising his enemy, his fame is correspondingly lessened. The true position can only be understood by remembering how great a naval power the French represented at this time.

Moreover, Napoleon cannot then have estimated his peril from the English very highly. To understand the isolation of England and the general political situation in Europe in 1798, it is necessary to glance briefly back at the war of the first Coalition between 1793 and 1795. In the autumn of 1793 the French armies, victorious though they were, had suffered seriously in morale. Muddle, indiscipline and corruption—apparently inseparable con-comitants of revolution—had impaired their qualities more gravely than any hostile arms. The Coalition, had it been able really to combine, might easily have overcome the young republic. But instead, faltering and self-interest prevailed. Prussia devoted her strength, and her British subsidy, to reducing Poland. England and Austria failed to act with decision. Carnot was given time to address himself to his brilliant achievement of creating, or rather improvising, a new French army. In its essentials the machine which he built has endured to the present day. The corps of Carnot became, a century and a quarter later, the army of Foch, an army which is to-day the finest military organization in the world. Robespierre was too busy " primly presiding over the Terror " to concern himself about such trifles as the public, or even the national,

*After De Louthenbourg*

THE BATTLE OF THE NILE—THE BLOWING UP OF THE FRENCH FLAGSHIP "L'ORIENT"

safety ; Carnot, therefore, received a free hand. He was by no means beloved of the Terrorists ; they doubted his revolutionary zeal. But with a logic little displayed in most of their activities they recognised him as the perfect man for the work he had undertaken ; they permitted him to work in his own way. He prepared the ground for Napoleon's later glory : without Carnot, Napoleon's star would never have risen into immortality.

The British Army in Flanders in 1793 and 1794 was not in every way excellent. A certain youth of twenty-five, Colonel Wellesley—better known to posterity as Arthur Wellesley, 1st Duke of Wellington—recorded with some severity that, " when wine was on the table," his fellow-officers would " fling aside despatches to await such attention as they might be in a condition to give them when they had finished the bottles." By the summer of 1795 the French had driven this bibulous force out of the Netherlands, an ignominy for England which was crowned by the tragic farce of the Quiberon revolt.

Much of England's martial effort against France was concentrated at this time in the West Indies. Pitt thought of these islands as wealthy, vital to our trade, and a key to the domination of America. Nor was he alone in his opinion of the relative importance of the western and eastern spheres of war ; most of his contemporaries agreed with him. Like other isolationists, he never thought of England as an important military power on the Continent of Europe. In his view our part in any such international struggle should be to use our navy and our subsides to assist the other members of the Coalition to hem in the enemy. This policy of comparative isolation from the Continent did not begin with him ; nor certainly was he the last to uphold it. But pestilence carried off eighty thousand of our troops in the West Indies in three years, a high price to pay for isolation.

K

In 1795 Prussia left the Coalition. Spain did the same and, a year later, entered into an alliance with France. The man most responsible for the change in Spain's attitude was a handsome young guardsman named Godoy, who had risen to be the Spanish King's minister by virtue of his command over the Queen's affections. Then in 1797 Austria, having been expelled from Italy and threatened with invasion by Napoleon, also retired from the struggle. Consenting to the Rhine frontier for France, she received, as the price of her complacence, the former territories of the ancient Republic of Venice. It is not impossible that the contemplation of the old Venetian power in the Levant, and of the wealth which Venice's position as the virtual monopolist of the import of Eastern merchandise into Europe had brought her, may have helped to fire Napoleon's dream of Oriental conquest.

Thus, while in 1793 France had been fighting Europe single-handed, 1797 saw England almost single-handed against France ; with the rest of Europe either mildly neutral or else waiting for England's destruction with a certain hungry anticipation. Neither Pitt nor his Foreign Minister, Grenville, was sufficiently subtle to hold together our allies. Their callous and corrupt courts made peace with France at the first hint of danger, valuing their skins and their comfort even above Pitt's guineas. Worse still, there came at this moment two mutinies in the British fleet. The Spithead mutiny might be described as a strike of honest sailors against intolerable food and inhuman conditions. That at the Nore was more revolutionary in its nature, whether or not its participants were conscious of this. Fortunately for the future of England and her fleet, the Spithead munity succeeded, and the other failed. The concessions then wrung from the Admiralty have prevented the recurrence ever since of similar outbreaks.

Napoleon returned to Paris from his triumphs in Italy

at the end of 1797, and was appointed to command the "Army of England," a force organised and intended for the conquest of this island. His first interest was to probe into the chances of its success. He decided against it. He could see himself leading a force of threescore thousand men through Kent to London ; such a raid on a large scale was possible, but he saw no hope of permanent conquest with the materials then at his hand. He turned, therefore, to the project of an expedition to Egypt as a masterstroke against British prosperity, as the first step to further penetration into the East, and as a base for striking at India. In regarding the mastery of Egypt as a key to the world empire, Napoleon became one of a great line of far-sighted men, of whom it is enough to mention Alexander the Great, Julius Cæsar, Disræli and Lord Kitchener. Not less important a consideration, though one less picturesque, is his realisation that France's depleted resources could not possibly maintain large armies in her own territories ; these had to live abroad on the fruits of their conquests. And large armies were essential to France ; while only continuous and successful foreign wars could maintain the stability of the Directory.

Moreover, Napoleon knew that it was unhealthy for him to remain too long in Paris. He knew that the Directors feared him and his ambitions ; but he knew also that he was neither ready nor powerful enough at this time to replace them. And then too there was the spur of fame. He told Bourrienne that " This little Europe does not supply enough fame for me. I must seek it in the East ; all great fame comes from there. . . . If the success of a descent on England appears doubtful, as I fear it will, the army of England shall become the army of the East ; and I shall go to Egypt."

For all these reasons, then, the Egyptian expedition was inevitable. Napoleon set out his objectives in a minute

dated April 12th, 1798. They were threefold : to seize
Egypt ; to cut a canal through the Isthmus which separated
the Red Sea from the Mediterranean ; and to supplant
the British in all their Oriental possessions. How long
this would take, he did not claim to be able to judge. " A
few months, or six years—it depends."

The preparations for the expedition went forward
briskly at Toulon. So well were Napoleon's secrets kept
that the British could discover nothing certain about the
date of his departure or his destination. That he was able
to bring out his large armada undetected was a brilliant
piece of organisation and staff work. On his way to Egypt
he captured Malta. His task was made easier by his having
previously sent a " commercial agent," one Poussielgue,
to corrupt the Knights of St. John, who controlled the
island. This conquest, however, was shortlived ; a few
months later Nelson recaptured Malta and made it British.

How came Nelson into the Mediterranean ? In the
autumn of the previous year, 1797, Pitt somewhat tardily
decided to reassert the policy of British naval supremacy
in the Middle Sea. Nelson, who had been gloomily brood-
ing on the prospect of the Admiralty's having no further
use for " a left-handed admiral " and of becoming a burden
to his friends and useless to his country, was chosen as the
most suitable officer, by reason both of his skill and his
dash, to command a fleet whose purpose was to discover
why Napoleon was collecting the vast expeditionary force
at Toulon and to oppose its object. When Napoleon
slipped out of Toulon, on May 19th, Nelson had already
been eleven days in the Mediterranean, scouting for information. Two days later he learned that Napoleon had
sailed. Nelson hastened to Naples, and heard that the
French were near Malta. He dashed to Sicily and Alexandria, drew blank, scoured the Levant, returned to Sicily.
But Napoleon's fleet had passed him in the dark, and in

the dark Nelson remained.  At last in Greece he learned
that the French had been seen sailing south-east from
Crete : his first guess had been right ; Alexandria was
Napoleon's destination.  On August 1st the long search
came to an end, when he sighted the French fleet in Aboukir
Bay.

During these nine feverish weeks Nelson had founded
the " band of brothers " tradition with his captains.  It
was most unusual, and often most embarrassing for an
admiral to live among his captains, but he insisted on this.
His remarkable personality made the experiment succeed.
The result was that, while he learned to know the strength
and the weakness of the individual men under his command
and was able to instil into their minds the new code of
tactics in which he believed, they for their part learned to
know and to trust him and to co-operate with him and
with each other.  There is another side too to the " band
of brothers."  Nelson's nature required that he should
have an audience.  Flattery, as Emma Hamilton afterwards
discovered, was as necessary to him as air and prayer.  He
was a good comrade ; except for occasional outbursts of
furious petulance, soon past, he was a genuinely sympathetic, kindly and companionable man.

Meanwhile Napoleon, after a week in Malta—during
which, with demoniac energy, he established a whole new
system of government and even found time to revolutionise
the university—had reached the Egyptian coast on July 1st.
He landed his army at once at Marabout and took Alexandria by storm next day.  Two days later he set out into
the desert.  Though his troops suffered horribly from heat
and thirst, for the wells had been filled with stones to delay
his advance, he reached Cairo and fought the battle of the
Pyramids, defeating a Mameluke army of more than twice
his strength.  Exactly three weeks after landing, he occupied
Cairo.  The first part of his great enterprise was achieved.

He set to work to establish French rule over the country. With characteristic cunning he sought to conciliate the Egyptians by false protestations of sympathy with the Mohammedan religion, just as the Kaiser was to do a century and a quarter later. He told them that he had fought Islam's battles in Europe. Had he not vanquished the Christian Pope ? Had he not overthrown the Knights of Malta, whose creed it was that they were appointed by God to destroy the Mohammedans ? A more doubtful account tells us that he consulted the chief priests of Cairo upon the possibility of admitting his army into the Moslem faith. There were, of course, two difficulties about this. First, there were certain formal preliminaries ; but these the priests were inclined to agree with him in regarding as superfluous. Much more serious was the question of wine-drinking. Napoleon argued with mock sincerity that, coming as they did from a cold country, his men could hardly be expected to abandon their national beverage. If the story may be believed, the priests, with ingenuity comparable with his own, suggested that this obstacle too might be overlooked, if the French soldiers demonstrated their attachment to Islam by a sufficient quantity of good works. At this point the negotiations appeared to have rested. Napoleon had more serious matters to concern him. Nelson had at last discovered the French fleet.

Napoleon had left his ships anchored in seeming safety, fifteen miles east of Alexandria, between the island of Aboukir and the Rosetta mouth of the Nile. Any other admiral but Nelson might have feared to attack a fleet so snugly protected. But he, without a moment's hesitation, signalled battle. Possessing no charts of the bay, he had to sound his way through the narrow entrance in the failing light of evening. Ship by ship he grappled with the French. By morning the French fleet was annihilated. Its commander, Brueys, was dead ; Nelson himself had been wounded in the forehead. The Battle of the Nile, as it came to be called, was one of the two most decisive naval engagements ever fought. Never before in history had a whole fleet been destroyed by another of similar strength. Even Trafalgar, seven years later, had not so over-whelming a result. The Battle of Tsushima in 1905, between the Russians and the Japanese, is the only other which equals it. The military effect of Nelson's victory was as decisive. Napoleon was cut off in Egypt.

Nelson, triumphant but convinced that his own wound was fatal, sailed for Naples. Maria Carolina, Queen of Naples, was obsessed with one ambition, to crush revolu-tionary France, and revenge her unhappy sister, Marie Antoinette. She possessed much of the resolution of her mother, Maria Theresa ; but her husband was an Italian Bourbon, and by no means a very prepossessing specimen of that eccentric family. Sir William Hamilton was the British representative at Naples ; his wife Emma, the Queen's most devoted friend and adherent. Emma threw herself at Nelson's glorious head ; he fell victim to her radiant if mature charms and thus, at second hand, became the Queen's instrument. I think it an understatement to say that the senile Hamilton was complacent of his wife's affair with Nelson : he probably connived at it, for he doted on her to the degree of sharing her delight in Nelson's amorous fervour. In that strange triangular household we may now leave Nelson and return to Egypt and Napoleon.

With his communications destroyed by the destruction of his fleet, Napoleon was now no longer wholly master of the Egyptian situation. The first move against him came in September, when the Turks, the nominal suzerains of the country, collected an army to attack him. Simul-taneously a rising broke out in Cairo, where the " good works " of the French had seemingly not wholly convinced the priesthood of their devotion to Islam. Suppressing the insurrection, Napoleon marched north-eastwards into Syria to face the Turkish attack. It must be remembered that a subsidiary purpose of his Eastern expedition was to overthrow the Turks with the aid of the Greeks and other Balkan Christians and, seizing Constantinople, to " take Europe in the rear." Now that he no longer could hope to " see myself, having founded a new religion, on my way to Asia, mounted on an elephant, a turban on my head, and in my hand a new Koran composed entirely according to my own ideas " ; he threw off the mask of sympathy with Islam, and bethought himself of his attack on Constantinople.

At first he was completely successful ; he swept through the desert of Jaffa and captured it, shooting the captives whom he could not feed. But when he reached the port of Acre he found himself confronted by two foes whom he could not so easily overcome.

One was the plague, or whatever went by that name. It ran through his army like a devouring beast, nor could even his prestige withstand the blow it dealt to the unhappy Frenchmen's spirits. They died like flies ; the survivors, terrified and weakened by privation, faltered. And inside Acre was Sir Sidney Smith.

This young man—he was only thirty-three ; Napoleon was twenty-nine—had already shown himself possessed of remarkable courage and initiative. He had distinguished himself at the battle of St. Vincent, at Chesapeake, at the Leeward Islands, and at Toulon. Captured by the French in a vessel which had run ashore on their coast in 1796, he was imprisoned for two years in Paris. He made a sensational escape from the Temple, and managed to cross the Channel to England. He was at once sent out to Constantinople to join his brother, the British minister. With a small naval force he hastened into the Levant to oppose Napoleon. Defeating the French ships which covered

BATTLE OF THE NILE—THE ATTACK AT SUNSET. NELSON'S FLAGSHIP "THE VANGUARD," WITH SIGNALS FLYING

the town, and capturing the siege-train which they were transporting, he occupied Acre in the middle of March, 1799, just in time to use Napoleon's captured artillery and to set it in some defensive shape against the invader. For two months the inspiration and courage of his leadership forced the Turkish garrison to hold out against the plague-stricken French ; on May 20th, Napoleon raised the siege. Sir Sidney Smith's exploit, following upon Nelson's victory at the Nile, was a turning-point in history. By preventing Napoleon from conquering Constantinople, he diverted the whole course of the future Emperor's career. Napoleon learned that, on land as well as on sea, the English were destined to be his most dangerous and relentless foes.

Returning to Egypt in June with his exhausted and bankrupt army, he destroyed at Aboukir on July 25th a Turkish army thrice as large as his own ; but, though this victory removed an imminent menace, it came too late to rekindle his ambition to found a new Eastern Empire. His one thought was to return to France.

During these amazing months in the Levant, Napoleon became definitely transformed into the man whom history knows to-day. Eager to reach France simultaneously with the news of his victory at Aboukir, which would, he knew, efface the impression of the Battle of the Nile and the failure at Acre, he embarked with a few members of his staff on August 22nd in two frigates, leaving the Egyptian command to Kleber. Avoiding the British fleet near Malta, he touched at Ajaccio, in his native island of Corsica, and reached Fréjus, near the mouth of the Rhône, on October 9th. The stage was now set for the eighteenth of Brumaire. Napoleon had left Toulon in June, 1798, a popular and successful young general, ready to seize any possible opportunity to advance his career. He returned now, sixteen months later, the man of destiny, the victor

of Aboukir, the father of his army, the self-assured saviour
of France, the Napoleon of legend. His countrymen could
not foresee that Kleber would be murdered only eight
months later, and his successor be utterly routed by the
British very soon afterwards. Though Napoleon must
have realised that his great Egyptian army was doomed,
he took good care not to say so. He had left it in the
lurch ; it now became his aim to secure such triumphs on
European soil as would make impossible any impression
of failure in Egypt on the minds of his countrymen. It
is a reasonable argument therefore that Nelson's victory
in the Battle of the Nile and Sir Sidney Smith's gallant
resistance at Acre assisted Napoleon's ambition.

The immediate result in Europe of Nelson's triumph was
the formation of the Second Coalition. Naples, protected
by his victorious fleet, began to make inroads upon the
French conquests. Suvarov, the brilliant but half-insane
Russian general, commanding a mixed force of Russian
and Austrian troops, retook most of the French gains in
Italy. Nelson snatched Malta from the weak French
garrison which Napoleon had left there. The Second
Coalition was encouraged to proceed upon its fateful
enterprise.

To the people of France, before Napoleon's return, the
situation must have looked desperate. The Egyptian
expedition was far away across the sea ; the news of early
Egyptian victories meant little to a country which feared
invasion at home. Nelson and the English fleet were loose
in the Mediterranean, planning, it must have seemed, to
descend on the coast there and repeat on French soil the
horrors perpetrated by the Neapolitans. Suvarov's army
too might turn from Italy upon France at any moment.
The French were aghast with gloomy forebodings. Then,
at this psychological moment, Napoleon, the magic leader,
reappeared at Fréjus. There followed Brumaire, a story

to be more fully told in the next article. The Directory fell ; he was installed as First Consul with all the powers of a dictator.

In itself and its achievements, the Egyptian expedition counts for little. Except that it created the myth of an especial French interest along the Nile—resurrected as late as the day when Major Marchand faced Lord Kitchener at Fashoda ; even to-day not wholly dead—it established nothing. The flower of French manhood wilted under the scorching Egyptian sun ; and England acquired a supremacy over that country which even to-day she has not wholly lost.

But the Egyptian campaign begot Napoleon the Emperor. It brought him for the first time into direct conflict with the greatest of his adversaries, England, and the greatest of his rivals, Nelson. It was the first act in that momentous historical drama which ended in the climax of Waterloo and in the tragic epilogue of St. Helena.

# THE 18TH BRUMAIRE

## THE UNEARNED INCREMENT OF EGYPT

"NAPOLEON found the crown of France in the gutter and picked it up on the point of his sword." Whether, in any sense or degree this trite saying may be true, there is universal agreement that the *coup d'état* of Brumaire not only affected Napoleon Bonaparte's career more than any other event in it, but did in fact determine his destiny.

It is outside the matter to argue whether any other man at any other period could have been matched with an equal opportunity or how far in a critical hour luck and his brother Lucien helped Napoleon or whether the pear was ripe and ready to fall into his mouth ;—the broad fact remains that in that hour of crisis, he was steady and strong enough to found a rule which was to lead France along levels of glory such as no one but himself could have dreamt of.

The opinion of a schoolboy as to his master, of a soldier as to his officer, and of a republic as to a leader, can generally be assumed as fairly correct even if such opinion is due to intuition rather than information ; the originator of a ghastly failure in the Near East set foot again on French soil to be greeted with a popular enthusiasm to which history can scarcely offer a parallel, and with an official chilliness for which frequent and even recent parallels can be easily quoted. The line between the award of a Victoria Cross and a court-martial for technical disobedience to orders is believed to be sometimes rather a narrow one ; the arrest of Napoleon for returning without his army was the alternative to the rapturous reception of one whose coming it was firmly held—if a little loosely argued—would cause the face of France to smile again. And while France *portrait le deuil du pays* Paris had been about as unhappy as it was possible for Paris to be, and a sort of gloomy inertia had been punctuated by spasms of fear that worse things were perhaps in store for her.

The vendors of newspapers hoarsely and defiantly shouted their sensational, if unveracious, stories, groups of unemployed gathered about the Porte Martin, suicides and murders abounded, the ill-lit streets were being infested with thieves and prostitutes who were allowed to pursue their grisly calling while inoffensive individuals were pounced upon by police and military. Social entertainments were rare except for the receptions given by Barras at Grosbois, the Opera had closed its doors and only the theatre, that institution indispensable for every Frenchman, remained active or in any sense agreeable.

The man of the moment was quick to read what was expected of him in the face of the folk who flocked on board his boat at Fréjus defying, and enabling him to defy, quarantine regulations with the cry that Austria was much more noxious than any plague, in the towns illuminated to honour his passage through them, in the delirious joy of the crowds at Lyons, in the displays of national colours which marked every mile of his journey. Travelling at full speed and leaving his luggage a prey to prowling brigands, he missed Josephine who had tried to intercept the last stages of his journey and to bring all her coquetry and feminine wiles to bear on him, and to crave his pardon before he had fully steeled himself against her. He arrived in the early morning to find himself alone in the little house, *entre cour et jardin*, in the renamed Rue La Victoire with every empty room redolent of a faithless spouse.

A day in which to rest and refresh himself in the company

of Madame, the mother, whose stern care for her children never tired and whose strong maternal love never varied, and then an unabashed culprit, knowing himself to be a popular idol, paid his respects to the Directoire who sat specially to see him and perhaps considered that as their first messenger had never landed in Egypt, his mission to summon Napoleon home might be considered as cancelled. The costume which Napoleon selected for the occasion was—and perhaps deliberately intended to be—a little peculiar :—a felt hat of an indescribable shape, an olive green tunic with a Turkish scimitar attached to the said tunic by silken cords. When he appeared the guard presented arms, some of the old soldiers standing about were moved to tears, and the soldier whom they would have followed to the cannon's mouth recognised, or pretended to recognise, many of them and pressed their hands with fervour. Gohier was the President and he gave the accolade on behalf of his colleagues with some carefully chosen phrases of welcome which drew from Napoleon an ardent declaration that his sword would never be drawn except in defence of the Republic and of the Government. A huge and very vocal crowd hung on his heels when he emerged and paid their homage as if he were scarcely a human being like themselves, little thinking that all the time a very human thought of Josephine was gnawing at his heart-strings. Napoleon had loved his wife with much of the romance of a boy and all the passion of a man. His love had only been tinged with jealousy when he had sailed for Egypt, but his brothers—more especially Lucien who had managed to keep up a fairly steady flow of letters—had left no stone unturned to foment that jealousy into rage, and had spared no effort to inform him of his wife's delinquencies, and to urge on him not only the propriety but the necessity of a divorce. The story of a conjugal *raccommodage* is an oft-told tale.

Josephine returns to find the door of her husband's room shut against her ; tears, cries, entreaties, prolonged for hour after hour, Eugène and Hortense adding their own to their mother's sobs and supplications until suddenly the door opens, the outraged husband relents, cooing and coaxing are redoubled, and the reconciliation is an accomplished fact ; Josephine resumes her place at her husband's table and in his bed, and, what was more important still, in his confidence. The husband may be rightly charged with conjugal weakness but at the back of his mind there lurked the notion that reconciliation might be very timely ; Josephine might be very useful in his new and great adventure, her birth and her connections meant something, just the something that he could not adduce for himself ; she could bring just the touch of gaiety and sparkle so necessary to make attractive the programme which he had sketched out. The programme, as a matter of fact, was a simple one—to do away with the Directoire and take over for himself complete charge of the State. " *L'état, c'est moi* " must be even truer for him than on the lips of a Bourbon king.

Now a free rein could be given to ambition, whether patriotic or personal, and there is no lack of advice, support and encouragement. " Do you think the thing is possible ? " Napoleon would ask, to be told that the thing was not only possible but three parts done. More especially the soldiers were heart and soul with him ; officers would chance getting leave of absence in their hurry to pay him homage while of course many out of a job and a good deal out at elbows repaired to him to retrieve their fortunes.

A General without an Army or a military post, in what for anyone else might have been a very false situation, is " the General," his family, his friends and the public know him as such. But neither now nor at any other time is there any trace of an eager soldier being unduly elated by popularity. He knew, no one better, that the open-mouthed approval of all except really good men is the precise measure of their possible hostility, and he would value applause at precisely its right worth and by not a grain over. He even declined to receive a military deputation lest some breach of military discipline should be attributed to him or them.

While his satellites were circling round him hungry for notice if for nothing more, Napoleon was at grips with the situation. He must first set himself to learn what he did not know—and outside Lucien's letters he knew very little—of internal events in the last eighteen months. He would know that Russia, England, Portugal and Austria had linked hands against France and that French commerce had been swept off the seas by Nelson, but he perhaps was to discover that the national purse was scarcely fatter than when Louis XIV handled it, that religious schism was rife, and that so far from Royalist feelings being stifled, there had been recurring revolts on behalf of the Bourbons. It needed but a rapid survey of the situation for him to decide, if he ever had any doubt on the subject, that his immediate duty lay at home, and his determination to oust the existing authorities and institute a stable government would be facilitated by evidence that France was tired of the hymn of hate which she had chanted through ten long and stormy years. Difference of opinion, honest or otherwise, as to the best means of saving the country, had sown bitter discord, but now people were weary of quarelling and Napoleon's own recent successes were doing much to bring men to preserve France from foreign aggression ; Bonaparte would consolidate what the Generals had done and at the same time set his country's internal house in order. Liberty, victory and peace, he said, would place the French Republic where she had stood in the eyes of Europe. A place which nothing but ineptitude or treachery

THE CAPTURE OF THE BASTILLE

*From a drawing by Prieur*

should cause her to lose. He knew that he must lean in one direction or another before acquiring supreme power, but he made up his mind that as soon as that power was acquired, he would rise above all political parties and create a government which would make direct appeal to the national goodwill and remake a France rich in material resources, impregnable from assault, and mother of a united family.

Something in the nature of a revolution was required but it must be something very velvety and as far as possible automatic ; the public was satiated with violence. The troops must only be called in at the last resort and on civilian requisition. The illegality must be carefully veiled and the change of government must be so smoothly effected that the thing would hardly be felt until the new powers had shown of what kindly stuff they were made.

His first idea was to get himself made a member of the Directoire, then to dominate and dissolve it ; the blow might be more easily and more lightly struck from within than from without. One of the Directors would surely make room for the man who was being universally and almost hysterically acclaimed ; the technical irregularity of his being ten years too young for the post could be easily brushed aside. But either because the constitutional scruples of Gohier and Moulin weighed with him or because he mentally refused any form of divided authority he decided to place himself nowhere than absolutely at the head of affairs but with the minimum of anything like force.

The great point was to win over the Abbé—and sometime Vicaire Général to the Bishop of Chartres—Sieyès. The newspapers had already intelligently anticipated something of the sort and had adumbrated a duumvirate to preside over the destinies of a regenerated Republic. " Fréjus where Napoleon landed is the birthplace of Sieyès," was a favourite expression of the journalists.

Lucien, now President of the Council, professed himself

L

all willing to act as intermediary between the professional soldier and the still professing if no longer practising priest. A few years earlier, with fraternal frankness, Lucien had written " Napoleon seems to me to have a strong inclination to be a tyrant, and I believe he would be one if he were king, and that his name would be for posterity and for the sensitive patriot a name of horror." But now Lucien inclined to a duumvirate, only he, and not Sieyès, was to be the peer of Napoleon ; he would see to the civil side of affairs while his brother would be engrossed with the army. But the immediate task was to hoist the hero into high office, and with that in view Lucien would lend himself to any arrangement. He would conduct negotiations with possible supporters, preside over social meetings, and make himself generally useful. Napoleon hesitated for a moment ; he and Sieyès were in character as the Poles apart ; the one, with all his faults, crystal clear, the other pedantic, dogmatic, and invested with a sort of " got up " mysticism. Then, while whole-hearted republicanism was a *sine qua non* of the projected coup, Sieyès was a little under suspicion for a certain, real or imaginary, Royalist tendency. For three days the two kept apart, each professing to consider that the first visit should come from the other, Bonaparte meanwhile coquetting a little with Barras, who however was wholly indisposed to contemplate himself as " brilliant second." But there could be no doubt as to Sieyès having the better and much stronger following, and whatever his handicap there was no real question as to which of the two men was the better adapted to Napoleon's purpose.

How often it happens that an important arrangement comes near to being spoilt, and is finally facilitated, by some trifle. Napoleon's aide-de-camp called at Sieyès' house to announce that the General would pay him a visit next morning at a certain hour. Sieyès was out at the time and on his return, wishing perhaps to hang back a little, sent his brother to say that the hour named would not suit him as he would then be at a meeting of the Council. Napoleon flew into a temper, roundly scolded the unhappy A.D.C. for giving an incorrect message, and declared that he would call on no one. He was the " glory of the nation " and it was for others to call on him. Happily Talleyrand came to the rescue, spoke straight words to an angry soldier, and a day or two later the newspapers could announce that Bonaparte had paid a special visit to the Directors Sieyès and Ducos and that the visit had been promptly and politely returned. The first interview began a little awkwardly but Napoleon quickly changed his tone, compared the recent *malentendu* to a couple of Duchesses quarrelling about their tabourets, and while underlining with every observation his own strength, shaped every phrase to charm and attract. Sieyès expressed himself as quite willing to back the movement provided the object were really to save the country and lay deep the foundation stones of liberty ; he moreover had a plan of his own which might be useful and which he would presently disclose. So things stood for the moment ; the two men affected in public a certain coldness towards one another, while their mutual friends kept their hands together, Talleyrand suggesting how things and Rœderer what things should be done.

The plan which Sieyès propounded commended itself wholly to Bonaparte who never evinced any wish to pull up a plant in order to look at the roots. The main idea was to let the existing authorities destroy themselves and to overthrow the Constitution quite constitutionally. The Ancients enjoyed the right to shift, if necessary, the venue of the sessions, and to St. Cloud the sessions should be transferred where it would be easier to extract from the two Assemblies a vote in favour of a revision of the Constitution and the creation of new powers. In the discussions which ensued Napoleon displayed infinite tact ; he allowed Sieyès—who seemed to have disliked putting pen to paper —to ramble on about future organisations and committed himself to no word which might infer that their co-operation would be continued or which might in any degree fetter his own ambitions or give anything less than full play to his own genius. And by tacit consent the two men agreed that for the next days they must remain hand in hand, and that they would avoid going too closely into details lest any disagreement should arise between them. Napoleon only insisted that the secret of the plan—he declined the word plot—should be kept as close as possible ; only a select few, such as Talleyrand, Rœderer and Cambacérès were admitted to inner knowledge, the others only being informed as to the parts they might be called upon to play. Napoleon's " manners " were never more gracefully employed than in winning over a couple of hesitating Generals ; Jourdon succumbed to an invitation to dinner with a heart-to-heart talk afterwards ; Moreau yielded to a jewelled damas and a few such phrases as : " General, I had several of your Lieutenants with me in Egypt, and, needless to say, they highly distinguished themselves." Murat was of course amenable from the start and eventually available to lead the Grenadiers into the orangery at St. Cloud and dissipate the Council. Berthier, Lannes, and Leclerc were willing helpmates and something more ; Bernadotte could scarcely be approached—still less reckoned upon—after his outspoken advice that any entertainment to Bonaparte should be postponed—" till he accounts in a satisfactory manner for having abandoned his Army " ; Bernadotte's renewed adhesion was however only to be a matter of time and opportunity. Fouché could, and did, make himself extremely useful by arresting any Deputies who seemed to threaten danger and by rendering services which only the police—and perhaps only Fouché's police—

LAST VICTIMS OF THE REIGN OF TERROR

could accomplish.  Josephine, whose good looks were still
more than equal to the test of candle-light, brought to bear
on the circumstances, with perfect correctitude, all the
richness of feminine attire and all the resources of feminine
attractions.  The little house in the Rue de la Victoire was
a recruiting station of the most sumptuous but practical
kind ; soldiers and savants were made equally welcome,
and if the women were few, they made valuable contribution
to the soirées.  Napoleon himself was the centre of every
gathering, leaning easily against the chimney-piece or
moving from one group to another, he talked pleasantly
but authoritatively on a variety of subjects but managed
to make each one a peg on which to hang an emphatic
protest against any idea of his wishing to do anything
contrary to law and order.  He went out very little and
scarcely at all in the evenings ; few *salons* could boast of
his presence but he frequented the Institute of which he
had been made a member and talked philosophy and science
with men like Volnay.  Through these days of trial his
demeanour was irreproachable ; he was frank, simple, and
entirely conciliatory, and his abstinence from general
society only caused interest in his every word and deed,
real or imaginary, to increase with every hour.

It is a commonplace how often brave and brilliant
soldiers are at the same time devout and earnest Christians.
Napoleon, if not a " pratiquant," was avowedly a " croyant "
and was imbued with a sense of reverence for sacred things
and it will always remain a matter for surmise how far he
resented—he quite certainly regretted—the insult offered
to the Holy Church in the banquet spread within the walls
lavishly decorated for the festivity of St. Supplice.  The
function was originally to have been a tribute from both
Chambers to Bonaparte and Moreau ; it dwindled into an
affair got up by a few of the Ancients who were now Bona-
partists almost to a man.  The chief guest did what he could

to make the feast as lively as a funeral ; he said little and ate less, and only asserted himself by toasting in wine specially provided by Duroc, " Harmony of all the French." Did Sarah Bernhardt remember this little exhibition when in reply to the health of France, insolently offered by the Prussian Minister at Copenhagen not long after the confiscation of Alsace and Lorraine, she rose to her feet with the cry : " Yes, let us drink to France and the whole of France " ?

A few days earlier Sieyès had agreed with Bonaparte that the outline of the perfected Constitution should not be laid before the Council but should be submitted to a Committee ; having so done he surrendered any measure of direct authority in the " plot " leaving Moreau, who had entered Paris almost surreptitiously, and Napoleon, who had entered in a blaze of triumph, captains of the hour. The draft which the Abbé had submitted laid down that the Councils of the Ancients were, quite constitutionally, to pass three measures as a preliminary of upsetting the Constitution itself. The sessions of both Councils were to be fixed to take place at St. Cloud, and Bonaparte was to assume command of the troops in Paris ; at St. Cloud Sieyès and Roger Ducos were to tender resignations which would be accepted, and lastly Gohier, Barras and Moulin were to be compelled into resignation, and a provisional triumvirate would be formed. Bonaparte, Sieyès and Roger Ducos, needless to say, would carry out the work of reconstitution.

The nerves of the conspirators were a little strained and it required Napoleon's iron nerve to be calm when the clatter of a cavalry escort disturbed a midnight talk he was holding with Talleyrand in the Rue Taitbout. A hurried exit was about to be made through a convenient back door when the cavalry was discovered to be only engaged in escorting a game-house keeper with his spoils from the Palais Royal.

On the morrow of the banquet it was decided that the blow should be struck on November 10th : the Ancients were to be assembled on the 17th Brumaire and to fix a session for both Assemblies for the 18th at St. Cloud. This might of course give rise to a certain amount of citizen excitement but it would be comparatively unimportant if the temper of the troops were all right, and this was a consideration which had to be reckoned with, but could be reckoned with cheerfully. The soldier is usually quite incorruptible for political ends, but the soldiers of France just then had a long bill of complaints which they expected Napoleon to settle for them. Their rations had been scanty, their tobacco had reached vanishing point—one pipe per company would be passed from mouth to mouth—their pay had been a little more than sketchy. " If there is one thing in which the soldier excels it is in comment " : so runs a line in a recent war play. The comment on French soldiers' lips just then mostly took some shape as : " The ―― have kept us for six months without pay and boots ; if only Bonaparte were at the top ! "

In the course of an all-night session on the 16th-17th Brumaire the Ancients voted that Bonaparte, in order to carry out their decree, should be appointed Commander of the Paris Garrison as well as of the National, and their own Guard. Napoleon's own night was scarcely less wakeful, and with the dawn all the Generals, except Jourdan and Augereau, who were not invited, came to his door. Bernadotte yielded so far to his brother-in-law's blandishments as to put in an appearance but declined to put on uniform. Lefebvre, however, who was still, so far as he knew, Commander of the Paris Garrison and who regarded himself as a pillar of the Republic, had donned uniform but had been a little startled on his way to the Rue de la Victoire, to see troops moving without his orders. Bonaparte checked any hesitation and choked any protest with a beau geste : " See here is the sword I carried at the Pyramids. I give it to you as a mark of confidence." " Into the river with the lawyers ", came the reply on more forcible lines than even Sydney Smith's famous remark.

The ground was now thoroughly if cautiously prepared for the Ancients to transfer on the 18th Brumaire (November 9th) the session of both Councils to St. Cloud under the rather flimsy excuse that a Jacobin plot threatened the peace of Paris ; these worthies also plumped for placing the troops in, and near, Paris under Bonaparte who at the Tuileries adroitly avoided taking the usual and formal oath of fidelity to the Constitution. Here he was no less adroitly backed by Lucien, who offered the somewhat specious plea that as the sessions had been transferred to St. Cloud, no oath could be taken anywhere else than there.

The next morning, curiously enough, when the French temperament and all the *va-et-vient* is considered, there was little sign of any disorder. Was there a feeling difficult to define but impossible to deny that a master hand was about to grasp the helm? Moreover, the Jacobins only now suspected that the overthrow of the Constitution and not its reform was the order of the day ; St. Cloud of course buzzed all the forenoon with eager talk, discussion, contradiction and prophecy. By two o'clock the Five Hundred were mustered in the Orangery on the ground floor, the Ancients upstairs in the Hall of Apollo, while Bonaparte, his heart beating high if his pulse was beating a little unsteadily, was closeted in a bitterly cold room with Sieyès whose courage now showed signs of oozing between his fingers. The Ancients proceeded to pass a vote to postpone consideration of the proposal to entrust Bonaparte with the conduct of affairs, giving as a reason that unless the Directors were present, their action might be illegal. Just as the Secretary announced that four of the Directors

had resigned and the fifth was under control, Napoleon
appeared at the door. It was now four o'clock and he
could bear the suspense no longer. " The wine is decanted
and one must drink it. Hold your tongue ! " he said in
the tone of a man who is more accustomed to give orders
than to take advice, to Augereau who tried to restrain him.
But from the moment of his entrance into the great hall
he was at once nonplussed by having to stand not as he
wished facing the President, but a little on one side. The
historian, however, will perhaps always find it difficult to
account for the complete breakdown of a man who was
generally apt to be a master of himself no less than of all
his subordinates. Soldiers, however brilliant with the
sword and clever with the pen, are said to be at a grave
disadvantage in argument, to fail altogether in anything
like oratory, and thus to become an easy prey to the politician. Napoleon, who was admirable in direct appeal to
individuals and masterly in his military proclamations,
had little experience of addressing Assemblies and perhaps
no gift for swaying civilian crowds. Superadded to this
disability and to some degree of nervous exhaustion, there
was possibly the feeling that, having always boasted of
being as good a citizen as he was soldier, he was now setting
himself defiantly against the law. He wanted to be ardent
and convincing ; he only alternately blustered and hesitated.
" You are on a volcano ; let me speak with all the frankness
of a soldier " :—then with that egotism which later on
was sometimes sadly to cramp him, " I was quietly in Paris
when you called on me to carry out a change of power ;
you talk of Cæsar and Cromwell and a military government ;
if I had wanted a military government should I have rushed
to support a national representation ? Remember that the
god of battles and the god of victory are on my side." (The
last phrase was really a réchauffé of what he had said at
Cairo.) He was pulled up short by a voice : " What about

the Constitution ? " Napoleon then tried to enunciate some rather wild accusations until his friends sought to intervene and prevent him from any further sorry exhibitions. There was to follow the odious scene which bid fair to overthrow the whole scheme of Napoleonic redemption when with the entrance of a party of Grenadiers, some of the Deputies lost all self-control, rushed at Napoleon and shook him until his teeth chattered in his head. The successor to Alexander and Julius Cæsar, stammering and nearly fainting, must be led out of the Assembly by two soldiers in a state of physical and mental collapse. The situation, within a shred of being lost, was saved by the superb sang-froid of Lucien. Calm, cool, under perfect control, he contrived by little less than a miracle of combined energy and tact, to restrain his yelling assailants and to make himself heard. In stern, cutting tones he refused to put the vote of outlawry, and with a gesture, a little suggestive of the Porte St. Martin, cast off his official robes, threw his insignia of office on the desk in front of him with the exclamation : " Let me be heard as the advocate of the man whom you rashly and falsely accuse." Further disturbance was cut short by a party of Guards whom Napoleon had so far recovered himself as to send in, and who without further parley escorted Lucien to where his horse awaited him in the inner courtyard. Never did magistrate give fuller play to his magisterial powers than Lucien proceeded to do. Lucien swung himself into the saddle, and in sonorous voice called out : " General Bonaparte, and you soldiers, the President of the Council announces to you that factious men with daggers have interrupted the deliberations of the Assembly. He authorises you to use force against these disturbers. The Assembly of the Five Hundred is dissolved." Then perceiving a slight hesitation among the troops he draws his sword with a shout : " I swear to plunge this sword into the bosom of my brother if he ever should aim a blow at the liberties of France." A further bright idea occurred to him. " The majority of the legislature," he exclaimed, " are honourable men, but in the room from which we have come are a few English hirelings, assassins, who hold the others in terror." There was a movement in the line. " Let us go back to the hall, and if they resist, kill," murmured Napoleon hysterically. " Keep quiet," was the brother's reply. " Do you think you are talking to the Mamelukes ? " The word of command rang out, the Guards advanced, and in a few minutes the room in which the disorder had reigned was empty. The coup had been brought off.

Where the soldier had for once in his life failed miserably the citizen had succeeded gloriously. If from the November 9th, 1799, can be traced the rise of Napoleon's imperishable fame, the success of the day must in large degree be attributed to Lucien. Curiously enough, it also sowed the seeds of distrust between the brothers, a distrust which expanded into discord and finally into a quarrel so acute as to render it necessary to separate them. Did the word gratitude not exist in Napoleon's vocabulary or did he then remember that not only was Lucien strong when he was weak, but that it was Lucien who quickly consolidated the work of the soldiers, it was Lucien who quickly procured a decree which named Bonaparte, Sieyès and Ducos as provisional consuls while a commission was formed to deal with the necessary changes in the Constitution, and lastly that it was Lucien who collected a group of the younger deputies to cloak with legality the happenings of a day when parliamentary government fell under the military sword ?

# SHERMAN

THE American Civil War was, as everyone knows, one of the decisive wars of history.

Contemporary judgments as to the probable event were usually discordant.

Even the issues were not clearly discerned. It was, as we realise now, a struggle between two divergent and indeed inconceivable conceptions of social and political life.

All the military odds were in favour of the North whose numbers and industrial resources had determined the result of the war almost before the first gun thundered. And there was always latent behind these advantages the moral strength of those who revolted against the view that man should legally be the purchased and abusable chattel of man.

On the other hand the languid graces ; the unquestioned gallantry ; the stubborn resistence to an overwhelming balance of strength ; must always win sympathy and enlist the admiration for the struggle of the South.

The result of the war was decisive. It brought into existence that great homogeneous nation whose giant growth—with all its extravagances—is the most amazing portent of the last two hundred years.

Sherman was almost the most remarkable of the military leaders who achieved this result. He was one of the great civilian soldiers ascending at times to the company of Cromwell and Clive and always exceeding in stature the majority of professional soldiers. The work of Captain Liddell Hart upon the subject of this memoir is therefore extremely welcome.

His pen has been both busy and fruitful but surely it has seldom been more attractively and usefully employed than in sketching—with a well-filled-in background—the career, and in exhibiting the character, of William Sherman. The writer's military accuracy is for the most part unimpeachable and if some of his dicta lay themselves open to comment there is nothing to disturb the authority of a very valuable book.

As was the case with so many other American Regular officers, Sherman, after a brief bout of fighting against the Seminole Indians, enjoyed a long spell of civilian life which was roughly broken into by the call to arms for a civil war. In this respect it may not be uninstructive to remember how many distinguished warriors on land and sea have been summoned from retirement, or half pay, to speak effectively with their country's enemy. Nelson passed many years eating out his heart ashore ; Rodney, through the generosity of a French nobleman, was released from his creditors in Paris, to win the great victory off the Saintes ; Lee was living the life of a country gentleman ; Stonewall Jackson was a Professor in a Cadet School ; Grant was a somewhat unsuccessful business man ; Kitchener was British Agent at Cairo ; and Hindenburg was in something more shadowy than retirement when the summons to active service reached their ears. Yet, to quote no others, Nelson reigns on a pinnacle all his own ; Lee was to prove himself one of the greatest masters of strategy who have joined an honoured page in military history ; Stonewall Jackson was to furnish material for a biography which is perhaps without parallel ; Grant was the founder of the attrition school of war ; Kitchener was to create the New Armies which crushed into dust the " accursed system of Prussianism " ; Hindenburg was to shed none of his prestige even in the dark cloud of catastrophic defeat. It would seem that a period wholly free from the monotony of peace-time soldiering, given to steady thought and contact with men of all professions, may be no bad preparation for the grave duties which the exercise of high command in the field or on the sea must always involve.

As the United States Army of seventy years ago consisted of some 1600 men scattered over small posts and detailed to deal with Indian frays, Sherman, when the great trial of strength came, had never seen, far less manœuvred with, any large body of troops and, unlike Lee and Jackson, he had missed any share in the Mexican campaign. Nor did the intellectual side of war seem to make any direct appeal to him. He read little and wrote less on military subjects, and it is fair to say that the Civil War in which he was to find lasting fame, found him a normal, hard-headed, home-loving, money-acquiring American.

It was at Bull Run that in command of a Brigade he made a distinct, and distinguished mark, but the fight itself has generally been given the character of a collision in which luck, and the initiative of local commanders, were the leading features. The Southern Army acting on the defensive and with a larger proportion of Regular officers capable of thinking and acting for themselves, was better equipped than the Union forces and won a victory which in a sense was more unhappy for them than defeat. For the South in a glow of optimism thought her cause to be quickly and already won, whereas the North, taught by disaster, stamped her great foot and set herself to organise a real army.

The result of Bull Run did something to stimulate popular sympathy in England for the Confederation of the South ; Palmerston the Prime Minister, and several of his colleagues had a distinct bias in that direction, whereas the Queen and the Prince Consort inclined slightly, and unobtrusively, to the opposite side. Mr. Gladstone's own indiscretions gave rise to the malicious accusation that he was actually a subscriber to a Confederate loan. But he must be judged by his own words : " A friendly correspondent," he writes to the Duchess of Sutherland, " is sorry the South has my sympathies. But the South has not my sympathies except in the sense that the North has them also. I wish them both cordially well ; in both I see the elements of future power and good." Mr. Gladstone's biographer is not slow to suggest that in his reflections on the struggle the statesman curiously forgot that it was not a political contest but a social revolution that was at stake ; that secession meant not an official split but the erection of a barbaric State moulded on a system which was to keep the labourer in perpetual bondage, and yet for ever to be contiguous to that of a nation founded on free industry and political equality. Was it lack of insight which caused a statesman usually very circumspect to utter the famous phrase at Newcastle which described Jefferson Davis as " founding a nation " ? Thirty-four years later Mr. Gladstone was to write of that phrase : " This declaration most unwarrantable to be made by a Minister of the Crown, with no authority other than his own, was not due to any partisanship for the South or hostility to the North. I really—though most strangely—believed that it was an act of friendship to all America to recognise that the struggle was virtually at an end ; that my opinion was founded on a false estimate of the facts was the least part of my fault." Never perhaps, as Mr. Gladstone so frankly and disarmingly admitted, were future military events so entirely to belie a politician's registered opinion.

No narrative of William Sherman should omit the story of that officer after Bull Run who complained to Lincoln that Sherman had threatened to shoot him, and of the President's reply: " Well, if I were you and he threatened to shoot, I would not trust him, for I believe he would do it."

Sherman's call was now from the West where Robert

Anderson in Kentucky, dealing with the situation which oscillated between "secesh" and "anti-secesh" tendencies, cast about for capable assistants. Sherman and Thomas were his choice, and no better choice could have been made. The conflict of opinion between Easterners and Westerners, which reasserted itself in the Great War, has often served as a text to illuminate military controversies, and there have been military writers to assure us that the struggle between Lee and McLellan, Hooker, Meade and Grant in the East were of less decisive importance than the passages of arms in the West. Here as elsewhere the cooler view would probably be that military events in the Eastern and Western theatres of America interacted on one another, and that a long drawn out war must be studied as a whole rather than in respect of its various fronts and phases. In that grim conflict it was not a point of occupying this or that territory or of defeating this or that commander, but of crushing the spirit of revolt in the Southern States, and this could only be done by exhibiting to the general mass of the Southern people the military power of the Union as an overwhelming reality. "Your real enemy," said Kitchener to Haig, "does not consist of the men in front of you but of the German people behind them." His meaning was that so long as Germany could put in a fresh man at arms to replace every man killed, wounded or missing, so long as she could replace with a fresh gun every gun lost or destroyed, no victory—however showy— could be decisive.

Initial advantages lay immensely with the North; her population was nearly four times as great as that of her adversary; she monopolised the industrial resources of the Union; she had command of the sea. On the other hand the Southern States were a vast area, thinly populated, largely self-supporting as regards foodstuffs, inhabited by a fiery-tempered people full of sectional patriotism, and heartily hating the North. The people south of Mason's and Dixon's line were in many respects a race alien to the North, and curiously enough the " poor white " class was even more fiercely sectional than the wealthy planter. Apart from the rather overdone slavery question, an economic point strained to an issue, the South wanted Free Trade, liberty to buy manufactured goods from the cheapest markets, and resented as an exploitation for the benefit of Northern manufacturers the demand of the North for high Protection. This to be or not to be between Free Trade and Protection had great international reactions. Both for France and Great Britain the triumph of the South involved a definite economic gain by opening the Southern States as unrestricted markets for their goods. Naturally then Lincoln was keenly alive to the loss of prestige which any threat against Washington would involve, and conversely never forgot that the fall of Richmond would banish the fear of foreign intervention ever sub-latent in his mind. If one gives full importance to the Eastern theatre of the war, one must realise that no other policy than that of the slow strangulation of the Confederacy could have achieved finality. The distances to be traversed were too great and the enemy's resistance too stubborn to admit of any procedure save that of a slow sapping of Southern strength. The cruel and disabling weakness of the Confederacy lay in its lack of capacity to manufacture arms and munitions, and in the great river lines which opened the way to her fairest and most fertile regions. These streams gave to an enemy access in roadless regions ; once in control, for instance, of the Mississippi, he could cut the Confederacy in twain, move his forces from point to point and supply them, with a fine contempt for railways.

The campaign for the re-conquest of the Confederacy— for it mounted to no less—had for its main points the blow

M

at Richmond, the blockade, and the fight for control of the Mississippi. McLellan's thrust at Richmond, however directly unsuccessful, tied down the East Confederate leaders to the defence of the Southern capital, and thus weakened the resistance to Grant. The blockade gnawed at the vitals of the Southern people ; the cotton in the fields rotted where it might have been bartered for guns and rifles ; coast shipping, which played so great a part in the social life of the Southerners, languished more and more. The Federal blockade thus brought about stagnation by its strangle-hold and it is within just surmise that Sherman's march to the sea would have been an operation alike perilous and uncertain had Georgia not been segregated from her sister States. The effort of the South to break the blockade by building the *Merrimac* has been much embroidered ; this much advertised ship could scarcely deal any paralysing stroke. She was a shallow-water craft useful only in rivers, and the Federal ships which she sank were at anchor. *Monitor* which opposed her was also a shallow-water boat and foundered ultimately at sea. The suspicions with which naval officers regarded Ericsson's design were not ill-founded, and the celebrated duel between *Monitor* and *Merrimac* was scarcely *à l'outrance*, as neither ship was competent to challenge or defend the command of the sea. The seizure of Forts Henry and Donelson by Grant in February 1862, was a brilliant overture to the campaign in the West, the full points of which were lost owing to the divided control and to Halleck's hesitations. With the South everywhere on the defensive, Jefferson Davis, who had been a pupil at a military academy, insisted on keeping the supreme military control in his own hands, and even to men like Lee and Joseph Johnston nothing like a free hand or free head was given. Not for the first or last time in military history the amateur as a strategist was to prove a disaster to his own side.

Captain Liddell Hart " produces " very ably his chief actor ; it must, however, be conceded that the strategist has, on the whole, done so oftener ; and on a larger scale— twice wounded and with three horses shot under him—in the bitter battle of Shiloh, which, at the outset a Confederate success, ended, largely owing to the death of Albert Sidney Johnston, in a Confederate disaster. The Battle of Shiloh has been fought out over and over again on paper, and criticisms have been freely lavished on Grant, Johnston and Beauregard, with insufficient excuse for their in-experience in handling large bodies of troops, and with perhaps insufficient recognition of Beauregard's skill in extricating his exhausted and bewildered forces from the grip of an enemy powerfully reinforced by fresh troops. What Sherman did and dared at Shiloh may well be studied afresh, and could not be better explained than in the narra-tive at every stage absorbing, which Captain Liddell Hart offers us. Sherman, now a Brigadier, was given an oppor-tunity of displaying that spirit of loyalty without which military merit is little worth but in which soldiers are often extremely deficient. Rumours—largely to be traced to disaffected stragglers from the battle—brought Grant into ill odour at Washington, which his own frank report was not able wholly to dispel ; so energetic indeed was the mud throwing that but for Sherman's dogged insistence to the contrary, the resignation of a most valuable soldier might have been tendered and accepted. The same advice may be offered in relation to the Seven Days in the East and the succession of bloody struggles which culminated in the Confederate invasion of the North, and the hotly contested, yet indecisive, battle of the Antietam. The next great event in the West was the reaching out for Vicksburg, which started not too happily. With Sherman in an attempt to seize Chickasaw Bluffs, Grant assumed command, mainly to surpass McClernand who was now to conduct the operations over Sherman's head. Before Vicksburg fell to Grant's bold and skilful manœuvres, there must be noted the not unusual crop of intrigues, quarrels with the Press, distorted communiqués and heated controversies, in pleasant contrast to which comes Sherman's generous and spontaneous admission that " Grant is entitled to every bit of the credit for the campaign. I opposed it. I wrote him a letter about it."

Parallel with the campaign of Vicksburg, which fell on July 4th, 1863, was Lee's attempt indirectly to relieve the pressure on the West by that renewed blow at Washington which brought about the Battle of Gettysburg. The observation has been made that this critical action exposes the reverse of the medal as regards raids, area-warfare and so forth. Stuart's cavalry, absent on a raid, deprived Lee of " eyes and ears " at a moment when those members were of first rate importance to the body ; Longstreet's gospel as to the superiority of defence over attack took some of the heart from his support of his Chief's plans, and if for a moment the victory which would have ensured foreign recognition for the Confederacy was within Lee's grasp, the opportunity slipped through his fingers, not to be recovered. After the fall of Vicksburg, Grant assumed supreme command in the West with Sherman as his trusted Lieutenant ; move and counter-move brought Rosencrans and Bragg to face one another south of Murphreesboro. Rosencrans struck at Bragg who recoiled and then hit back at Chichamaug, and after one of the fiercest battles of the war drove Rosencrans into Chattanooga and invested him there. With Grant's concentration to relieve Rosencrans, occurred an episode which invites reminiscence. Sherman was carefully surveying the enemy's position and cogitating his plan of attack ; he suddenly shut his long glass with a snap and turned to W. F. Smith, the Chief Engineer, with the crisp words : " I can do it."

WILLIAM T. SHERMAN

On July 20th, 1812, just fifty years earlier, Wellington, on the morning of Salamanca, had come down from his observation post on the Arapile for some breakfast in a farmyard when an A.D.C. brought him word that an important movement was taking place in the enemy's lines. Wellington took a peep through his glasses ; " By God," he said, " that will do." With his mouth full he galloped back to his post of observation and after examining the enemy, shut up his glass, turned to the Spanish attaché, and exclaimed : " Mon cher Alava, Marmont est perdue " : he had detected an evolution which would separate the French left wing from the centre and one of his big opportunities had come.

Despite difficulties of terrain and inco-ordination in attacks, the Federal superiority sufficed to push back the Confederates, and Chattanooga had serious strategic effects. The battle was fruitful in controversy but Captain Liddell Hart is perhaps a little censorious in remarking that " everybody knows that amid the uncertainties of war mistakes must be made, but nobody knows the General who admits that he has made one." The inner story of the experience of most famous soldiers reveals the frequent admission of errors of judgment, and one of the great leaders in the Great War was heard to say of the day's operations that many mistakes had been made but no one had made so many as himself. Has the author forgotten, too, the bitter regret expressed by Grant for the Battle of Coldharbour ?

At Chattanooga Grant thought, and said, that Sherman's position during a phase of the battle implied a certain lack of judgment. Whether *post hoc* or *propter hoc*, President Lincoln, weary of special pleadings to explain individual failures, and conscious that the handling of men in battle is a highly specialised trade, decided to put one General in supreme command, to refrain himself from interfering with that General, and to suffer no one else to do so. It may be remembered that his example was wisely followed twenty years later by Queen Victoria who insisted that no mandate from Downing Street should affect Lord Wolseley's plans for crushing Arabi's rebellion. Grant, crowned with the laurels of Vicksburg and Chattanooga, was Lincoln's choice ; the office of Lieutenant-General, dormant since the days of Washington, was revived for him, and he repaired to the East to grapple once and for all with Lee. Sherman took over Grant's duties in the East, and to read his correspondence at this period is to recognise anew his military sense and devotion to duty, and yet to admit a little unwillingly that his outlook was somewhat lacking in breadth. The commander in the West seemed to see things as in a picture, whereas the Generalissimo saw them as in a plan. " As to the future," Sherman wrote, " I now exhort you to come out West. . . . From the West when our task is done, we shall make short work of Charleston and Richmond, and the impoverished coast to the Atlantic." Grant thought otherwise. The loss of Washington would certainly have been as disastrous to the Union as the loss of Paris to the Entente in the Great War. " I will stay with the Army," he wrote to his Lieutenant, " of the Potomac, and operate directly against Lee's army wherever it may be found. . . . You I propose to move against Johnston's army to break it up and to get into the interior of the enemy's country as far as you can, inflicting all the damage you can against their war resources." The helplessness of Napoleon's Generals when confronted with sudden difficulties was largely due to their Imperial master's method of laying upon them orders in too much detail. Had Grant this in mind when he added : " I do not propose to lay down for you a plan of campaign, but simply to lay down the work it is desirable to have done, and leave you free to execute it in your own way."

With subsidiary orders to Banks for operations against

Mobile, and for Butler to strike at Richmond we have the outline of Grant's plans for 1864. It was not to be a matter of East or West but of concerted action and unison of effort against the common foe. Grant could not only reckon on his numerical superiority—the Union troops in the field were little short of 1,500,000 men—but on the rock fact that his army, man for man, was better equipped and better trained than the men he had to meet ; Halleck, whatever his deficiencies as a strategist, was a good administrator and had built up a solid system of training. The South were suffering from the effects of the blockade, the Federal control of the river lines, the disrepair of their railways, and the ragged and barefoot condition of their soldiers. Wade Hampton's cavalry, armed in many cases with flint-lock, muzzle-loading horse pistols, or ancient carbines, faced mounted armed men with modern revolvers or Sharp's repeating rifles. Their one advantage lay in the enormous distance to be traversed by an invading army whose strength was constantly drained by detachments, while, of course, opportunities were offered for skilful leaders to penetrate gaps in column and strike at flanks.

Captain Hart's fine eulogy of Sherman's Atlanta campaign is sure to be contrasted with the rather chilly estimate made by Hamley in the 1866 edition of his *Operations of War*. Anyhow the struggle between two Generals, both as bold as they were skilful, is a fascinating study. Johnston would entrench a position which Sherman, with a very much larger and better equipped force, would approach ; he would examine Johnston's lines, decide them to be too formidable to attack, and dividing his army in two—each half being nearly equal to Johnston's whole—would remain facing his foe with one moiety, while the other would make a detour to threaten the opponent's flank :—Johnston would then retreat and take up a position further back. Resaca, Calhoun, the Allatoone Hills, were all won in this fashion,

Sherman being unable to ensnare his antagonist, while that antagonist was unable to hit back. On June 27th Sherman found himself forced to an attack on the Kenesaw Mountain sector ; the coup failed, but he was able later to manœuvre Johnston's still unbroken army across the Chattahoochee.

Now came into play Jefferson Davis's personal antipathy to one of his most brilliant Generals. He had insisted on retaining military control, he had always disparaged Johnston, and now seized the opportunity of forced retreats before a vastly superior force to supersede him with one of his own henchmen, General Hood, who in a badly-conceived and worse-managed attack, was very roughly handled. Hood's further counter-strokes were scarcely less clumsy, and it has even been thought that in Jefferson Davis Sherman found a friend rather than an adversary, and that, if Johnston had remained in the field, his expulsion from Atlanta would anyhow have been at a far heavier cost. A comparison is made between Grant's " failures " in the East against Lee with Sherman's triumph over Hood. Measured in territory won, there was not much difference in Grant's advance to Richmond and Sherman's advance to Atlanta. Grant had 119,000 men against Lee's 61,000, while Sherman had 98,000 against 50,000 under Johnston, but while Sherman was lucky in the substitution of Hood for Johnston, Grant was throughout up against the most formidable of the Southern Generals.

The march to the sea was at once the most spectacular episode and the most dreadful duty of Sherman's career. How far the duty to be done involved the dreadfulness imparted into it may always be an open question, but at least it is to Sherman's credit that after leaving Atlanta, the towns of Georgia were leniently treated, while at Savannah he was immediately concerned to issue supplies to the people. Sherman's object is thus stated. " I propose

LIEUT. CUSHING BLOWING UP THE CONFEDERATE RAM "ALBEMARLE," OCTOBER. 1864

to demonstrate the vulnerability of the South and make its inhabitants feel that war and individual ruin are synonymous terms." His scheme was to leave Thomas to hold the line of the Tennessee, thus forbidding a Confederate thrust at the territory already won, while he himself would stride from Atlanta to the Atlantic, living on the country in the widest sense of the term. He could of course gather confidence from his overwhelming numerical superiority ; he estimated the strength of the Southern Army at 40,000 men, and he could leave Thomas to hold his line with 73,000 men while he himself would have 60,000 well equipped soldiers to follow him. How often can we read of a commander who was able to divide his forces and leave each half so superior to the enemy's whole as to avoid any danger of anything like a real defeat ? The Russians, when in August, 1914 they hazarded an analogous but much less dangerous manœuvre, paid a ghastly price at Tannenberg. Sherman's plans were of course based upon a careful estimate of his enemy's character as well as of the means at his enemy's disposal, and he could the better afford to take risks because he would not be measuring swords with a Johnston or a Lee.

The march through Georgia was to throw a lurid light on what Sherman had written earlier with regard to feeling in the South. " I doubt if history affords a parallel to the deep and bitter enmity of the women of the South. No one who sees and hears them but must feel the intensity of this hate. Not a man is seen ; nothing but women, with houses plundered, fields open to the cattle and horses, pickets lounging on every porch, and desolation sown broadcast, servants all gone, and women and children bred in luxury, beautiful and accomplished, begging with one breath for the soldier's rations and in another praying that the Almighty or Joe Johnston will come and kill us, the despoilers of their homes, and all that is sacred." It is possible to suggest that the policy of Hoche in La Vendée in France affords a happy contrast to the process of reducing the South in America.

It were as foolish to belittle Sherman's famous march and allude to it as a walk-over as it would be to deny the Red River Expedition because Wolseley never fired a shot, but the march might wisely be compared, not to the disadvantage of the latter, with Bolivar's passage of the Andes in the war of South American independence. And if Sherman in his own hand has recorded his expression of regret for his policy of " making a circle of destruction and of devastating the land," it can never be said of his troops as was said, exaggeratingly, fifteen years ago that to spoliation was added deliberate cruelty to helpless women and children.

In happy contrast to happenings in Atlanta, Georgia and the Carolinas is Sherman's treatment of Johnston when that great Southern leader—too late recalled by Jefferson Davis to command—finally laid down his arms. Both Grant and Sherman were apprehensive that the Southern armies might dissolve into guerilla bands, and far-seeing policy, no less than magnanimity, marked their attitude to their still high-spirited opponents. Just as it only needed a word from Botha to prevent or postpone the peace of Vereeniging, so it only needed a call from Lee or Johnston for the Southerners to reaffirm the righteousness of their cause, reject any half-hearted adherence and renew operations adapted to their wide arena and loose organisation. The closing scenes of a great struggle are perhaps those which throw the most welcome light on the captains of both sides, and in the volume to hand they are unfolded with excellent taste.

" The war is over, occupation's gone," was Sherman's brief comment to his Staff when he really knew the weary warfare was accomplished. Thirty busy and useful years

were however in store for him. It has been said of many
military commanders that their careers would have closed
on a higher point of excellence had they succumbed to the
enemy's fire in the hour of victory ; of Sherman it can
surely be said that in the civil paths of life he was later to
tread, he did nothing to dull the gold of the reputation he
had won on the battlefield.

Whether or not Captain Liddell Hart's work will be
accepted as a text-book for the military student, one thing
at least can be claimed for it. In a play just now greatly
in vogue the hero, an author, draws a distinction between
books which when once you have taken up you can scarcely
put down, and those which, however quickly you put down,
you never pick up again. To the former category *Sherman*
most surely belongs.

# INFLUENCES FOR GOOD OR BAD IN THE GREAT WAR

A DISTINGUISHED authority has lately assured us that History is not worth reading unless written with some bias. The phrase if misleading has at least this vein of truth in it, that a wholly passionless judgment may postulate a clear knowledge of matter but preclude anything like quick sympathy with man.

To be—as distinct from passing for—a learned man, one must have studied with some eagerness men as well as circumstances ; to be an authority on the game of life one must have taken some part in its rough and tumble, and not merely have stood a cool and unruffled spectator. The historian who is no more than an accurate compiler of a mass of facts, however skilfully marshalled, and who misses the human side of the problem he sets himself to solve, is likely to find the circulation of his works the reverse of brisk, and to find himself sooner or later condemned to enforced and dusty repose on the library bookshelf. The writing of history is an art rather than a science, the art of compelling human figures to stand out from dry documents and musty folios, and to tell, as far as possible, and for all that it is worth, their own story. Henderson may or may not have idealised Stonewall Jackson, but his hero has not only touched the minds, but over and over again has done much to affect and stimulate the careers of British soldiers. For it is certain that, be he soldier or statesman, priest or poet, a man's worth and work will be measured not only by the labours of his brain and hand but by the influence, for good or ill, which he brought to bear upon the events of his day.

There is little doubt that one of the chief exercises of the student of the future will be to examine some of the special and conspicuous influences in that quarter of a century within which was embedded a period when the civilized world stood desperately to arms. How far will such students be able to determine whether in the absence of this or that personage events would have been directed into some quite different course ; whether if this, or that, counsel had been adopted, this or that temper more carefully studied, a different or an earlier term might have been set to a mighty conflict ? Here will be a fascinating and not unfruitful field for speculation : here will be a theme eagerly snapped up by Debating Societies.

There is every indication that the war story, from which a dozen years ago the publisher shrank, and the war play from which the theatrical manager recoiled, are daily becoming more and more marketable and profitable goods. *A fortiori* then, when the Great War has become pure history, the men who played parts of first-rate importance will grow in stature as they recede into the past, and may go far to displace in interest, statesmen and soldiers who preceded them. Meanwhile there may be names which leap to the lips, even of Lord Macaulay's proverbial schoolboy, and whose characters it may be worth his while to consider.

Prominent, if not predominant among the men whose names will be bound up with the Great War, must stand the man who sought to bring it about. It will always be a subject of contention even among those who admit Germany's war guilt, how far the country, and how far the Monarch, was responsible. German pacifist writers inculcate the doctrine of a peace-loving people, unwillingly called to arms by a ruthless ruler. During the War the Kaiser figured in something like the sinister form of Bonaparte during the Napoleonic Wars, without of course being credited with the military genius which even those who detested the " Corsican ogre " were forced, however grudgingly, to concede.

The Kaiser, ageing prematurely, egocentric, self-righteous, maimed, dogmatic, thanking God that he was not as other men, played a part in plunging the world into war which has been the subject of controversy but as to which the evidence urged is clear and irrefutable. The war-time legend which depicted him as deliberately plotting since early manhood the struggle, may be distorted and is certainly exaggerated ; but his foibles were such as to emit the sparks which produced the explosion as surely as flint scatters sparks when struck by steel. His was emphatically the " Great I " and " little you " temperament. *Gott mit uns* was *Gott mit mir ;* in international no less than in domestic affairs he must play the leading part ; and at times admittedly he played it with striking if boomerang effect, as in the downfall of M. Delcassé. He saw the world as a stage and was determined that he would have all posterity for his audience.

Thus when the crisis came, nothing was further from his mood than a compromise ; the mere thought of changing characters with Austria and playing the part of " brilliant second " which he had assigned to his Ally would be anathema ; his must be the flashing sword to avenge his murdered friend.

The searcher after truth will always find it difficult to put his finger on the moment, or even the period, when a great Autocrat registered mentally his decision to pit his forces against the Entente Powers, nor will it ever be easy to decide how far a purandiac patriot—for to do him bare justice Wilhelm was nothing less and nothing else—

honestly believed he had his quarrel just ; Serajevo he may have regarded as a great opportunity, or the dark crime may have come to him in the course of events as a great impetus, but whether an opportunity or an impetus it served his purpose.

Queen Mary, we are told, was determined that, whether Protestant or Catholic, Cranmer should burn ; public documents go to prove incontestably that whether Serbia were to accept or resist Austria's haughty demands, the Kaiser was sure that the hour had struck for a trial of strength. And of the issue he harboured no doubt.

Reviewing the magnitude of the fearful results which sprang from the imposition of an individual will, it is strange to reflect that whereas the historian will continue to point to one man as responsible for a vast calamity, within a week of that man's demise the journalist will have no use for him as " copy." Napoleon, twice deported and drawing his last breath within a narrow prison, shed nothing of his fame. Wilhelm with his passage through ignoble flight, into ignominious, if unfettered, exile, surrendered everything which could suggest in any way, or in any degree, the heroic.

A rough estimate of all that led to the definitive breach of European peace will probably set out the Austrian ultimatum as the chief factor. It may always remain difficult to attribute the authorship of that Ultimatum to any single person, for although it was actually drawn up by Freiherr von Musulin, it was repeatedly altered in successive Cabinet councils. The phraseology in which its demands were put forward can be traced to Count von Hotzendorf in whom was burnt the conviction that war was inevitable and that, if it were delayed, Austria's great chance would grow rather worse than better.

It would however be a mistake to regard Count Berchtold as a weakling, still less as a tool in the hands of more active men. The assassination of Archduke Franz Ferdinand came as the culminating point of a period of relations strained to a snapping point between Austria and Serbia, and a campaign of propaganda against Austria was generally held to make Serbia morally if not legally responsible for the crime. The failure of the Serbian Government to initiate vigorous measures of enquiry undoubtedly played into the hands of the Austrian war party, and Berchtold told a friend of the present writer, that at the time when he drafted the Ultimatum, he did not believe that Russia would take up arms on behalf of her puny friend. His belief on the contrary was, that if Russia should show signs of proceeding to extremities, Austria would be able to draw back (*zurückziehen* was the word actually used). This sounds rather naïve, but much evidence goes to show that while Austria reckoned with the possibility of measuring swords with Russia, she did not regard this issue as a probability, and that it was the influence of the Kaiser and of von Moltke which caused Austria to stiffen her neck in the face of Russian intervention.

Berchtold complained to my friend that at a critical moment the Prussian General took negotiations out of Austrian hands. " Austria must at once mobilise against Russia, Germany will mobilise," he telegraphed to von Hotzendorf early on the morning of July 31st. On the same day the Austrian Military Attaché in Berlin wired : " Moltke says the situation is critical unless Austria mobilises at once against Russia. Refuse England's new peace offer. Germany unconditionally with you." Then later on the same day : " Will Austria leave Germany in the lurch ? " The contradiction between Bethmann's telegrams and those from Moltke naturally bewildered the Austrian statesman : " Who is in command ? Moltke or Bethmann?" he exclaimed. Austria was no doubt determined to punish Serbia, whose promises of amendment she wholly distrusted.

Even if she had no special wish that her Ultimatum should be accepted, there is no real evidence that war with Russia was her purpose, and it was the intervention of the German General Staff at the critical moment which precipitated the crash.

Thus as regards the responsibility of a leading Austrian statesman for happenings which brought down his Emperor's grey hairs with sorrow to the grave, it is not unfair to suggest that it was his unhappy indecision rather than any registered resolve which influenced the trend of events.   In a sense he was the incarnation of the state of Austrian nerves which reacted on the nerves of Russia, each equally concerned as to the mobilisation of the other.   Had Berchtold been resolute enough to warn his Imperial master that war would mean, not the preservation of the Dual Monarchy but its almost immediate disintegration, the great European war-cloud might for the moment have drifted across the sky.

The Kaiser having determined—or it having been determined for him by his worst advisers—that a great hegemony of Europe was within the order of the German end, it remained for certain leaders of men in the countries of the Entente to thwart that maleficent purpose, and by force of arms to crush a system which for over fifty years had been a constant threat to European peace.

History has not yet claimed two outstanding patriots, and History may be left to appraise rightly the concentrated genius of Mr. Lloyd George, and the cool calculations based on pitiless logic of M. Poincaré who, alone among statesmen, was from his high office astride the whole situation from beginning to end of the struggle.   As these lines are being traced, there has passed into the Grand Peut-être the fiery spirit whose contribution to the War was predicted with precision in the War's earlier stages by the President of the Republic : " So long as victory is on the cards Clemenceau might spoil everything ; when all

N

seems lost he is capable of saving France to the uttermost."
In November 1917 the situation in France was perhaps
dark enough for Georges Clemenceau to be the only man
to save it.  His immediate declaration of a " moral mobilisation of France " must still vibrate in the ears of every
Frenchman ; the title of Père La Victoire with which the
soldiers labelled him as he trod their front trenches was to be
justified but a short year later.  Victory, complete and final,
nothing else and nothing less, was the decision he registered
in his mind with the sound of the enemy's challenge, and
to ensure that victory Georges Clemenceau spared nothing
and shrank from nothing when once the reins of office were
in his iron grasp.

Count Sazonoff's whole career, honourable in the highest
degree, was so eloquent of schemes as brilliant in conception as they were hopeless of execution that it may
hereafter be found difficult—apart from his share in Russian
mobilisation—to charge him with any special occasion of
making up his mind and carrying out his design.  On the
other hand, although large military decisions, even in the
very conduct of war must always be subservient to international, if not national, politics, it is possible to attribute
to the Grand Duke Nicholas no less than three other
soldiers resolutions taken without civil sanction which
bore the weightiest and most pregnant fruits.  Joffre's
will to deal with the enemy on the Marne which issued in
a battle described at the time by Lord Kitchener to the
writer as nothing else and nothing less than " decisive,"
the masterly stroke—the secret of which he locked in his
bosom—delivered by Foch on the 18th of July, 1918, and
Haig's determination to secure victory before the autumn
suns of that year should set, were all instances of how a fine
military brain can be usefully exercised when a military
executive is for the moment wholly unfettered by considerations of policy.  Then it has been suggested that the

archives of our national history might be ransacked to find evidence of any step of more cardinal importance than that taken when Mr. Asquith authorised the ultimatum to Germany which Sir Edward Grey announced to an excited House of Commons on the 3rd of August 1914. The Prime Minister is constitutionally only *primus inter pares*, but his counsel and influence are stuff of no flimsy material. To deal with Mr. Asquith's war services is to enter a path thorny with controversies and punctuated with " ifs " and " ands " and " might have beens."

The broad outstanding fact is that at a moment of supreme crisis the Chief Minister of the Crown took the responsibility, which he alone could take, of advising his Sovereign to accept a challenge as arresting as it was formidable ; that advice was given in the teeth of opposition no less sharp because it was friendly, and that the man who gave the advice swept with him into the battle arena a people and an Empire with purpose as earnest as it was national. Few phrases have been more belittled and disparaged than Mr. Asquith's " Wait and see " ; few phrases have shown greater practical wisdom. Mr. Asquith —unlike Mr. Balfour with his gifted faculty for seeing both sides of a question—would recognise without any real hesitation or reservation the right path to tread, and would not refrain from setting out on it when once he believed that the moment had occurred for the adventure.

It is possible for an unfair critic to think that in the same position Mr. Winston Churchill might have hurried up too quickly to take the glove, or that for the moment Mr. Lloyd George might have declined to take it up at all. In those first days of an unforgettable August Mr. Asquith may have paused, but he did not postpone for a moment the awful hour in which to exchange diplomacy for warfare. The same may be said when two years later he introduced the measure of General Service which as we now know, ensured that our warfare, however weary, would be victorious in the end.

If the Prime Minister's responsibility for the declaration of hostilities stands alone, scarcely less onerous was the burden shouldered by his nominees at the War Office. "Everyone knows," Lord Grey very wisely said, " the mistakes made while Kitchener was at the War Office, nobody knows the mistakes which would have been made had he not been there."

" The war will last three years if Russia stays in, four years if she goes out," was Kitchener's recorded comment on the day when he took over the seals of office ; the decision which he based on that surmise was that whether British troops advanced, retired or held their ground, it was not a question of reinforcing a perfectly equipped but miniature army but of creating a real army which should in time—although it was not to be in his time—dispute finally with the forces of the German Empire.

The War Secretary at once laid down his own plans for creating an army of 70 Divisions, coolly and quite correctly calculating that its maximum strength would be reached at the beginning of the third year of the War. But for this resolve and but for the immediacy of this resolve—clean contrary though it ran to all hitherto accepted ideas—the leaders of the British and French troops have agreed that Germany would have been victorious.

The writer may be excused for recalling the occasion when, as Director of the Press Bureau, he submitted to the Secretary for War the communiqué as to the issue of the Battle of the Marne. The epithet used to describe the allied success was " important " ; Kitchener ran his pen through it and substituted the word " decisive."

From resolution—and irresolution—savouring in an odd way of virility, it is not a descent to bathos to remember the vast influence of the feminine sex in—and for the matter of that after—the War, and to recall with honour a woman on whom, year in and year out, obloquy and reproach were at one time freely cast.  It is not within public knowledge when, or precisely why, Mrs. Pankhurst determined in her mind that she would do all, risk all, and if necessary suffer all, in order that there should be established those women's rights which have assumed a complexion and meaning in curious contrast to what was once the object of scornful, and as I still think of justifiable wrath. Is it to stretch a point too far to suggest that by the militants' movements—reprehensible though they may have been in themselves—the women of England were brought to the frame of mind which was to make so effective their war work and to mark them out before all other women as helpmeets to their men ?

During the red years Frenchwomen tilled the fields— perhaps only an extension of their peacetime hard labour— while the women of Germany were swept up by the relentless machine of over-Government ;  in England, where the centuries-old subordination to the male had already been challenged, the woman rightly and quickly heard the call. Their work in the factories at home, valuable though it was, is questionable in its effect ;  we have been faced, and are still being faced with the wage problem said to produce male unemployment.  Moreover, long before female labour had become effective, far too many fainéants were wearing blue dungarees rather than field khaki, and such were rather difficult to capture even by a tardy and perhaps too tender comb.

In actual service departments the employment of female labour was perhaps more readily appreciated ;  no forces employed a larger subordinate staff than our own.  Statisticians have worked out that it took a man and a half to keep a man in the fighting line ;  yet the great majority of men employed on Staff duties are (on paper) sabre or bayonet men, and reduce by their absence effective fighting strengths. The formation of certain Corps had an immediate effect on the front line ; packs were dug out from dusty corners and strapped once more to backs that were being rounded from over much sitting at desks. Cook-houses and messes of Reserve battalions were invaded, onslaughts were made even on the traditional Army cook shops, and smart young drivers were wrenched from the wheels of Staff cars and their places taken by equally smart and capable young women of the new breed.

There was too a moral aspect to the affair more effective than was possibly appreciated at home. There was something inexpressibly cheering to the man at the front in the appearance of his own womenfolk so close behind the line. Men came back to billets after foraging or short leave to the little towns of the war area to tell comrades of the khaki-clad girls of England tramping the pavements in twos and threes. There was not perhaps too much of sex feeling as normally comprehended. The girls were on the whole treated as comrades, comrades whose advent was all the more welcome because unexpected, or at all events unheralded. The women of the French countryside —small blame to a race of tried heroines—were rarely ornamental. In the workmanlike—yet still feminine— appearance of his own girls the British soldier found yet further cause for the national pride which was his mainstay. In the heat and hurry of current events the chronicler may have been a little sparing in his tribute to the lofty, and lasting, effort of women in four and a half years of blood and agony ; with the flux of time the historian may be trusted to do them full and righteous justice.

# THE COMING OF THE BOLSHEVIST

THE first two and a half years of the Great War left Russia badly shaken, but by no means broken. It has been customary to assert that Russia was "war-weary." by the beginning of 1917. A notorious article in the *Encyclopædia Britannica*, for example, declares that "whereas most of the leaders of the Duma were dissatisfied because the War was not better conducted, the mass of the people were dissatisfied because it had not long ago come to an end." Such statements are meaningless. Of course the Russian people were dissatisfied that the War had not long since come to an end ; but so were the English people and the French people and the German people. There was no nation in Europe which was not "weary" of the long-drawn-out hostilities and the lack of any decisive result. But this is not to say that any nation was yet ready to throw up the sponge and acquiesce in the ignominy of defeat. The military spirit in Russia was actually much better in March 1917 than it had ever been before. The crude optimism of the first days in 1914 had been shattered by German resilience and counter-attacks ; the deficiencies of command and supply had long since become apparent, and, as was the case in every other fighting nation, the whole fighting machine had been overhauled and vastly improved. It remains true, certainly, that the home front in Russia was poorly organised, by comparison with those in the West ; even so, the natural resources and the incomparable wealth of that vast empire balanced a weakness in administration and communications which must have been fatal elsewhere. The outbreak of the revolution cannot be understood unless it is recognised as a symptom less of " war-weariness " than of a determination to rid Russia of bonds which were stifling her hopes of victory.

The day has not yet come for a full valuation of all the evidence about the upheaval in Russia which destroyed the ancient rule of the Tsars and reduced a proud and prosperous empire to the murderous filth of Bolshevism. But at least it may be pointed out that the ruin of Russia was not a single, inevitable progress. It was the result of a series of errors and accidents. No more remarkable example exists in history of the degree in which the fortunes of an empire depend upon the personality of a single political head. A Cæsar, a Napoleon or—I name him advisedly—a Lloyd George could have made the Russian revolution the most potent instrument of victory ever forged ; in the incompetent hands of Kerensky the bright sword of a national renaissance was turned against those who should have wielded it.

It would be unjust to blame Kerensky for every political folly which marked the course of the first and only popular government which has ever ruled Russia. Others too bear part of the blame, but his must always be the main share. For he had it in his power at almost every period during those eight fatal months of his ministerial career to arrest his country's decline and to mend the fissures which had appeared in her political edifice. He failed utterly, because he was too vain, too unskilled in government, too timid of the duties of responsibility, too avid of its outer show, too incapable of transforming brave words into bold deeds.

We know now that, in every issue which led to the destruction of Russia, his real opinion was one which, if stoutly upheld and nobly persevered in, might have saved the day. But a lack of moral courage ; an unwillingness or

inability to distinguish between rhetoric and command,
between demagogic idealism and the stern if unpopular
statement of purpose, paralysed him, and set in his place
a gang of maniac, sadistic murderers who at least pursued
whole-heartedly a single definite purpose.

The first revolutionary Ministry was formed in the
middle of March, with Prince Lvov, a colourless Liberal,
as 'Prime Minister, and with Kerensky as Minister for
Justice ; the latter's real function being to act as a link
between the new administration and his Socialist colleagues
in the Soviet. These "workers' and soldiers' councils"
were mushroom growths, which had sprung up overnight
in the excitement of the Tsar's overthrow. At that time it
would not have been difficult—even later, it need never
have been impossible—to subordinate the Soviets to the
central Government. To Kerensky's credit it must be
said that this was always his wish though he never dared
to act with sufficient foresight or decision.

The chief weapon in the hands of the anarchic section of
the population was a notorious Order, issued by a handful
of irresponsible demagogues in the Petrograd Soviet, which
undermined the authority of the Army officers. Though
the Order was rejected by the Government, the fatal step
was taken of conceding certain of its privileges to the ranks
of the army at a time when only a whole-hearted insistence
on tightening up the bonds of discipline could have repaired
the damage. Then Lenin and his parasites were sent in by
Germany to poison the minds of their compatriots. Here
too was an opportunity for Kerensky to show himself a
statesman. He fought Lenin with words in the Soviet and
beat him, but, typically, he failed to follow up his advantage
by arresting and executing the handful of men who, he
well knew, were endeavouring to organise mutiny in the
army and sedition at home. The measure of his public
failure may be gauged, paradoxically enough, from his

personal success. Within a few weeks he had become Premier and the outstanding political figure in the country —the whole political platform had slipped far to the left, and Lenin's authority had increased with his own. Heroic efforts, however, by the officers at the Front restored a semblance of discipline to the armies. Fired by these men's courage and by the real eloquence of Kerensky, an advance was made against the Austrians on the south-west front in July ; it was soon stopped but it was an earnest of what might happen if a strong man controlled the political situation in the capital. The Bolshevists were horrified at such a possibility ; they organised an armed rising in Petrograd. It failed ; Lenin and Trotsky went into hiding. We shall perhaps never know whether or not Kerensky could have arrested them ; we may, however, feel certain that, even at this state, he would not have dared to execute them. Even so, fate gave him another chance, a last chance. It was still in his power to save his country by overawing the Soviets through which Lenin and his fellows exercised their influence.

One of the most distinguished officers in the Russian army was General Kornilov. Born in the hut of a poor Siberian peasant, this remarkable man had raised himself to high military rank. Before the War he distinguished himself by remarkable journeys in Central Asia ; after July, 1914, he was the hero of a brilliant rearguard action which saved an army but left him a prisoner in Austrian hands. The story of his early escape thrilled his countrymen, and, when the revolution broke out, he was the universal choice to command the restless Petrograd garrison. This task, and the even more ungrateful duty of acting as gaoler to the deposed Imperial family, disgusted him and he returned to the Front. There he, more than any other man, was responsible for the advance against the Austrians in July. When his army wavered, he did not hesitate to reintroduce the death penalty, which had been removed by the silly idealists in Petrograd. The July fighting and the unsuccessful Bolshevist riot in the capital raised him and Kerensky far above their compatriots.

Just as Kerensky was certainly the only politician who could at that time save the Government, so Kornilov was the only commander who could save the Army. Had the two men combined, Russia might to-day be a happy and flourishing nation. Their quarrel, which I am about to describe, made inevitable the coming of the Bolshevists. Yet, as will be seen, this quarrel was, in its nature, one of the most ridiculous incidents upon which the life of a nation could hinge. Only a creature of Kerensky's infinite vanity and stupidity could have permitted it to happen. Whatever the rest of his sad record of futility, Kerensky's failure to co-operate with Kornilov at this moment marks him out as the most nerveless imbecile in modern history.

To envisage the scene, one must note the different atmospheres which prevailed at Petrograd, where Kerensky was Prime Minister, and at Army Headquarters, where Kornilov was now Commander-in-Chief. Kerensky and his clique frothily endeavoured to reconcile the needs of the moment with the outworn futilities of their Socialist professions. They declaimed, they debated, they talked incessantly ; they never acted. At headquarters, on the other hand, the officers, doubly menaced by the enemy and mutiny, dared not speak out. Their regiments and their messes were honeycombed with prying commissaries of the Soviets ; to talk of duty, or to plan patriotic action, was equally likely to invite personal disaster. In consequence such officers as could trust one another formed secret societies ; they sought means to save Russia and to rid her of the pests which sought her destruction. These " conspirators " were disciplined men ; they trusted Kornilov, their Commander-in-Chief, and obeyed his orders unhesitatingly. They certainly did not trust Kerensky far, though even the most embittered of them must have realised that, in intention if not in act, he too sought the salvation of their country. But Kerensky was stupid enough to believe—or, as now seems more possible, to pretend to believe—that these officers' associations were deliberately conspiring to overthrow his civil government and to replace it by military rule. Doubtless a few of them were ; but he must have known that these could never have taken any decisive step. The danger of a " *coup d'état* from the Right," about which he made so many windy speeches, was negligible.

It was his plain duty at this point to establish such an understanding with the army command as would allow him, with its aid, to stamp out the pestilential Soviets and remove the Leninist stain. Indeed he went so far as to ask Kornilov to send a Cavalry Corps to Petrograd to stiffen the garrison there. But then, as usual, he faltered and hesitated.

A strange personage now took a hand in the game, one Vladimir Lvov—not to be confused with his namesake, the prince who had been the first Premier after the revolution. This Vladimir Lvov was a country landowner and a minor politician of quite staggering incompetence, who by some unfortunate accident had lately been given the post of Procurator of the Holy Synod. This advancement seems to have persuaded him that he was a statesman of genius ; he now decided to mend the fortunes of the country, and, by a trick, to bring about the collaboration of Kerensky and Kornilov which every patriotic man knew to be desirable. He therefore paid a call on Kerensky on September 3rd, 1917, and, speaking with studied vagueness, assured the Premier that he had been " sent " to him to discuss the question of strengthening the Government. Kerensky has told us that, beyond an unsuccessful enquiry as to who had " sent " Lvov to him, he paid no heed to his fantastic colleague. But three days later Lvov suddenly appeared at G.H.Q. in Moghilev and, demanding an interview with Kornilov, told him that Kerensky had despatched him there with a confidential mission. It appeared, according to Lvov's statement, that Kerensky, realising the critical position in the country, was willing either to join Kornilov with himself as joint dictator, or to serve under Kornilov's dictatorship.

Kornilov, who had little respect for the new Government and was used to the most extraordinary emissaries from Petrograd, believed Lvov's tale. The latter then returned to Petrograd and obtained another interview with Kerensky. " I have to make you a formal offer," he said. " From whom ? " asked Kerensky. " From Kornilov." He then told the Premier that Kornilov insisted on martial law being proclaimed throughout Russia, on his (Kornilov's) appointment as Dictator, on Kerensky's becoming his Minister for Justice and leaving at once for G.H.Q., where alone his life would be safe in the change of regime. Kerensky, thoroughly alarmed at what he imagined to be an army plot against his authority and his life, required Lvov to put Kornilov's alleged demands in writing. Lvov wrote :

General Kornilov proposes :—

(1) That martial law shall be proclaimed in Petrograd.
(2) That all military and civil authority shall be placed in the hands of the Generalissimo.
(3) That all Ministers, not excluding the Premier, shall resign, and that the temporary executive power shall be transferred to the Assistant Ministers till the formation of a Cabinet by the Generalissimo.

Kerensky declares that " as soon as Lvov began to write, my last doubt disappeared. I had only one desire, one overmastering impulse : to check the madness at the outset, not giving it time to blaze up, and preventing the possible breaking out of its partisans in Petrograd. . . . All instantly shone clear in a very brilliant light and merged into one clear picture. Certainly I could not then prove every point, but I saw everything with extraordinary clarity. In those instants, while Lvov was writing, my brain worked intensely." But unfortunately he did not trouble to reflect that, had Kornilov decided to act, he would surely not have choosen Lvov as his intermediary. He certainly suggested to the man that he might be the victim of a practical joke ; but this Lvov energetically denied. Kerensky then set himself to confirm his fears, and arranged to communicate with Kornilov by direct wire in the evening. The following conversation then took place on the Hughes tape-machine :

KERENSKY : " Good day, General. V. N. Lvov and Kerensky at the apparatus. We beg you to confirm the statement that Kerensky is to act according to the communication made to him by V. N."

KORNILOV : " Good day, Alexander Feodorovitch (Kerensky): good day, V. N. Confirming again the description I gave V. N. of the present situation of the country and the army as it appears to me, I declare again that the events of the past days and of those that I can see coming imperatively demand a definite decision in the shortest possible time."

LVOV : " I, V. N. Lvov, ask you whether it is necessary to act on that definite decision which you asked me to communicate privately to Kerensky, as he is hesitating to give his full confidence without your personal confirmation."

KORNILOV : " Yes, I confirm that I asked you to convey to Alexander Feodorovitch my urgent demand that he should come to Moghilev."

KERENSKY : " I, Alexander Feodorovitch, understand your answer as a confirmation of the words conveyed to me by V. N. To do that to-day and start from here is impossible. I hope to start to-morrow."

KORNILOV : " I beg you earnestly not to put off your departure later than to-morrow. Believe me, only my recognition of the responsibility of the moment urges me to persist in my request."

KERENSKY : " Shall we come only in case of an outbreak, of which there are rumours, or in any case ? "

KORNILOV : " In any case."

KERENSKY : " Good day. Soon we shall see each other."

KORNILOV : " Good day."

This whole conversation demonstrates the stupidity of Kerensky and the innocence of the Commander-in-Chief. At no point did Kerensky attempt to discover, either directly or by inference, whether or not Lvov had been authorised to deliver an ultimatum to him, or why Kornilov should suddenly have opened negotiations through so unpromising a channel. Instead, having convinced himself that Kornilov was plotting against him, he sparred for time. His promise to go to G.H.Q. was a blind ; the moment he left the apparatus, he took measures " to cope with the rebellion at its very commencement." One would have thought that even a Kerensky must have realised the fatal folly of breaking with Kornilov at such a moment. Even if Kornilov had been seeking, as Kerensky wrongly supposed, to seize the central government, it would have been simple prudence for Kerensky to use every possible means to counter him except that of declaring an open breach between the Government and the Army. The moment such a breach occurred, Russia was doomed. Any alternative must have been better. But Kerensky's vanity was hurt.

He arrested Lvov, sent a telegram to Kornilov, ordering him to surrender his command and come at once to Petrograd, and issued the following proclamation :

## A MESSAGE TO THE POPULATION

I hereby announce :

On August 26th, General Kornilov sent to me the member of the State Duma V. N. Lvov with a demand for the surrender by the Provisional Government of the whole plenitude of Civil and Military authority, with a view to his forming, at his personal discretion, a New Government for administering the country. The authenticity of Deputy Lvov's authorization to make such a proposal to me was subsequently confirmed by General Kornilov in his conversation with me by direct wire. Perceiving in the presentation of such demands addressed to the Provisional Government in my person, a desire of some circles of Russian society to take advantage of the grave condition of the state for the purpose of establishing in the country a state of authority in contradiction to the conquests of the Revolution, the Provisional Government has found it indispensable to authorise me, for the salvation of our country, of liberty, and of Republican order, to take prompt and resolute measures for the purpose of uprooting any attempt to encroach upon the Supreme Authority in the State and upon the rights which the citizens have conquered by the Revolution.

I am taking all necessary measures to protect the liberty and order of the country, and the population will be informed in due course with regard to such measures.

At the same time I order herewith :

1.    General Kornilov to surrender the post of Supreme Commander-in-Chief to General Klembovsky, the Com-

THE COMING OF THE BOLSHEVIKS

mander-in-Chief over the armies of the Northern front which bar the way to Petrograd ; and General Klembovsky to enter temporarily upon the post of Supreme Commander-in-Chief, while remaining at Pskov.

11. To declare the city and district of Petrograd under Martial Law, extending to it the regulations for the localities declared under Martial Law.

I call upon all the citizens to preserve a complete tranquillity and to maintain order, which is so indispensable for the salvation of the country. I call upon all ranks of the army and navy to carry on with calmness and self-abnegation their duty of defending the country against the external enemy.

A. F. KERENSKY,

*Prime-Minister, Minister of
War and of Marine.*

Kornilov at G.H.Q. was thunderstruck by this seeming change of front. So Kerensky had deliberately tricked him ! That the general was actuated, like Kerensky, by hurt pride is not to be supposed ; such was not his nature. He now in turn issued a public proclamation :

The Premier's telegram is in its first portion a lie throughout ; it was not I who sent Deputy Vladimir Lvov to the Provisional Government, but he came to me as the Premier's envoy. Deputy Alexis Aladin is a witness to this.

A great provocation has thus taken place, which jeopardises the fate of the fatherland.

People of Russia !

Our great country is dying. The hour of its end is near. Being compelled to come forward in the open, I, General Kornilov, declare that, under the pressure of

o

the Bolshevist majority of the Soviets, the Provisional Government is acting in complete accord with the plans of the German General Staff, at the time when enemy troops are landing on the Riga coast ; it is killing the army and shaking the foundations of the country.

A grave sense of the inevitable ruin of the country commands me at this threatening moment to call upon all Russian people to save the dying country.

All you in whose breast a Russian heart is beating ; all you who believe in God and in the temples, pray to the Lord to manifest the greatest miracle of saving our native land. I, General Kornilov, the son of a Cossack peasant, declare to all and sundry that I want nothing for my own person, except the preservation of a Great Russia, and I swear to carry over the people, by means of a victory over the enemy, to the Constituent Assembly at which it will decide its own fate and choose the order of its new State life.

I cannot bring it upon myself to hand over Russia to its hereditary enemy, the German race, and to turn the Russian people into slaves of the Germans, but prefer to die on the field of honour and battle, so as not to see the shame and infamy of the Russian Land.

Russian people, the life of your country is in your hands !

GENERAL KORNILOV.

It was too late. The Soviets, now thoroughly alarmed to discover the peril in which they lay, mobilised their strength. The Bolshevists took heart. The Cavalry Corps was stopped before it reached the capital. Kornilov, at the special request of the Government, retained technical control over the Army until General Alexeiev took his place. Two months later the Bolshevists drove out the miserable remnants of Kerensky's government, and the Army disintegrated.    All this because a foolish, self-opinionated windbag could see no further than his nose, and trusted a half-witted colleague in preference to Kornilov.

The future of the two chief protagonists in this fantastic but catastrophic episode may be briefly told. Kornilov escaped from arrest at the end of the year and with General Alexeiev founded the Volunteer Army whose first campaigns against the Bolshevists in the Caucasus are among the most romantic episodes of the whole War. So inspiring was his leadership of his force of hungry, ill-equipped ex-officers, Cossacks and schoolboys, that they used to attack enemy detachments not ten times but literally a hundred times stronger than themselves. The culminating triumph of this brave campaign, the capture of Ekaterinodar, the chief town of the Kuban, was darkened, however, by the death of Kornilov, who was killed by a stray shell. He was secretly buried by General Denikin, his successor, but the body was afterwards found by the Bolshevists who, with instinctive hatred for a hero and a patriot, played football with his head.

As for Kerensky, he still flutters vapidly (but, one imagines, still eloquently) through the capitals of Europe, despised by all except a small knot of ill-informed sympathisers—a living monument to vanity, folly, futility and cowardice.

# SOME MILITARY HAPPENINGS OF 1918

THE final year of the War dawned upon a world unaware of its portent. The great mass of the people—in Great Britain at all events—were thoroughly grounded in the policy of " carrying on," which had been theirs throughout the struggle. Whatever the confusion and fears in the realms of high politics, whatever the friction between civil and military departments, the temper of the nation, whether at home or in the Field, was much the same as it had been in 1914. Gone, indeed, was that superb contempt of a monstrous foe which had made people look for victory " by Christmas," and in its place there was a grim tenacity of purpose lightened only by that peculiar British sense of humour which, by its deceptive face value, has lured so many foes to destruction. It never even entered the head of the people that it was in any way possible to lose to Germany.

The man in the trench, the driver of the ration lorry, the waiting mother and the munition girl, knowing nothing of policies and diplomacies, were steadfast in the belief that the British " team " must win the greatest match of all time.

In the Field there was a certain lull. The noise of Cambrai had died down, and the soldier, never permitting himself the useless agony of looking ahead, occupied himself with filling yet more sandbags, or with pulling down houses, which he could do without, to make roads, one of his great necessities.

England had its air-raids and alarms. Yarmouth was

honoured with a naval bombardment, and forty-seven Londoners were killed in one January air-raid. To add to other discomforts, the restrictions on food were increased in severity. Yet London, and with it England, laughed. It is safe to say that never did the soldier let the civilian know the real horrors of war, nor did the civilian let his brother-in-arms realise to what extent he was tightening his belt, that the stream of supplies for the Front might not diminish in volume.

If the people of France had not the saving grace of British humour, they were yet nerved by a grimness instilled by their casualty lists and the thoughts of the shattered communes of the War zone. As some compensation for their losses, it may fairly be stated that the rigours of life in the civilian communities were hardly as harsh as in England. Supplies were expensive, but not nearly so unobtainable in Paris as in London. Moreover—and the French gave full praise for this to their anti-aircraft defences—Paris appeared almost unassailable from the air. It was in March that the long-distance shelling of the French capital commenced, but the shells were of such small calibre and infrequency that Paris heeded them not at all.

Little was realised—through the haze of a well-censored British press—of the continuance of the naval war. The public had a vague idea that the German High Seas Fleet was safely bottled up at Kiel. This was, roughly, true, but there were—and were bound to be—leakages of raiding submarines, and even of surface craft of the lighter sort.

Of the success of the anti-submarine campaign there can be little question. Over two hundred German submarines were included in the British " bag " for the whole War. In spite of this there was always toll being levied. In January the *Louvain*, in February the *Tuscania* (with a loss of 166 U.S. troops), and in March the *Calgaria* and *Guild-ford Castle*—the latter a hospital ship—proved by their loss that there were still teeth to be drawn. To the very end Allied shipping was falling victim to enemy under-water craft.

On the other hand there can be little doubt that the naval blockade of the Central Powers by the British and Allied Fleets was having its effect on the population of the countries affected, in spite of the vexatious limitations imposed by the presence of neutral seaboards. In this way the ground was being prepared and the seed sown for the internal uprisings which were to work more changes in the map of Europe than the conquests of armies.

Comparatively clear as the general situation may have appeared to the " man in the street "—or in the trench— there were big forces at work behind the scenes of every belligerent Power. The general tendency was a seeking of peace. That no such peace could be found was due to the fact that no country was in any wise prepared to admit defeat.

Perhaps it was that statesmen on all sides at last found leisure in which to word sonorous manifestoes, declarations of their aims and aspirations. For over three years they had been honestly at work, first in placing armies in the field and recruiting reserves, and then in organising their respective countries for modern war, both from a military and a civil point of view. The wheels of war had now, apparently, been sufficiently well greased to run nicely on their carefully laid tracks, and the traffic directors of the world were able to get back to their board meetings.

As early as in October, 1917, Count Czernin, the Austro-Hungarian Foreign Minister, had expounded his peace views. He foreshadowed, mainly, a general disarmament, and a League of Nations. His main argument, however, was financial. No nation, he claimed, could afford the continuance of modern war—its scale was too vast.

Hertling, however, the new German Chancellor, fortified by Caporetto, displayed in November much the same mixture of " Gott mit Uns," Imperialism and pure sabre rattling as of yore. " Nothing can, nothing shall, be changed in the foundation of our imperial constitution." The War, he maintained, was still a measure of honourable defence of German frontiers.

Still, in the month of November, 1917, appeared the Lansdowne Letter. Lord Lansdowne, although not a member of the British Government, was yet an old and honoured statesman, and as such received universal attention. It is the more to be deplored that his letter should have contained statements extremely distasteful to the fighting man, and so lukewarm in sentiment as to have appeared to enemy minds almost a confession of defeat. It was, indeed, as one writer expresses it, " an echo from a past age, a vanished age of sedate, diplomatic bargaining, when peace was made between combatants by a little give and take of territory, and a few concessions to national pride."

American and British statesmen were at one in declaring that no terms could be discussed with the present rulers of Central Europe, and early in January the Prime Minister issued a statement which could be fairly described as embodying the peace aims, not only of the Home Government, but of the British Dominions beyond the Seas. No destruction of Germany or of Austria-Hungary was sought, but a complete restoration of sovereignty to the overrun countries ; a restoration of Alsace-Lorraine ; the establishment of a Polish State, and a freedom of self-determination to be accorded to old submerged nationalities. Further afield, we were prepared even to allow Turkey to retain Constantinople. But the Dardanelles must be opened, and the nationalities of the Near East allowed independent government.  The old German Colonies must be allocated in the best interests of the native populations ; reparation must be made for the grave breaches of international law perpetrated by the Central Powers.  Finally the birth of a League of Nations, having as its aims limitation of armaments and diminished possibilities of war, was foreshadowed.

Mr. Woodrow Wilson's famous " Fourteen Points " were next in the field.  This document was, to a far larger extent than was generally conceded, a reiteration of the British statement.  The main difference lay in two directions.  Mr. Wilson laid great stress on a " freedom of navigation in Peace and War," and gave prominence to a League of Nations which Mr. Lloyd George had only issued as a tail-piece.  It was, in short, a document peculiarly designed to meet the needs of American policy in general, and Mr. Wilson's university mind in particular.

Whatever was happening beneath the surface, whatever might be partially concealed behind the proscenium arch of diplomacy, the outstanding events of 1918—perhaps the only two that the retrospective mind can recall without the aid of books of reference—were the German offensive of March, with its subsequent ebb at the command of Marshal Foch, and the Armistice of November.

It is curious to discover that peace in 1918 was nowhere —with one single exception—hoped, or even striven for. Armies and peoples alike were resigned to their desperate fight ; statesmen relied on blockades and propaganda, which they knew were weapons slow in action ; even the military leaders opined that the end was not yet.  Lord Kitchener had declared that the War would be won by the country which could place the last million trained men in the Field.  Those who accepted the dictum of the great man were now almost universally resigned to the thought that the last million must be soldiers of the United States. The solitary exception was Sir Douglas Haig.

That quiet fighter and thinker was confident that the end could be reached in the year 1918, and was determined that his every effort should be made to that end. His considered military opinion was reinforced by his humanitarian instinct. He refused to let the British Expeditionary Force—his Expeditionary Force, the Force he had played a leading part in creating before 1915—sit tight and be destroyed by ceaseless erosion, whilst waiting for as yet problematical Americans to arrive. He was, almost vehemently, supported in council and in action by the sovereign. There are many who, even to-day, are obsessed by the thought that victory was unnecessarily hastened. To His Majesty of England and Earl Haig is due the energetic pursuit of victory in 1918, and the termination of hostilities just as soon as the aims of the Allies had been realised. An insistence on overwhelming victory might have reaped very problematical additional rewards. It would certainly have been at the cost of many more thousands of empty British armchairs to-day.

It is false to describe the German offensive of March, 1918, as a last desperate throw of an almost ruined gambler. The High Command had every reason to believe that such an offensive could not fail. The Russian Revolution had been as the lifting of a huge weight from the bent backs of the German armies. Central Europe was now the main mass of Europe, bordered on the East by the new protectorates set up at Brest-Litovsk. Beyond these protectorates was chaos, but a chaos which was incapable of offence to Germany. Russia, indeed, had become the Hinterland of Europe.

Regarded in terms of mere figures, the Allied lands of France, Italy, Portugal and Greece, with an area of 390,000 square miles, and a population of 85,000,000 was opposed by a Central Europe of 1,065,000 square miles, populated by 203,000,000 undefeated enemies, hardly any of whom had experienced the pangs of foreign invasion.

Russian troops had not, for many months, taken a greatly active part in the War, but they had only to be even super-ficially in battle array to keep a vital proportion of the armies of Germany and Austria-Hungary on their menaced frontiers. The Revolution and Brest-Litovsk had finally eased the Central Powers of their Russian anxieties and disintegration of the Russian forces had removed every slight remaining cause of apprehension. A great tide set in. The men of Austria-Hungary marched south, Turkey faced the presumptuous Britishers in her strength, and Germany was enabled to transfer seventy per cent. of her Eastern forces to the all-important Western Front. Surely now was the moment for victory.

In so far as the civil needs were allowed to dictate to German military considerations, these, too, clamoured for the victory which seemed so easy to grasp. The success of the Allied blockade and the futility of the submarine war needed some palliation. Finally, no one realised better than the High Command that the day must come when the presence of America would definitely be felt. There was every reason to believe that that day could be anticipated, and made too late to benefit the Allied cause.

Those responsible for German military policy were still convinced, apparently, that Britain ranked as Germany's chiefest foe. The coming offensive was planned with that idea in view. The immediate object of the offensive was the destruction of the British Expeditionary Force, which would be the most easily accomplished by an isolation of that Force with the Channel at its back. The underlying idea, therefore, of the first great series of attacks, was one in which the occupation of Amiens, or even of Paris itself, was to be a mere incident—the driving in of a great wedge at the junction of the French and British lines, and the rolling up of the latter to the northwards.

This plan having failed—by what narrow margin it is even now terrifying to contemplate—a second plan was evolved having the same end in view. A direct frontal attack was made on the British lines of the Second and First Armies, having its storm centre at Armentières, and involving a piling up of yet more horrors on the festering sores of the Salient.

Nor could the state of affairs in the British lines prior to the attack have been described as entirely happy. The adoption of a defensive policy had been forced upon the Allied commanders. They realised to the full the dire importance of the Russian defection, and knew that weeks or months must elapse before serious help could be expected from America. There were other points which militated expressly against the well-being of the British troops. In detailing these points the British Commander, in his despatch dated July 20th, 1918, insists in a marked degree on the fact that he was governed rather by the overhead arrangements of the Home Government than by his own considered opinions. The first was an extension of the British line by twenty-eight miles southwards, " pursuant to a decision of the British Government," and " after considerable discussion on the subject." This relief, planned in September for December, did not finally become effective until the end of January, at which time British troops held 125 miles of active front. It was the new stretch of British Front that was to see some of the fiercest fighting of the coming offensive.

A change, again audibly deplored by Haig, and as actually by those under him, had also taken place in the interior organisation of the fighting division. The Army Council had decreed that the division of infantry should be reduced from thirteen to ten battalions. To quote the dispatch verbatim, " Apart from reduction in fighting strength involved by this re-organisation, the fighting efficiency of units was to some extent affected.  An unfamiliar grouping of units was introduced thereby, necessitating new methods of tactical handling of the troops and the discarding of methods to which subordinate commanders had become accustomed."

The great battles of 1917 had severely drained British resources.  Reserves in France were at a low ebb, and the battalions were given no time to train their new drafts to warfare in general, or their whole selves to the new policy of defence.  That reserves were few did not entirely indicate an actual shortage of man-power in the nation.  The old bogey of a German invasion of England still kept many folk awake o' nights, and a large—and to many minds an unnecessarily large—force was maintained at home to ward off the invading heel from the sands of the East Coast. Not until the darkest days of the offensive was a proportion of this force released to go to the aid of its comrades on the battle front.

The actual force in France had also been sadly weakened —this even prior to Cambrai—by the sending of divisions to Italy, much against the will of the C.-in-C.  Finally, when every private soldier knew that a great enemy attack was imminent, the Cavalry Corps was weakened from five to three divisions by the sending of the Indian Cavalry to Egypt and the dismounting of regular and Yeomanry Regiments who must have, if left alone, vindicated the élan of their army equally with those of the remaining three Cavalry Divisions in the retirement.

The coming attack, suspected throughout the winter, became evident towards the middle of February, 1918. By March 21st, the actual day of its opening, the number of German divisions on the Front had increased from 146 to 192, and the massing of troops and guns opposite the

British Third and Fifth Armies was sufficiently marked to leave no doubt as to the position of the danger zone for the Allied Forces.   British Headquarters had, however, no simple task in the disposal of its available forces.   The Ypres salient, responsible for the safety of the all-important Channel ports, should at this period of the year have been impassable ground.   An unusually dry winter had, however, robbed it of such facility of defence.   Enemy activity in that sector was, moreover, distinctly disturbing, and subsequent events proved that Haig was right in maintaining his line at that point in all its old force, at any rate, while he possibly could.

All necessary precautions having been undertaken elsewhere, the British C.-in-C. was still able to mass approximately one half of his available infantry and the whole of his cavalry on the immediate danger zone in front of Amiens. Even so, statistics would claim that his force was woefully inadequate.   Von Hutier was able to *open* his attack of the 21st with sixty-four infantry divisions, a force greater than the entire British Army in France at that time, and containing many divisions which had spent the whole winter in training for just such an event.   Sir Douglas had distributed his forces in depth, the actual front being a chain of lightly held posts, backed by positions of increasing strength and with a strong mobile reserve able to move swiftly by mechanical transport to any threatened point. This in addition to the three divisions of cavalry which were so ably to give the lie to those who thought that the day of *l'arme blanche* was past.

The British soldier had long maintained that the weather was invariably on the side of the enemy.   On March 21st Von Hutier had a dense white fog as his chiefest ally, which enabled his foremost divisions to overrun the British outpost line almost immediately.   Although many strong points held out for days, they were able to play no part in an organised delaying action, being, except in the case of those equipped with wireless, completely out of touch from the very commencement.

German casualties were heavy. Von Hutier had fallen back on the massed attack, Prussian-beloved, which had long been discarded. In spite of the casualties suffered at the hands of British rifles and guns firing at point blank range, he had by midday reached the main defensive positions along almost the entire lengths on the Third and Fifth Army Fronts, and at points pierced this line. He claimed, on the first day alone, 16,000 British prisoners and 200 guns. By the 25th the entire line attacked was admittedly in retreat. Péronne and Ham were lost, and on the following day the Germans more than regained the whole of their Somme losses in territory, reaching in a week a total of thirty-five miles advance.

Although it has above been stated that Amiens was to be an incident of the advance, the capture of that city would have signalled a definite breach between the French and British Armies. The town was vital as a junction of lines of communication, and soldiers will readily recall the severe dislocation of traffic which endured all the time that Amiens was in the actual war area, with the enemy but a mere twelve miles from its gates.

Individually and in formation the British troops fought as stoutly as ever, but formations were disjointed, and battalions were bereft of the direction of their higher commands, which alone could take that broad view of the situation necessary for their tactical employment to the greatest common advantage. Many serious gaps occurred in the line, and the strong bridgehead at Péronne, of which great things had been hoped, had to be abandoned.

It was here that the value of the cavalry divisions was amply demonstrated, and the views of the C.-in-C. himself vindicated. The cavalry alone could supply mobile forces independent of country. Cavalry commanders had long ago abandoned a rigid adherence to shock tactics, and the cheerful quitting of their cattle when they had served their purpose, allowed the regiments to be everywhere employed to the fullest advantage. Throughout the dark the mounted men found scarce an hour's rest, and, too late, frenzied efforts were made to remount the Yeomanry Regiments that had recently been withdrawn from the Corps. The best that could be done was to destroy valued regimental tradition by using Yeomen as drafts to the regular cavalry units. The Dispatch reads, " Without the assistance of mounted troops, skilfully handled and gallantly led, the enemy could scarcely have been prevented from breaking through the long and thinly held front of broken and wooded ground before French reinforcements had had time to arrive."

In an army from the first almost destitute of reserves, desperate expedients had to be adopted. Such a need gave rise to the strangely constituted " Carey's Force." Never, in the space of such a short history did an irregular body (for it could be described as little more) give a better account of itself.

Commanded by the general from whom it took its title, this force was composed of details, stragglers, schools personnel, tunnelling companies, Army troops companies, Field Survey companies and Canadian and American engineers—in fact, of all those men, who, necessary and vital in a war of position, found their occupation gone at such a time. Gallantly did they ply the rifles of which they might have been imagined to have lost the knowledge. To such a pass had matters come that these were, at one time, literally the only reserves on the Fifth Army Front.

Reinforcements were at last forthcoming from several sources. Generals Plumer and Horne, of the British Second and First Armies, selflessly parted with cherished divisions from their own lines. French troops were hurried up from less harassed positions in the South. Divisions were at last spared from the precious Home Front itself. Finally, relinquishing for a time their ideal of placing an American Army, as such, in the field, the American authorities permitted their battalions in France to be brigaded into the French and British Forces.

While the French and British lines on the Somme were being so hardly held, General Gough, whose battered Fifth Army had been replaced by the weak army of reserve, the Fourth, under its old leader, Rawlinson, was feverishly reconditioning the old Amiens lines of defence. It was on these lines that the German waves dashed in vain. The German Command made vast efforts to prevent the Allies from stabilising themselves in their ultimate defensive positions, a loss of which would almost definitely have forced a resumption of purely field operations, with a tremendous German bias. By April 4th the British Commander was definitely satisfied that Amiens would not fall, and the German Command also was compelled, reluctantly, to concede the point.

The second phase of the German attack, namely, the frontal assault on the British Second and First Armies, was no less anticipated by British Headquarters than the first. The anxiety, however, was by no means so great. It was realised that it would hardly be undertaken before the failure of the Amiens drive was certain. Moreover, such was the situation that Sir Douglas had always felt that he had, in the North, ground " up his sleeve," as were ; ground which he could conveniently surrender should it at any time appear advisable. This, the ground on the Lys to the south of Armentières, he now decided could be given up, were its possession seriously challenged, until the troops which Plumer and Horne had sent south could be replaced. Some anxiety was felt less the enemy

should attack at Vimy. Such an attack would almost inevitably have undone the whole work of the Arras battle
of April, 1917, and must have been regarded as yet another
drive at Amiens. Vimy, and with it Arras, was fortunately
to remain comparatively quiet.

The position in the North was sufficiently serious. It
must be realised that only twelve British Divisions in France
had not taken part in the fighting before Amiens, and large
drafts from home were not considered conducive to efficiency on the grand scale. Loath as one must be to comment
on the troops of " Our Oldest Ally," the presence of
Portuguese troops in line before Merville was not happily
regarded by some authorities. Indeed, the Portuguese had
experienced a long spell of trench duty and needed rest. It
was while arrangements for their relief were pending that
the blow fell, on the morning of April 9th, again shrouded
in thick fog.

The British line fell back on the Lys, which was crossed
by the enemy at several points, notably at Estaires. The
attack on a twenty-mile front was largely successful,
although it is certainly true that much of the ground was
that earmarked for surrender in the British plan. Armentières itself was evacuated, not without a gallant defence
worthy of its war history (and legend) together with Estaires
and Merville. By the third day the Germans claimed
14,000 British prisoners. It was on April 13th that Haig
issued his famous " Back to the Wall " order. Although
the northern offensive was not generally so seriously
regarded as its forerunner, the very issue of such an order
to British troops by a commander so phlegmatic as Haig is
significant enough. But the attack had reached its zenith,
and it seemed a happy omen that on the following day
public announcement was made of the conferment of the
supreme command in France upon Marshal Foch.

From mid-April there recommenced on a robust scale

P

counter-attacks by British, French and Belgian troops along the whole length of the Front, although months were to elapse before it could be claimed that a real offensive had opened.

Meanwhile Austria was gambling violently. On June 15th, the Italian line from Assiago to the sea was attacked. Certain successes were gained on the Piave, but the Italians, strengthened by a large British force under the Earl of Cavan, had no lack of reserves. Heavy rains came to their assistance, and the Austrian offensive ended in sheer disaster before the end of the month.

Although ultimate victory was to be granted to the military, such victory could not have been achieved by Armies alone. Military aggression became really effective in July ; the stranglehold continuously and unchecked had been applied in all directions, by land, sea and air. It is more difficult, in spheres other than military, to point to definite incident. The attack on the Mole at Zeebrugge and the subsequent closing of the harbours at that place and at Ostend appeal to the imagination. When such glories fail to appeal England will have fallen low indeed.

Ludendorf called upon his men for one last effort in mid-July, when he attacked on a fifty-mile front at Rheims. But the attack had lost its sting, despite initial success and even a crossing of the Marne. Foch was at last to reap his reward. Throughout four months of battle, with his troops of both nationalities continually on the defensive, he had remained cool, ably seconded by the impassive Haig. On July 18th, the very day following the collapse of the German attack, the Generalissimo calmly unleashed the Allied Forces.

The main difference in method between Foch and Von Hutier was, that while the latter preceded his massed attack by a dense artillery preparation, Foch sent his supple lines forward unheralded, but stiffened by many tanks.

Moreover, the Allied advance was soon seen to be continuous whereas the German attacks, formidable though they were, consisted of disjointed series of rushes, which became more and more isolated as time went on.  In the first rush of victory the Allies re-entered, and were this time definitely to retain, the towns of Albert, Bapaume and Noyon.

All was not over ; but so many incidents, such victories and dashes were to be crammed into the next four months that it seems, looking back, but a step to the Armistice itself.  Actually, six weeks were to elapse before the offensive became even effective, by the breaching of the supposedly impregnable Hindenburg Line.

The accomplishment of such a task by the Allied troops was the severest blow that could have been struck at German prestige.  It sounded the general advance.  British and French swarmed once more over familiar ground, and on to cities that had for four years awaited their coming. The Americans gained a first independent victory in the flattening out of the long-established St. Mihiel Salient. On September 28th, King Albert headed a combined British and Belgian advance on a line reaching from Dixmude to Ploegsteert.

Meanwhile not an Allied army on any front was allowed to idle.  Some sort of poetic justice decreed that the army of Salonika which had fretted for action since 1915, should be the first to reach a culminating triumph.  After a short but brilliant offensive, lasting fifteen days, the men of Salonika received the unconditional surrender of Bulgaria. Serbia's King regained his old capital on November 1st. The case of Austria was now hopeless.  French horsemen swept up the Danube ; the Italians pressed not only from their home front but from Albania as well.  On November 3rd, what was left of an Austro-Hungarian government capitulated, and the death-knell of the old Holy Roman Empire was sounded.

Of the complicated but ever glorious Palestine Campaign little may be here described. It was brilliantly conceived and gallantly executed. Allenby's difficulties had been serious, and mainly arose from circumstances which did not arise from the actual campaign itself. Many of his tried troops had been filched from him for other purposes. He had lost nine regiments of Yeomanry and the equivalent of two divisions of infantry. For many months he was compelled to halt his men on their position outside Jerusalem until the arrival of troops, mainly native, who had been released from France by the reorganisation of the cavalry corps, or from India by the brilliant termination of the Border wars, put him in a position once more to assume the offensive.

His force was one that would have caused the Crusaders of old to have raised pious hands in horror. There were Arabs, Moslems, representatives of all the creeds and races of India, and even Jewish battalions, pledged and destined to free the Holy Land at last. Allenby's total force never exceeded 57,000 rifles, 12,000 sabres and 540 guns, a small enough number to subdue the Ottoman Empire, but its composition was such as to commend it to its leader. Nor did his estimation of its fighting value play him false.

On September 19th he opened his offensive. By nightfall of the same day his leading horsemen were plunging through the hills of Samaria. On the next day the Turkish Army was in full flight. The remainder of the war was a mere record of towns occupied. One infantry officer has described the advance as " cavalry rushes, and then waiting till we could catch up." Damascus and Aleppo were both surrendered, and Marshall moved through Mesopotamia to Mosul. When he entered it he was unopposed. Turkey had bowed to the inevitable and laid down her arms.

The end was now definitely in sight. Germany stood alone and reeled rather than stood. War on the Western

Front degenerated almost into comedy. Hard fighting, regular battalions raced to be in their 1914 positions before the end, and often succeeded. Huge bodies of Germans went about pathetically begging to be taken prisoner.

St. Quentin, Osten, Lille and Douai all fell in the first days of October. Afterwards the debacle, until the day when—Kaiser and Crown Prince fled—the German delegates sullenly surrendered to a grimly waiting Foch.

# THE TRIUMPH OF THE FIFTH ARMY

IN the early morning of March 21st, 1918, the greatest
military attack in history was launched by Germany
upon the British Front in France. It was destined
to decide the Great War.

Three and a half years had elapsed since the first German
advance upon Paris. Since then the Central Powers had
broken several of their enemies. Roumania was crushed
in 1916; in the following year the Italians were overwhelmed at Caporetto, while the culmination of the Russian
revolution in a Bolshevist triumph permitted the Germans
to transfer the most effective of their troops from the
Eastern to the Western Front.

In spite of the great reinforcement produced by this
removal our enemy's affairs were at a crisis. President
Wilson, after perorating for nearly three years, had at long
last been forced by the declaration of unrestricted German
submarine warfare to lead America into the War. It is
probable that, had the Germans delayed a month before
issuing the submarine orders, these would never have been
issued; since the Russian Revolution gave Germany an
indisputable chance of victory, whereas the entry of America
into the War presented a very definite risk of eventual
defeat. And indeed the U-boats, though they had achieved
much, had not done all which was expected of them. The
fact that American troops could be transported in ever-
increasing numbers to France made it certain that, before
long, the Germans must act on the defensive. The attack
of March 21st, 1918, therefore, represented Ludendorff's

last bid for victory. He told the Kaiser that the battle would be "the greatest military task that has ever been imposed upon an army. It will be an immense struggle that will begin at one point, continue at another, and last a long time ; it is difficult, but it will be victorious."

To this it need only be added that if time had been the only element involved such a victory was in fact attainable.

No attack on so vast a scale had ever before been planned. The Staff work of the Germans was beyond all praise. To the student of military history the most remarkable feature of this tremendous enterprise was that, for all its vastness, despite the certainty which existed in the minds of all that an attack was imminent, it actually recaptured the element of surprise, which had seemed almost excepted from the tactic of this war. But this surprise lay partly in the audacity of the whole conception of rapidly moving forward an enormous mass of divisions (about seventy) with guns a distance of three or four marches, and launching the most powerful attack in history without any preliminary bombardment or other warning ; and partly in the fact that, the Germans having the means to prepare for an attack on a long extent of front from Bethune to Rheims, the configuration of this front enabled them, by central concentration of their troops, to send support and reinforcements to whatever spot they wished even at a very late moment in their preparations, to make their chief striking point.

I propose to examine here why the attack failed—a failure which was the prelude to Germany's final defeat. Having staked all on its success ; having put all his remaining strength into this one crushing blow ; Ludendorff's failure meant that a decision before the arrival of the Americans became almost inconceivable. This involved the eventual certainty of Germany's defeat and in consequence impelled her to a desperate attempt later in the year to break through to Paris, in the vain hope that a decision might be snatched even from despair.

The principal force of the attack was delivered against the British Fifth Army, under the command of General Hubert de la Poer Gough, of whose career I may give a short account. He joined the Army at an exceptionally early age and was the youngest boy of his time at Sandhurst. He was posted to the 16th Lancers in 1889, when he was still only eighteen ; and was promoted to captain after less than five years' service, becoming the youngest captain in the Army. It is not perhaps uncharacteristic of his energy that he won the regimental point-to-point in his first year of service. He saw active service in the Tirah campaign, as commissariat officer to the Second Infantry Brigade. Then he passed, high up in the list, into the Staff College.

A year later he increased his reputation in the South African War as a brilliant young officer. Given command of a regiment of mounted infantry at the age of twenty-nine he took part in the final battle of the Relief of Ladysmith, and was the first man to enter the city. Later in the war he attacked Louis Botha's advance-guard under the impression that he was dealing with the Boer General's whole force ; was overwhelmed by his main body and taken prisoner ; but managed to escape in a few hours. Botha's son was present at that action as a boy of thirteen ; in the Great War he became Gough's aide-de-camp, and they discussed the incident together.

The end of the War found Gough severely wounded in the arm. On his recovery he became Brigade-Major to the cavalry under General Seobel, and then went to the Staff College Staff under General Rawlinson. He next commanded the 16th Lancers for four years, and was then appointed to the command of the 3rd Cavalry Brigade at the Curragh. The last of the three years during which he held this command was enlivened by the confused dispute between the Curragh Command and the Liberal Government into which I need not enter here. Tension was relieved on the Curragh as elsewhere by the outbreak of the Great War.

Gough took his men straight into action at Mons and Le Cateau. Within a fortnight he was put in command of the 2nd Cavalry Division, consisting of the 2nd and 5th Brigades, and took part in the Battle of the Marne, the advance to the Aisne, the Battle of the Aisne, and the first Battle of Ypres.

In April, 1915, he was given command of the 7th Infantry Division and fought in the two battles of Festubert. In the later stages of the War he was attacked for a ruthless expenditure of men at the Battle of Passchendaele. Mr. Churchill said of him that he was " a man who never spared himself or his troops, the instrument of costly and forlorn attacks." Yet it is on record that, on more than one occasion, Gough refused to make an attack which he considered to lack the prospect of success ; notably when he was ordered to renew an attack with the 7th Division at the first Battle of Festubert, which had just led to the bloody repulse of the 8th Division. It is only right to add, to the credit of General Rawlinson, who was then Gough's Corps Commander, that he never resented this display of initiative. Gough thus showed that he could spare his troops on proper occasions, even to the extent of accepting the grave responsibility of disobeying orders.

From November, 1915, until April, 1917, he commanded the First Army Corps, and with General Rawlinson's corps fought the Battle of Loos. In May, 1917, he was given command of the Fifth Army, and took a considerable part in the Battle of the Somme. It may be noted that in a review of the Somme fighting issued by G.H.Q. in December, 1916, definite proof was given that the Fifth

Army had been more economical than the Fourth Army on the basis of results achieved, not only as regards casualties of all kinds incurred, but also in proportion to the material and troops placed at the disposal of the respective commanders.

As regards the Battle of Passchendaele, letters exist commencing early in August, 1917, and continuing at almost weekly intervals, addressed by Gough to G.H.Q., which express his views that every reasonable objective of attack had been achieved, and that the right course was to break off the battle.

On December 18th, 1917, Gough's Fifth Army took over—at the extreme south of the British line—thirteen and a half miles of front from General Byng's Third Army, which remained on his left flank. The defences of this front had been somewhat neglected. It had been captured only in the Spring of 1917, and, in view of the French attack on the Chemin des Dames and Champagne, and our own on Arras and Passchendaele, a German attack in this area seemed most unlikely in 1917. The line was thinly held and, in view of the projected Cambrai attack, the Allies hoped soon to advance beyond it. For these reasons the trenches and defences were in many places almost derelict. Very little wire existed ; and in some places the Third Army had actually demolished the wire of the defences in the rear. Conditions were little better on the twenty-eight mile front which General Gough also took over from the French on his right at the beginning of the New Year. Here, it is true, there was a good front system of trenches ; but little or nothing had been prepared in the rear in case of attack.

Gough's whole force to hold this long front of forty-one miles opposite St. Quentin consisted of fourteen infantry divisions and three cavalry divisions. (The three latter approximated in numbers to one infantry division.) General

Byng on Gough's left had no fewer than nineteen divisions to hold a front of about twenty-six miles. In other words Byng had almost double the strength of Gough, and was, of course, nearer to such reserves as G.H.Q. disposed of in the North.

When Gough took over his new front, he quickly came to the conclusion that there was an imminent possibility of a strong German attack—a possibility which became a probability when he found General von Hutier placed opposite him. He called his subordinates together and urged upon them the importance of endeavouring to dig and wire as much as possible, especially behind the front line ; all purely military training was to be subordinated to this major task of defence. About the end of the first week in January he sent a memorandum to G.H.Q. pointing out the Fifth Army's deficiency in men, labour and materials to hold so great a front. He had in fact paper strength of about one infantryman per yard of front in the line, and one infantryman to three yards of front in reserve ; in the latter figure are included the Cavalry Corps and the Division in his area in the G.H.Q. reserves. (This statement is confirmed by Sir Douglas Haig's despatch of August 20th, 1918, which states that, on the whole front of this army, the number of divisions in line only allowed of an average of one division to 6750 yards of front. Since nine infantry battalions, excluding pioneers, formed a Division, this meant that there was only available one battalion to every 750 yards of front, or one man to a yard. If the three divisions in reserve are included, and the Cavalry Corps is taken as equal to nine battalions, this represents on the same numerical basis one infantryman to three yards. Thus in line and in reserve Gough had only four infantry-men to every three yards of front.)

G.H.Q. replied to his urgent memorandum that, in the absence of effective reinforcements, the Fifth Army, if attacked by the Germans in overwhelming strength, must be prepared to fall back fighting ; but he was supplied with some additional labour corps, including Chinese.

A word is necessary to explain the reason why Gough's front was so weakly held.  The fifth Army was the farthest south of all the British Army on this front ; its neighbours on the right were the French.  It lay thus farthest from what G.H.Q. rightly considered the most vital portion of the British line, namely, that which covered the Channel ports.  The line was held with progressive weakness as it stretched south.  It is true that a break through by the enemy in any part of the line would be dangerous ; but a break through in the North would be fatal.  It was Gough's duty, as both G.H.Q. and he saw it, to act as a buffer to any German attack which might be launched upon him ; to repel it if he could with his weak forces ; but, in any case, to delay it and, if possible, exhaust it, swinging back as slowly as possible without losing contact with the rest of the British forces on his left.

The principles of this strategic conception of Sir Douglas Haig were sound and are old-established.  But it is questionable if Sir Douglas measured the tasks he imposed on his army commander with sufficient judgment.  Gough's task being to fight a delaying action, the forces placed at his disposal should admittedly have been as few as possible. But there is a considerable difference between a bare sufficiency and an insufficiency ; and Haig would seem to have approached perilously near to leaving Gough with insufficient troops even for the delaying operations he was to undertake.  He thus threw an immense, an almost impossible, burden on the commander and on the officers and men who had to carry out this great, and what eventually turned out to be, decisive task.

By the middle of March it became clear that the Germans were about to attack in enormous strength on the front held by the Fifth and Third Armies. They massed forty-three Divisions against the Fifth Army and twenty-four against the Third Army, under General Byng, making a total of sixty-seven Divisions. Of these, all forty-three divisions were launched against the Fifth Army on March 21st, and eighteen against the Third Army.

The latter attack was aimed at the centre of Byng's line to the North of the Flesquières Salient so as to break in there and cut off all his troops in the salient. In this the Germans almost succeeded, although Byng had sufficient troops at his disposal to bring eight divisions into action during the day on a front on which the resources of the Fifth Army nowhere permitted more than three divisions being employed.

It is a coincidence that, on the previous occasion when the Germans attacked Byng, in the latter phases of the Cambrai battle in November, 1917, they had also seriously threatened his position in that salient : they broke in on the South, captured a hundred guns, practically the same number that he succeeded in capturing from them, and created for a time a very threatening situation for troops of his army who had advanced to Bourlon Wood.

On Wednesday, March 20th, Gough visited his four corps commanders, warned them of the imminence of the attack and discussed for the last time the preparations made to receive it. Shortly before dawn next morning German artillery set up the most terrific barrage which had ever been experienced on any part of the Front since the beginning of the War. They brought over 5000 guns into action, not counting a large number of trench-mortars. By 9-30 their infantry began to come over to the attack. The morning was misty, a circumstance which has usually been regarded as one of the causes of the early success of the German attack. So up to a point it was ; for it prevented the British defenders and many machine-gun posts from putting up a more effective resistance. On the other hand, it may be questioned whether the mist was not equally, or even more, serious for the Germans. They would certainly have broken through the Fifth Army's thinly manned line in any weather ; but the mist complicated, and even broke down, their communications. The usual view that the weather of March 21st, 1918, helped the Germans may, on the opinion of very high authority, be discounted.

The German attack consisted of sixty-four divisions. As many as forty-six of these were thrown against the Fifth Army (with its fifteen divisions and forty-one miles of front) ; and only eighteen against the centre of the Third Army (with its nineteen divisions and twenty-six miles of front) north of the Flesquières Salient.

Gough realised that there could be no hope of holding or regaining his front, and that a serious menace was presented by the almost entire absence of reserves to man his weak defences in the rear. In consequence of his early grasp of the real situation that faced the Fifth Army, he issued a " directive " about noon to his four corps commanders, laying down the general lines on which the fighting was to be conducted, namely, that the Fifth Army was to fight a retiring action—delaying and holding up the enemy everywhere as long as possible, but without running the risk of allowing the line to become involved in a decisive struggle and thus of being overwhelmed. The main object before him, as he had no reserves, was to maintain a line however ragged and thin always facing the German advance. If the enemy broke through his thin line of troops, they could have pushed quickly down the road in large bodies and, establishing themselves behind the British, captured the detraining stations and started a panic, involving also the French, which might, and probably would, have thrown the whole front into chaos for a hundred miles, and conceivably have ended the War so far as the French were concerned.

Gough could not hope for speedy reinforcements. It will be remembered that one of the main controversies inaugurated by this attack, turned on the 200,000 reserves kept back in England, who might otherwise have played their part in this battle. And for reasons already explained, Haig could not risk weakening his position in the North until it was clear that the whole German attack was directed at the south of his line. Gough took a vigorous decision in regard to one of the divisions behind him, the 50th Division —some twenty-five miles to the rear—which was in G.H.Q. Reserve and not under his orders. He did not hesitate, however, to order it forward before 9 a.m. of March 21st, and to arrange for the necessary trains, informing G.H.Q. later of his action. This division was hurried into battle under very difficult conditions, but, if Gough had waited for G.H.Q.'s sanction, the delay would undoubtedly have added considerably to the very precarious position that had been created by the weight of the German attack.

As a result of the first day's fighting both British armies were driven in. It is interesting and important to compare the records of the Third and Fifth armies in this and the following actions. The Germans drove in the Third Army at the point of attack to a depth of five thousand yards, although the defenders were able to put eight divisions into action on this front of ten miles. The Fifth Army, overwhelmingly outmanned, lost in depth about the same amount of ground.

Next day the Germans continued their advance on both fronts. The Fifth Army was driven back and back, fighting with desperate courage. The Third Army too had to withdraw from the whole of the Flesquières Salient.

I do not propose to recapitulate in detail the course of this great battle, which has been described in many essays and books, not least effectively by Mr. Churchill. It is enough to say that by Sunday, March 24th, the Fifth Army was established behind the Somme. Gough had at last received two divisions of the reserves : the 8th Division arrived in line on the Saturday evening, and the 35th on Sunday evening. These two Divisions were all that Haig found himself able to send to the Fifth Army, though by this time the Third Army had been reinforced with four divisions. On Gough's right, the French had sent four divisions to take over a small section of the line ; but having been hurried up from a great distance they arrived without their artillery, and ill-equipped, and were therefore not very effective.

On the left the Third Army, reinforced now with four divisions—which gave it a strength almost equivalent to that of the invading Germans—nevertheless gave ground heavily. On the afternoon of Sunday the Germans broke through the right of that Army about three miles from its point of junction with the Fifth Army, capturing Maurepas, Combles, Guillemont and Flers, and established themselves some thousands of yards behind the front, thus placing Gough's left flank in great and evident peril.

By the morning of the 26th the Third Army had fallen back behind the Ancre, and was six miles in the rear of the left of the Fifth Army, which had, therefore, to fall back again some three miles to prevent the new salient becoming too pronounced. By the 28th the Third Army had fallen back still further. The bridge at Cerizy over the Somme had been left unguarded, so that the Germans were able to cross and still further endanger the left flank of the Fifth Army.

On his other flank Gough was hardly more fortunate. The French, in circumstances of admitted stress, fell back rapidly over twelve miles of country in a single day ; lost Montdidier and left the Fifth Army marooned far behind

GENERAL SIR HUBERT GOUGH, K.C.B., G.C.M.G., K.C.V.O.
The Commander of the Fifth Army

them. Not the least of Gough's anxieties was to retain contact with his retreating neighbours.

The Fifth Army, shattered but not defeated, continued to fight what must be regarded as among the most heroic rear-guard actions of military history. At one point Labour battalions were brought in to help stem the advance ; a corps of American engineers, who had been employed in building bridges over the Somme, first blew up their bridges and then took part in the defence of the line in front of Villers-Bretonneux ; innumerable other incidents not less remarkable if less picturesque, were recorded. By April 4th, the Germans had penetrated no fewer than thirty-eight miles behind the original British front ; they had captured more than a thousand guns and over 60,000 men. But their attack had lost its momentum. It was now flagging and sagging.

Gough called up on the telephone Sir Hubert Lawrence, Haig's Chief of Staff, to make his usual evening report of the position ; he was able to tell him that, in his opinion, the German attack had spent itself and was so far exhausted, that if G.H.Q. could send him three fresh divisions, he was sure he could throw the Germans on his front back across the Somme, a distance of about fifteen miles. But no fresh divisions were sent to him, and the Germans were not thrown back over the Somme until our great attack in August.

As the weather improved, the retreating British were able to oppose an enemy which was losing its first hopes of triumph and was dismayed and perplexed by the continued opposition offered to it. The attack ceased. And Germany's final defeat, six months later, became almost assured.

That this result was due principally to the courage and determination of General Gough and his Fifth Army would seem indisputable. On them fell the brunt of the attack. The Armies on his flanks did not hold as firm as they might

Q

have done. Gough had neither adequate rear lines of defence nor reserves. Yet with such tenacity and courage did he continue to oppose and muffle the enemy's advance that, after the first terrible fortnight was passed, the front still stood, and Ludendorff's last throw had patently failed. Amiens was saved ; so was Paris ; so were the Channel ports. So was France. So was England.

Whereupon Gough was recalled in disgrace.

He and his Staff had been, not unnaturally, elated at their success in turning what would otherwise have been the prelude to complete German victory into the probability of complete German defeat. To the amazement, however, of those who had fought under him, he was swiftly relieved of his command and placed on half-pay. It is known that G.H.Q. neither recommended nor approved this action, which was wholly due to pressure from England, where only the apparent success, and not the real failure, of the German advance was as yet understood.

On April 9th, Mr. Lloyd George, the Prime Minister, discussed the battle in the House of Commons. It is evident that the information which had been given to him was largely incorrect, for several statements which he made, implying discredit upon General Gough, were groundless.

He referred, for example, to " the way the Third Army held, never giving way one hundred yards to the attack of the enemy. . . . Their retirement took place in order to conform to a retreat on their right flank." But, in fact, as already explained, although the Third Army was more than doubly as strong in the man-power in respect to its length of front as the Fifth ; and although it was attacked on only a small portion of this front ; it was driven back along its whole front to the extent of nearly three miles on March 21st ; later, at more than one critical moment, under the pressure of attack it exposed the flank of the Fifth Army for several thousands of yards.

The Prime Minister stated that " The enemy broke through between our Third and Fifth Armies." This was incorrect. The Germans broke through the defences of the Third Army on March 24th, but never broke through the Fifth Army. On the afternoon of that day the Third Army reported to the Fifth Army : " The enemy has broken through our right and occupied Combles, Morval and Les Bœufs."

Mr. Lloyd George referred also to General Gough's " failure adequately to destroy the bridges." But within a fortnight of taking over the Front, Gough had arranged for the eventual destruction of about two hundred and fifty bridges, practically all of which were destroyed during the retirement, and none forgotten. But the Third Army left intact the important bridges at Cerizy and Bray.

Fourthly, Mr. Lloyd George spoke of the failure of the Fifth Army " to hold the line of the Somme at least till the Germans brought up their guns." Yet the Fifth Army held the line of the Somme for more than two days under heavy artillery bombardment ; until the Third Army fell back on its left flank, and the French on the right flank.

The picturesque episode of the organisation of the Labour battalions in the defence of Amiens was mentioned by Mr. Lloyd George in these words : " General Carey gathered together signalmen, engineers, and a labour battalion, odds and ends of machine-gunners, everybody he could find and threw them into the line, and held up the German Army, and closed up that gap on the way to Amiens for about six days." But General Carey was on leave in England when this force was organized. It was actually formed and organized by the Fifth Army Staff, under Gough's instructions. General Carey returned from leave two days after it was in position, and took over the improvised force from General Grant, the original commander, who, being the Chief Engineer of the Fifth Army, could not be spared for long from his own important duties.

Many members of the House of Commons appeared to think that Gough was in some way responsible for the Cambrai slaughter of the previous year. Mr. Dillon indeed definitely said this in the House, and was not contradicted by the Under-Secretary for War, who should have known better. Those operations were conducted entirely by General Byng, and Gough was never within a hundred miles of the scene of action.

Moreover, the Prime Minister, as well as Lord Curzon in the House of Lords, undertook that an enquiry should be held into the circumstances of the battle. It is certain that one of the questions which would have been asked at such an enquiry was why no reserves were available for the Fifth Army, although nearly a quarter of a million men were concentrated in England who were soon afterwards sent to France. Also why the British had taken over, with so few troops, a long stretch of front previously held by the French with greatly superior numbers. These two points would have raised critical questions of policy at a very difficult moment ; the reasonable apprehension of which possibly helps to explain why these promises were not implimented.

Although General Gough continued to press for an enquiry, he was informed by the War Office, six months after the Armistice, that none would be held. The official letter concluded with a personal compliment to Gough and the statement that " The gallant fight of the Fifth Army against such heavy odds, and in circumstances of extraordinary difficulty, will always rank as one of the most noteworthy episodes in the Great War."

Admiral Byng, it will be remembered, was shot after his failure off Minorca " pour encourager les autres." General Gough, though his punishment was less severe, has the satisfaction—if satisfaction it be—of knowing that he has been punished, not for failure, but for success in " one of the most noteworthy episodes in the Great War."

Perhaps these lines, written when the passion and confusion of the fight are past, may help, however humbly, to establish the truth about the magnificent action of the Fifth Army and its commander in those decisive days of March and April, 1918.  If one soldier more than another was directly responsible for our victory in that year, that soldier was General Gough.

# FOCH AND CLEMENCEAU

"THE Grandeur and Misery of Victory" is a voice echoing from a past, but a past so fraught with incident that it gains in historical interest as it recedes into distance. Georges Clemenceau was one of the last survivors of a generation which had seen Alsace-Lorraine torn from the side of the mother country ; he had seen France in the hour of her bitterest humiliation in 1870 as well as in the hour of her sharpest agony in 1914, and the experience had scarred his very soul. No thoughtful students will ever reduce Clemenceau to the ranks of a mere politician ; nearly all will rightly raise him to the highest place among statesmen ; whatever defects can be charged to him, no one will deny his magnetic personality, his intellectual power, his unfailing courage and his devotion to the cause of his country. He shared in the highest degree with so many of his countrymen the gift of eloquence, both with the pen and the spoken word, and there will be many to regret that his last literary work, even if it should be acclaimed as a work of genius, is more remarkable for general force than for the passionless care of historical detail. To quote one instance. To anyone at all intimate with the character of the British Commander, the dramatic story treating of him and the suggested unity of command is only inoffensive because known facts reject it, while the suggestion that Haig was disloyal to Foch as Generalissimo is a charge wounding to the memory of the great English soldier, and expressly rejected by his illustrious French contemporary.

Clemenceau selects for the target of his incisive style the greatest soldier whom France has produced since Napoleon ; his barbed arrows sometimes, by no means always, miss their aim. Of Clemenceau M. Poincaré said, and said with some truth, at the beginning of the War : " When everything is going well he is capable of losing everything ; when everything seems to be lost he is perhaps the only man who can make good." A phrase is none the less apt because it is threadbare, and it is a thousand pities that both these eminent Frenchmen, animated usually by pure patriotism, should not have remembered that *qui s'excuse s'accuse*.

The English soldier, remembering how often, and sometimes how rightly, military views differed from those of politicians, and the English politician who saw the soldier fling away thousands of lives in unintelligent butchery, will scarcely suppose that the disputes which arose from time to time here in England were in any way analogous to the posthumous accusations which Georges Clemenceau has laid against Ferdinand Foch. War is at best a period of great emotional strain, and just as one cannot reasonably expect the civilian to remain a purely passive spectator when events are occurring which threaten the very existence of his country, so one cannot be surprised if the General, absorbed in the problems of his active command, should be a little sparing in explanations of a purely technical character to his civilian masters. But such parsimony makes him a worse soldier. A certain amount of friction is bound to occur which nothing can heal except calm reasoning and mutual forbearance. But at a time when passions are raised to a boiling point and the fate of nations hangs on a hair, forbearance is a quality which is easier to inculcate than to exercise. In the opening passage of M. Poincaré's *Memoires* as he records the first and wholly unwarrantable invasion of Belgium and his own country, there is a tone of sharp resentment that the President of the Republic should be kept out of the complete confidence of the military chiefs, incredibly fatuous as their councils were. We get a moving picture of M. Messimy, the Minister of Marine, breaking down in Cabinet and bursting into tears when sharply questioned by some of his colleagues on points with which he had to admit that he was unfamiliar. The period in which Foch was Generalissimo of the Allied armies and Clemenceau was Prime Minister and Minister for War, marks perhaps the supreme crisis of the struggle which came at a time when resources had been expended and nerves strained to snapping point by four years of continuous and deadly fighting. To understand in any way or degree the difficulties of those days one must seek to measure them not in the light of their after-knowledge but as they occurred to men on whose decisions hung, not only the fate of battles, but the destiny of Europe. When for instance Ludendorff thundered down upon the West Front like some flaming Moloch of war, with positions considered to be impregnable cracking up under the onrush, with the Allied troops retiring under conditions which had all the appearance of defeat, can one wonder if there were civilians in France who were shrilly vocal in their cries for something to be done, while soldiers, fervently agreeing that something must be done, were themselves not quite uncertain what that something must be. The infallible soldier has yet to be found as much as the infallible statesman ; in every military operation, at least between reasonably matched opponents, however coolly calculated the plan, however excellent the " intelligence," however wide and precise the outlook, something must be left to chance, and disaster cannot be ruled out even when the plans have been most carefully conceived and scrupulously carried out. The great soldier is the man who leaves the least possible to chance, who keeps his head in reverse no less than in success, who risks weakness here to be strong

*Topical*

MARSHAL FOCH

there, who holds his own hopes high and who keeps his army tight in hand and refuses even to be discouraged when weaker minds yield to something like despair.

*The Grandeur and Misery of Victory* is in every sense a civilian's book ; it is powerfully and brilliantly written and its pungency of expression survives translation into our own tongue which is admittedly a less happy medium for the characteristic French *mot juste*. " The Parthian, as he fled at full gallop, loosed yet one more shaft behind. At the moment when he was swallowed up in the perpetual night of the tomb Marshal Foch seems to have left a whole quiverful of stray arrows to the uncertain bow of a chance archer." The " chance archer " is M. Raymond Recouly, and the " uncertain bow " may have some reference to the style of a writer who declares " I have reproduced with minute fidelity, with almost photographic exactitude, the words actually spoken to me by the Marshal. My memory is naturally excellent and enhanced as it is by long professional practice, I can easily retrace any conversations, however lengthly, word for word, without alterations or omissions." If these words mean anything they mean that M. Recouly wrote from memory without taking notes a book which comprises more than 100,000 words, and records conversations extending from the end of the War to 1928. No one will doubt M. Recouly's honesty and reverence for the fame of Marshal Foch ; but memories are often too seductive, and however excellent the memory of this scribe, the reader cannot resist the impression that variations—of course quite unintentionally—have crept into the text of an attractive volume, which Clemenceau roughly describes as " an impudent farrage of troopers' tales." Moreover it is an open secret that Marshal Foch during his lifetime, although possessed of a very slender private fortune, refused very large sums for his memoirs. He feared that however accurate and unprejudiced his tale might be, recriminations

would fall thickly upon his head, and flood-gates of comment would be opened which he would be wholly unable to
close. Those who hold dear the memory of Ferdinand Foch
ask, assuming the book to be a plain unvarnished record of
conversations, why was it published immediately after his
death, thus apparently cutting across his express wishes ?
But this is a matter for conjecture and if anything suggests
that Foch was cognizant of the intention.     Clemenceau's
indignation was flaming ; nor do I find it excessive. " What,
Foch, my gallant Marshal, are you so insensible to the
thrill of the great hours that you took ten years of cool deliberate meditation to assail me for no other reason than a
stale mess of military grousings ?   What is more, you sent
another to the field of honour in your place—which is not
done.   Were you so much afraid of  my counter-thrust ?
Or had it occurred to you that if, as was probable, I died
before you, I should for ever have remained, *post mortem*,
under the weighty burden of your accusations ?   My gallant
Marshal, that would not have been like a soldier."
    One can see the old man, tortured by his own growing
physical weakness and stung to fury by the suggestion that
he had hit below the belt. ". . . We did not always agree.
But the tilts we had at one another left no ill-feeling behind,
and when tea-time came round you would give me a nudge
and utter these words that were innocent of either strategy
or tactics, ' Come along !   Time to wet our whistles ! ' "
Clemenceau has got a grievance ; he is angry, and like all
angry men, refuses to admit it.   But is he angry without
due cause ?   If, so he seems to argue, Foch wants to
measure rapiers with him, why not do so openly under his
own name instead of employing the services of a second ?
But it should baffle imagination to think of Foch descending
to such means when alive.   But he is dead, and the hand
which was powerful to crush a perilous system is powerless
to prevent anyone from attributing to him opinions which

he may conceivably have never expressed or even held. But to hold this view is to brand his life-long friend as an impudent liar capable of defaming the illustrious dead.

What probably went further than anything else to exacerbate at the time the relations between the General and the Minister was the fact that neither could really feel himself master in his own house. As Generalissimo over the Allied armies Foch had to exercise tact and restraint no less than skill and courage. The following Generals who were *de jure* his subordinates were often seeking to persuade themselves they were *de facto* independent commanders, and the soldier in supreme control had to work under conditions which perhaps he alone wholly understood. Clemenceau, when he came to the Peace Conference, found himself in a somewhat analogous position. His stake was by far the greatest at issue for it meant nothing less than the security of France, but he could move no step unless President Wilson, Mr. Lloyd George and Signor Orlando kept step with him. It is within just surmise that had Clemenceau enjoyed anything like full sway at the Peace Conference, Foch would have found little cause for complaint. Thus the question of the Rhineland for instance was as close to the heart of one as of the other. The difference in fact between the two before the Armistice would have been entirely avoided had the army in the field been of purely French material. We meet then the paradox of two great men accusing one another of " weakness " when to have been " strong " in the implied sense might have been to undam a sea of dangers. To remember the intense ill-will between Moltke, Bismarck and Von Roon in dealing with the infinitely less complex problems of the campaign of 1870 is to understand how likely some controversy was to occur between the civil and military potentates in the World War ; the real marvel would have been if no disagreement had arisen. Nor must there be forgotten the resentment felt by two men—both of them too clever not to know how clever they were—at being, as it seemed to them, almost contemptuously set aside. Clemenceau when he attempted to speed up the use of the American troops undoubtedly thought himself snubbed by Foch and no less by Poincaré. " For me, the French Minister of War, who day by day saw our ranks grow thinner and thinner after sacrifices unmatched in history, was there any task more urgent than to hasten, as far as possible, the effects of the intervention of America ? " Then—according to M. Recouly's text, Foch complains of being " snubbed, put in my place, and curtly advised to busy myself with my own task of conducting the armies," and this he claims because he was anxious to hear something about peace projects when an armistice was almost within sight. But was this particularly his business ? It is curious but irrefutably true that vague imaginings breed ill-will far more than honest differences of opinion on points of principle. Like other warriors Foch in this greatest of all wars had to adjust his theories to facts and to learn lessons from his own mistakes. " I have looked through Colonel Foch's work on the Principles of War. I saw with utter dismay that there was not a single word in it on the question of armaments. A metaphysical treatise on war ! " Clemenceau in his haste to complete his work before drawing his last breath, perhaps confuses here two distinct publications, *The Principles of War* and *The Conduct of War*. For in the latter there is a very thorough and highly technical study of armaments. " What a difference of mentality on two sides of the Rhine ! In Germany every tightening up of authority to machine-drill men with a view to the most violent offensives ; with us all the dislocations of easy-going slackness and a fatuous reliance on big words." Here Clemenceau is almost equally just to Joffre, Poincaré, and Foch. The revival of the three years' service for France was an answer—as far

*Topical*

CLEMENCEAU

as an answer could possibly be made—to the German menace, and it scarcely suggests fatuous reliance on big words, whereas in matters of applied military science, Germany certainly showed herself scarcely superior to the French, or for the matter of that to the British Army. It is obvious to any careful reader of Foch's dicta that he did not at once anticipate trench warfare, and that he did not look either for a long or a world-wide war. But with the solitary exception of Kitchener his view was shared by almost every leading soldier in Europe. Germany at the outset had her mind set on seizing Paris and achieving a new and greater Sedan. The main factor which led to trench warfare was not " the power given to the defensive by modern weapons," but mutual exhaustion after the first battle of Ypres.

If a quality could be named which sharply distinguished Foch from the conventional Staff Officer mind it was the elasticity of his genius, his ability and willingness to scrap preconceived theories in favour of doctrines culled from practical experience ;—in much that he said and did he seemed to blend the pitiless logic of the Latin with the Anglo-Saxon-like contempt for purely academic theories. The French attack on the right of our own troops on July 1st, 1916, will probably receive close study in the future. The success of the French has been too lightly attributed to superior artillery, while it may be recognised hereafter that it was the minute preparations made under the ægis of Foch which were chiefly responsible for the deepest penetration of the enemy front made on that unlucky day. Maxse's 18th Division was under a commander who set himself to learn in the best French school and to pass on the lessons to others scarcely less successful or less costly comparatively speaking in life.

" Clemenceau is a domineering, dictatorial temperament and grew more and more irritated by the opposition he discerned in me," so runs a phrase of Recouly, and is one of the phrases, which whether accurately worded or not, roused Clemenceau himself to bitter resentment.  Yet one can hardly read *The Grandeur and Misery of Victory* without receiving the impression that the phrase has a ring of truth in it.  Clemenceau's picture of Foch is out of drawing and crudely coloured ; his picture of himself is little more flattering and suggests in places an actor shouting about the stage as he plays his part in the world's greatest tragedy.  History will surely be kinder to a famous Frenchman than he has been to himself in his last output.  When clamour of tongue, no less than clash of sword, has ceased there will stand out Georges Clemenceau's unshaken faith in victory and the noble part he played alike in summoning Foch, nearly twenty years ago, to the École Supérieure and in vesting him with supreme control rendered not only advisable but necessary by the desperate events of March 1918, by Pètain's anxiety for Paris and rendered easy by Haig's superb gesture of abnegation.

Clemenceau is far from fully recognising the initial difficulties which confronted the man he had pushed to his high place—difficulties which, on his own admission, he did a little to aggravate.  The British Army had in truth sustained actual disaster and drafts to strengthen it were tardy and barely sufficient ; the French Army was for some time still subject in many respects to Pètain rather than to Pètain's superior.  The Headquarter Staff was strictly limited in size and through the months of April and May, 1916, there was still to be established the actual mechanism of command over a strung-out chain of troops, and it was not until July that unity of command was a living and breathing entity.  Truly the Generalissimo needed (perhaps he did not always receive) the full support and sympathy of his civilian chief.

If the chapter devoted to the unhappy events on the

Chemin des Dames is the most unfortunate—one might say the most malicious—chapter in the book, the large bone of contention is to be found in the use—or, as Clemenceau would have it, the insufficient use—of the American Army. The conditions of the American Army are well-known now, but at that moment better known to Foch, perhaps, than anyone else. America, on coming into the War, passed a law for compulsory military service and planned to raise a distinctively American Army which should play the decisive part in the final fighting. Within a period of eighteen months she set afoot a grand total of 3,348,444 men, white and coloured, excluding officers. But the crisis on which the American Staff banked came sooner than was anticipated and Pershing was suddenly brought up short to face the situation that on the one hand the Allies were clamouring for immediate aid, while on the other American folk at home expected that their mighty efforts would issue in a purely American Army operating so as to fill American breasts with pride. Our own Dominions had the same justifiable feeling, but time was on their side to give it complete effect.

Clemenceau exhibits at times an irritating propensity to regard the international problem from a narrowly national point of view. General Pershing, we are told, " Owed it to the romantic side of America's intervention to form a self-contained American Army." Clemenceau's own theory as to the use to be made of American troops was simple enough—on paper. Small bands of American and infantry machine gunners sandwiched into veteran French formations could, he thought, be made effective much more quickly than in brand new American divisions lacking in trained staff officers or administrative services. Such an arrangement might have been workable between the British and American armies when a community of speech facilitated arrangements. But Foch, ever practical,

was acutely conscious not only of the friction which would
arise if the War Minister's proposals were forced on the
American Commander, but also of the consequent technical
military disadvantages, which may be summarised as :

(1) The danger that raw troops mixed with veterans
    might carry away the veterans in a moment of panic
    instead of being stiffened by them.
(2) The increased size of divisions would render them
    unwieldy.
(3) The obvious disadvantage of bi-lingualism.

Speaking of himself, Poincaré and Foch, Clemenceau
informs us, " We agreed on fundamentals, but disagreed
on methods of procedure . . . I went so far as to demand
that the Commander-in-Chief should give an order to the
American General."

The Minister's desire to get American troops busy as
quickly as possible was a healthy one and fully shared by
Foch and the President of the Republic, but the two latter
saw that to start by causing bad blood between Foch and
Pershing and between the American and French Governments would have done much to obstruct the path to unified
command. It is arguable though not clear that here
Clemenceau was trespassing upon ground outside his
province and that his influence at this particular moment
was a handicap rather than a help ; but it is, of course, not
surprising that Poincaré's hint to him to mind his own
business brought him to a frenzy of indignation, for which
his excess of zeal and inability to see things through other
than French spectacles must be his plea. Yet it is almost
unthinkable that on October 11th, 1918, when to both
Foch and Haig the end of the weary warfare was within sight
the Minister should go so far as to write in terms suggestive
of a desire to bring pressure upon President Wilson to

NEAR MONS, NOVEMBER 11TH, 1918

replace Pershing by someone more amenable and that he should solemnly invoke Foch with the sententious words : " Commander, it is our country's command that you should command." Happily M. Poincaré was strong to forbid the letter to be sent and Foch had sufficient sense of humour to treat the suggestion without gravity.

To enumerate the later " charges of military insubordination " brought by Clemenceau against Foch would be tedious, and briefly put, Foch who had contributed so powerfully to victory expected to be allowed some, perhaps even an excessive, voice in discussing terms of peace. Clemenceau who had not hesitated to intrude himself on purely military matters sharply repudiated any attempt of a soldier to open his mouth even when directly called upon as Chief Military Expert. Here, of course, the personal element prevailed. " The Tiger " was not the man to forget or forgive a rebuff, whether deserved or not, and his sense of being wrong over the matter of the American troops only stimulated his angry moods.

" In face of temptation," he writes, " this Soldier threw on the dung-heap that religion of discipline which he had himself practised and taught throughout his whole career." It is with surprise that one reads how this invective was due to the simple if rather surprising fact that Foch had given an interview to the *Daily Mail*, and had replied to a message of Birthday congratulations from Mr. Lloyd George, by thanking the British Prime Minister for his personal advocacy of supreme command.

There came the incident of Foch's alleged delay in telegraphing arrangements for the reception of the German Peace Delegation. Here, however, the General has a very distinct grievance of his own, for he had been promised an audience of the Council of Ministers before the arrival of the Delegates and the promise had not been kept. Foch believed, and said, that for the future permanent safety

R

of France the left bank of the Rhine ought to be annexed. Whether or no his opinion would have been acceptable or accepted, whether or no it would have conflicted too sharply with any notion of " self-determination " the fact remains that the soldier who had reaped victory might at least have been allowed to voice his views as to essential conditions of peace. Clemenceau gives some delightful sketches of the Peace Conference. Mr. Lloyd George's " bright two-fisted smile " ; Arthur Balfour as " the most cultured, the most gracious, and most courteous and adamantine man " ; Bonar Law " would have been a first-class Frenchman had he not been wholly British " ; Lord Robert Cecil " with a smile like a Chinese dragon " ; President Wilson " armoured in his fourteen points " ; Edward House, " a super-civilised person escaped from the wilds of Texas " ; Smuts " with his forced smile and spleen against the French."

Some further light is thrown in what is anyhow a very attractive volume on the period of wrangling which ended in the peace of Versailles, the fiasco of the Guarantee Pact, and the long weary road marked by fruitless attempts at an independent Rhineland, by the occupation of the Ruhr and Locarno. Against the French failure to secure the left bank of the Rhine and an independent Rhineland must be set partial successes in Upper Silesia, in Posen, Dantzig and elsewhere. But it is not unfair to suggest that what France scored she scored largely for others, and that the total blanks she drew as regards territorial gains in Europe might well exasperate her : it is possible also to think that had Foch been one of the Big Four instead of Clemenceau, he might conceivably have done better for his country ; his irresistible good humour, his constant ability to see the other man's point of view, and his honest longings for a permanent peace might have gone far to gather the fruits which he thought his own and his country's due. But I do not share

*Topical*

THE END OF "DURATION." TROOPERS HANDING OVER THEIR SERVICE KIT WHEN SIGNING
OFF AFTER DISMISSAL

this view. Obstinate, domineering, narrowly French, too often unsympathetic, and losing himself and others in a torrent of passionate words, Clemenceau was none the less the very man to conquer superable difficulty and there is some *naïveté* in his solemn rebukes to Poincaré and Foch that they wanted " the occupation of a territory by force of arms against the will of the inhabitants," whereas he himself sought the liberation of the peoples.

The Treaty signed, the issue justified the misgivings aroused in the minds of those who followed the course of negotiations. France saw herself abandoned by America, and for the moment—but only, we must hope, for the moment—estranged from England, dependent on herself with little States such as Poland directly dependent on her. Little wonder that Foch and men of his kidney accused Clemenceau of forfeiting the substance of victory for a nebulous peace ; little wonder that he said in an " interview " that " Clemenceau has lost the Peace " and that he dismissed the minister's visit to America as " a piece of personal publicity." That very impartial journalist, Mr. Ferdinand Tuchy, wrote at the time that Clemenceau seemed to have nothing to tell the Americans except that the French were worthy people and unjustly attacked, and the Chronicler gave a strong hint that the real purpose of the trip to the States might be found in the word " dollar." To which the answer is perhaps : " Why not ? you have it all ! " The military student will turn quickly to the portions in M. Clemenceau's book which deal with German disarmament and views on future war. As regards disarmament, if the writer overstates his case there is a solid gravamen of truth in his utterances. No one who has been allowed behind the scenes in Germany could deny the importance of the various semi-military organisations such as Stahl Helm, Consul, and others, or will shut his eyes to the various attempts to evade the disarmament clauses in the

Treaty.   Moreover, the very important experimental work being undertaken in Germany in connection with small arms has passed unnoticed in our own press, perhaps because just now we ourselves are busy in experiments with mechanisation and tanks.   The effort which at sea produced *Ersatz Preussen* is being actively pursued on land and well may have in store some unpleasant surprises in another European War.   But here again, to their own discomfit, we must admit an almost equal lack of vision in civilians and soldiers alike.   The civilian admits the soldier's foresight, and his own lack of it in ensuring the permanent safety of his country.   In warning his countrymen against General von Seeckt's praise of the " small professional army " as pure bluff, Clemenceau may be thought to display greater acumen than some " experts " on this side of the Channel who ignore the real trend of military thought in Germany, who disregard such matters as the determination to transform the Reichswehr into a Rahmen-Heer, i.e. frame-army, capable of being expanded into a great fighting force, and who assimilate open-mouthed whatever propaganda may suit their own easy-going convictions.

" The verdict on the Clemenceau-Foch controversy may well be suspended until there sets in the clearer light, as well as the calmer atmosphere, which posterity will enjoy. That verdict will anyhow surely run that both belonged to that rare category of men of genius who have spared nothing and shirked nothing in the tireless service of their country.   It is possible to think that when the name of almost every other politician has been buried in the dust of oblivion, Georges Clemenceau will live on in French as in British memories.   It is certain that in the eyes of the whole world no shadow will be allowed to rest on the shield of a soldier whose fame will surely grow and grow as he himself recedes into the past.

# POST-WAR ANXIETIES

### THE DANTZIG CORRIDOR

FEW towns have in the past been subject to more masters than Dantzig ; few towns to-day offer more food for argument and reform ; and it is not surprising that a little while ago attention, without as well as within England, fastened on an admirably written volume by Sir Robert Donald, the bare title of which, *The Polish Corridor*, was bound to be provocative. There were, of course, many who did not accept his standpoint ; there were not a few who regarded him as not a little unfair with respect to the legitimate Polish claims as opposed to their exaggerated pretension ; there will be scarcely anyone to reject the warning that the problem of the Polish Corridor does constitute a very real danger to the peace of Europe, and that to postpone its solution is only to increase its difficulty.

The Peace Conference at Versailles has been described as a battleground between dead hopes and live aspirations, the spirit of *realpolitik* rising phœnix-like from the ashes of vanquished empires to grapple with a very admirable if rather shadowy spirit of idealism. From this conflict there emerged a peace which was a Pandora's box, perpetuating old, and creating new, enmities; " self-determination," so far from being a universal solvent for the world's sores, was only an added irritant. And amid the chaos of personalities, politics, new States' mandates, minority treaties and plebiscites, there was born the bitter question of Dantzig. A

strange anachronism indeed ; a Greek city State in a twen-
tieth-century Europe linked by a strip of territory running
through the heart of an Empire in order to give another
Empire, alien in race and creed, access to the sea ; a
Sovereign State which is not a Sovereign State ; a port in
antagonism to the hinterland which it is supposed to serve ;
a city German in origin and in its economic ties, given
quasi-independence as a free city but under Polish suzerainty ; an open wound in the side of Germany ; a doubtful
gain for Poland. It is of no avail to blame the men who
drafted the Peace Treaty ; they were subject to forces over-
riding their own powers of guidance. Poland came to the
Peace Conference with strong claims, even if the claims
were largely based on sentiment. The wrongs suffered in
East Prussia by Poles, their forcible expropriation from
their lands to make way for Prussian colonists, the attempts
to Prussianise them in German schools, the law which
declared it a crime for a Pole to speak in his own mother-
tongue,—these were all forms of injustice familiar to every
reader of the public journals long before the War. And
behind all this there loomed the tragedy of the gallant little
kingdom which for centuries had asserted itself as the bul-
wark of Christendom against the Turk, forcibly dismembered
by the three Great Powers—Prussia, Russia and Austria ;
Polish pride ground into the dust, Polish people forbidden
to be a nation. Small wonder that democratic sympathies
were with a sorely-tried country, and that President Wilson's ear was open to the outpourings of Paderewski ; the
great artist pleaded the cause of his ravished fatherland.
Of all the peoples who fought and bled in a war to render
democracy safe for all time, what people had played so
tragic a part as the Poles ? Poland had been a battleground
for German, Russian and Austrian armies, and to add to the
horrors of war, the German-Pole must fight the Russian-
Pole, and there were indeed Poles from Austria who, if they

would preserve a shadow of freedom, must take up arms against Russia. It was not only sentiment which prevailed with President Wilson; there came in considerations of *realpolitik* which no less directly affected Clemenceau. With his clear, hard, logical Latin intellect the French statesman kept one object steadily in view, disarmament and dismembership of Germany. Who shall condemn one of his special outlook in this respect? In his mind's eye there was ever present the picture of France twice invaded within a generation, of fair lands befouled and fine buildings wantonly wrecked, of old men and helpless women treated in a way from which civilised folk are content to avert their eyes.

The only dissentient from the policy of giving the new-born Poland all she wanted was Mr. Lloyd George. A dis-membered Germany would, he thought, hinder a speedy and general economic recovery. There may have been latent a sense of sympathy for a vanquished foe, a reluctance that England should be unheard in vital European matters and a recoil from some of the inflated claims proposed by the Polish delegation. The Poles with many fine qualities have been scarcely distinguished by political *flair*, or sense of political proportion; having made but a slender con-tribution to the successes of the Allies, they were of all the new aspirants for nationhood the most vocal and far-reaching in their demands for territory.

Long before the Armistice President Wilson had declared as the thirteenth of his famous " points " : " An inde-pendent Polish State should be erected, which should include the territory inhabited by indisputably Polish populations, and which should be assured a free and secure access to the sea, and whose political and economic and territorial independence should be guaranteed by International Covenant."

Lord Balfour, as early as February, 1917, had touched

vaguely and more cautiously on the problem of a Polish State. " The stumbling-block," he said, " was the outlet to the sea." Clemenceau thought and said that it would be well to build up a powerful and prosperous Poland, and the more prosperous she could be rendered, the greater her value to France in a future war with Germany, which for France must be always something more than a mere hypothesis.

" There can be no other outlet," Lord Balfour went on, " except Dantzig. This would leave an Alsace-Lorraine to rankle and fester for future trouble." He thought that Dantzig might be made a free port and in that way satisfy Poland. Colonel House put in a cold water reminder that the Germans and the Poles would be antagonistic and apt to find grievances against one another. The Peace Conference was confronted by a point-blank demand for Dantzig. " Permanent peace," it was alleged, " will be impossible so long as the sources of the Polish national river are in the hands of the enemies of Poland and humanity." East Prussia was to be bodily incorporated in the new Poland save for a " Republic of Königsberg " which was to be united as closely as possible with Poland. Mr. Lloyd George emphatically opposed a " strong " Poland ; he feared that an exasperated and dismembered Germany would be a breeding ground for Spartacism. The claims of Poland suggest an attempt to get back the frontier of 1771 ; and though sanctioned by M. Jules Cambon's Commission on the Polish frontier, they were extreme. Apart from the forcible colonisations by Germans in East Prussia—an artificial movement on a small scale—there had been a natural inflow of Germans dating from the Teutonic Knights ; German tradesmen, merchants, artisans, manufacturers, so abounded that in many regions the urban population was predominantly German while the country-folk were almost entirely Polish. There resulted a linguistic

MAP SHOWING THE PROBLEM OF THE DANTZIG CORRIDOR

and ethnological tangle to puzzle the most philanthropic and philosophic travellers along the road of " self-determination."

In the Council of Four Mr. Lloyd George made a sweeping onslaught upon the recommendations of the Cambon Committee. He cut down Poland's territorial claims to the " indisputably Polish element " and originated the " Corridor " idea. Only the Corridor was to be drawn irrespective of strategic or transportation considerations so as to embrace the smallest possible number of Germans.

The creator of the Corridor was undetermined as to its width, and he must of course submit to the usual process of give and take. Thus Dantzig and the Corridor were the offspring of Idealism mated with *Machtpolitik*. Dantzig instead of being given to Poland outright was made a free city under protection of the League of Nations, and tacked on to Poland by a strip of territory. Here was to be found a crop of troubles for the future peace of Europe. Half-measures at the time may offer a refuge from action but action must sooner or later be faced, and if the cause be right there is seldom any advantage in postponing it. Thoughtful men have soberly considered that it would have been well to give Dantzig and its hinterland outright to Poland. Germany could hardly have complained ; she would have bowed to the fortune of war and an application of her own doctrine of *væ victis*. But she can scarcely acquiesce cheerfully in the settlement of to-day.

If territorially the Corridor is small, momentous problems of the eastern frontier attach to it with the naked issue of its ownership obscured by special pleading ; charges of atrocities and counter-atrocities, an interminable wrangling between international jurists ; an endless barrage of tracts, books, and professorial propaganda, all equally indigestible, and each side convinced of its own just cause.

Admittedly the question before the Peace Conference was this ; as the Allies of the Entente had promised to found a new Polish State with access to the sea, and as access to the sea *must* mean some form of control at least in the port of Dantzig, was Dantzig to go to Poland *totus porcus* or not ? Rightly or wrongly the Peace Conference chose the latter alternative. " Self-determination " is of course a phrase which can be twisted to mean almost anything. One can talk of the right of the inhabitants of Battersea to self-determination against the London County Council. Advocates of strict and literal application of " self-determination " sometimes forget not so much the problem of " linguistic islands "—which is a common-place of this discussion—as what might be defined as the gravitational effect of the racial mass and the " pull " due to this. This factor of " pull " is in reality not susceptible to logic ; sooner or later the argument resolves itself into which particular mass can exert the strongest " pull."

The whole history of Poland exemplifies this. Like Belgium, she has been the cockpit of Europe. Switched in between the oscillating racial masses, Germany and Russia, she has been " pulled " by each in turn, and it was the temporary collapse of both these masses which gave her a chance to suck in draughts of air, expand her lungs and breathe fully. Whether this will be a temporary respite, or whether it will come to a renewed pull-devil, pull-baker between Russia and Germany for the control of Poland, depends not only on what any Polish Government wishes or does, but upon the entire future constellation of European policy. There seems to emerge the point that Poland cannot afford to antagonise simultaneously Russia and Germany. She must be friendly with one or the other or with both. Friendship with present-day Russia is for Poland an impos-sibility ; a far-sighted Polish Government may recognise the necessity of friendship with Germany, a far-sighted German Government may recognise the need to meet Poland half-way ; on one of these contingencies rests the only possibility of an extension of the Locarno Pact to include Germany's eastern frontier and of a final unravelling of a clumsily but tightly tied knot.

The population of the Corridor is at present roughly one million ; it has an area of 16,295 square kilometres. The German census figures for 1910 gave :

| Germans | Poles | Cashubes | Bi-lingual |
|---------|-------|----------|------------|
| 603,821 | 545,846 | 104,474 | 17,433 |

The Cashubes though Slavs are descendants of the original inhabitants of the Baltic littoral. Before the war their sympathies were pro-Polish, and after the Armistice they welcomed the Polish troops. Expectations have been scarcely fulfilled, and in the last elections they are said to have voted considerably with the German minority.

The figures quoted exclude the Free City of Dantzig and give to the Slav elements combined a distinct majority ; on the other hand if Dantzig is included the figures are reversed:

DANTZIG 1910

| Germans | Poles | Cashubes | Bi-lingual |
|---------|-------|----------|------------|
| 315,281 | 9,491 | 2,124 | 3,021 |

The combined totals for Dantzig *and* the Corridor are :

| Germans | Poles | Cashubes | Bi-lingual |
|---------|-------|----------|------------|
| 919,102 | 555,337 | 106,598 | 20,456 |

Each side is thus in the happy position of being able to prove its case to its own satisfaction. The Poles can assert that the Corridor is preponderantly Polish and that they have in any case only the right of " usage " of the Port of Dantzig—which is not quite the same thing as the Free City.

The Germans maintain that the Free City and its hinterland must be counted together—surely an exaggerated claim. Where does the hinterland of a City end ? The *whole* Corridor cannot legitimately be regarded as a hinterland of Dantzig. There supervene charges as to bad treatment of Germans by Poles in the Corridor and elsewhere ; the forcible expropriation of Germans from their lands, denial of rights of citizenship, breaches of the Minority treaties of Versailles, and so forth. No doubt much of this is propaganda and no little of it may be true. The Poles have little experience of self-government as under German rule no Pole had a chance to acquire a responsible position without denying his own nationality ; under Russian rule they were no better off. Thus when it came to founding a new Polish State, the only *cadre*, whether of trained officers or officials, available to the Poles was composed of those who had held office or commissions in Galicia under Austrian rule. This limited *cadre* had to provide for the administrative needs of a state five or six times as large as any in their experience, and when sent to such regions as Upper Silesia, and Pomerania, they were strangers to local conditions and regarded with suspicion by the local Poles. Thus even when themselves honestly disposed to respect " minority " clauses, they lacked the means or authority to enforce their will ; they had to cope with unscrupulous elements stimulating the mass of ignorant covetous peasants to seize under colourable pretexts the goods of wealthy neighbours whom they deemed at their mercy.

But if the Polish State were too weak to prevent unscrupulous acts, must not Germany herself bear some of the blame ? Just because liberty was so unaccustomed a beverage it went to Polish heads. The real mistake, as regards breaches of the Minority Treaties, was the abrupt grant to these new States of full-blown rights of nationality. There might well have been a transition period—say ten years—with neutral judges to deal with breaches of these Treaties and an international gendarmerie to enforce their decisions. Then, when racial feeling had died down and the new Governments had attained to good working order, the neutral control could have been gradually withdrawn, and these States admitted to full nationhood. In 1919, given a firm will at the Peace Conference, means were undoubtedly available to provide such an international judicature supported by an international constabulary. But in the atmosphere which prevailed, this would have been a counsel of perfection. The tendency was to envisage the League of Nations as a sort of formula where would be found refuge from conflicting policies and interests. Mr. Lloyd George, almost at daggers drawn with M. Clemenceau over Upper Silesia, must cover retreat from an untenable position by referring the matter to the League of Nations; if not a matter of " saving face," it was a gesture of polite surrender. Other prickly matters protruded—and protrude—themselves, and the League of Nations functions with the dignity and sometimes the unfruitfulness of a Royal Commission. To the uninformed the Councils of Europe seem to be wrapped up in a cobweb of debate, and the cry is heard, as to what the League of Nations can actually *do* to enforce a Minority Treaty on any country determined to *break* it ? Is it to go to war ? None would recommend it, even if the League possessed any resources for this. What about the Kellogg Pact signed by its members renouncing war as a means of enforcing *any* policy ? Which side can talk of *self-defence ?* The side which breaks a treaty or the one which takes up arms to enforce it ? Is the League of Nations to enforce the Minority Treaties for which it is responsible by moral suasion ? What does any Polish, Roumanian or Czechist peasant, hungry for his neighbour's land, care about the moral suasion of Europe? What Government will make itself internally unpopular by insisting upon these treaties which they deem opposed to their own vital interest and to their natural instincts ? When German or Hungarian publicists drench us with complaints as to infractions of the Minority Treaties, they may not wholly exceed that truth. The reply is that having willed—and lost—the War, they must abide by the consequences and that the less they try to exploit political grievances, the sooner things may right themselves for everyone.

The lands which now form East Prussia and the Corridor, peopled by heathen Prussians, and offshoots of Poles, Lithuanians, Tartars and nondescript races, were forcibly converted to Christendom by the Teutonic Knights, whose motives were questionably religious. The then convention was that heathens could own no goods ; their lands, chattels, and their very bodies were at the disposal of the purchasers of their souls' redemption by " apostolic blows and knocks." First invited by the Polish duke Conrad of Masovia in 1230 to aid him against the surging pagans, mail-clad, schooled with a conventual discipline, they swept, a torrent of steel, into that region of fens, forests, lakes and rivers, pitting the land with their strongholds, ravaging, destroying, the vesper bell drowned by the call of trumpets and the pounding of horses' hooves. With law and order they brought serfdom and *herrenrecht ;* the monasteries were soon fringed by little knots of German colonists, artisans, craftsmen, all the flotsam which flows in the wake of an invading army, and these developed into towns, Thorn, Culm, Graudenz, Mewe, Neustadt, Konitz, and many others. The Order waxed strong and prosperous, controlling broad lands, fortified towns and villages. Grand Masters, such as Siegfried von Feuchtwanger, Conrad von Jungingen, ranked as temporal monarchs forging alliances with the Hanseatic League, compelling the English traders who had fought the League to negotiate a special treaty of commerce in 1388. There ensued in 1410 the disastrous battle of Tannenberg when

Poles and Lithuanians, united by the marriage of Queen Hedwiga to Prince Jagiello of Lithuania, turned on the Order hated by both alike. The Reformation was a crowning blow. Protestant Prussia was expanding East and in 1525 the last Grand Master, Albert von Hohenzollern, renounced the Order to become first temporal duke of Prussia.

The Corridor runs thus through the long-standing abode of enmity between Pole and Prussian, and Dantzig, an apple of discord, hangs on a branch of trouble. Originally one of the cities of the Hanseatic League, it was for two centuries under suzerainty of Poland though never a precise part of the Polish Kingdom and always a predominantly *German* city. It was to share the fate of all that part of Poland and to fall to Prussian rule. For the city itself this was neither a hardship nor a misfortune, for its economic ties were with Prussian ports and it shared in the general rise of Prussia to wealth and power. But Dantzig has always had an individuality and character of its own. There is inherent, something Scandinavian blending into its stubborn Teutonism, flavoured by a faint spicing of Dutch ; mediæval, picturesque and ultra-modern, Dantzig is at once a theme of present day controversy and one of the most romantic, fascinating and topsy-turvy cities in Europe.

The City State of Dantzig consists of the city of Dantzig, the town of Zoppot, and three rural districts. The population in 1924 was 383,994, a number obviously too great to be nourished by the tiny State territory, which entirely depended on trade with neighbouring regions. In this respect the Corridor, cutting across the lines of communication east and west and building across them a double wall of tariffs, is an undoubted grievance. Theoretically Dantzig should benefit in exchange by special access to the Polish market ; in practice this may depend upon the future development of Poland ; moreover the creation by the Poles of a special port of Gdynia, only a few miles away, should produce in time a formidable rival to Dantzig and one possessed of special facilities.

Common sense dictates, if the present regime is not to do injury to Dantzig, that there should at least be no artificial Customs barriers and that trade must be allowed to flow freely.

The Free City is the proud possessor of four Constitutions :

(i) that imposed upon it by the Treaty of Versailles ;
(ii) the Dantzig-Polish Convention arranged by the Allied Powers ;
(iii) the local constitution ;
(iv) the Covenant of the League of Nations.

There are six governmental authorities ; the Senate, elected by Dantzig herself, the Polish Government which controls foreign affairs, transit and Customs, the Harbour Board, half Poles, half Germans, with a foreign neutral chairman, the High Commissioner appointed by the League, who has the agreeable sinecure of interpreting the various constitutions and of settling disputes, the Council of the League which hears appeals, and the High Court of the Hague, the whole League of Nations, the suzerain superpower. In the literature of the League of Nations controversial claims of the various governmental bodies in Dantzig play an honourable and imposing rôle. The general result is a monument of protocols, decisions, interpretations, mounting steadily higher ; the output of printers' ink is enormous, learned jurists confess themselves " paper-assiers " with the piles of parchments, *plaidoyers, démarches*, appeals. The subject however affords one light in the dark hovels of unemployment ; from the learned jurist to the printer's devil so long as he can hold a pen there is generally an honest penny to be turned out of Dantzig.

The Free City is at the mercy of Poland by land and of the

Allies by sea ; she is a foundling adopted by a council of benevolent old maids spinning skeins at Geneva.

Of the five High Commissioners appointed by the League of Nations to rock the baby's cradle—three English, one Italian, one Dutch—General Sir Richard Haking deserves honourable mention as the one who saw her safely through her teething troubles ; applied the cooling plaster of admirable common sense and strictest impartiality to the racial passions which threatened to upset her infant system ; and laid a soothing hand when she screamed in convulsions. If the Poles, suffering from territorial indigestion, sought to Polonise Dantzig and to interpret any doubtful treaty clauses by *force majeure* to their own advantage, Dantzig herself was a lusty-lunged, peevish and fractious infant only too anxious to meet the Poles half-way in fomenting trouble. If anyone in modern times has shown the wisdom of Solomon and patience of Job in applying the light of human kindliness and calm common sense to legal disputes and quibbles, Sir Richard Haking is surely the man ; his decisions are still quoted in the interminable legal arguments which Geneva leisurely discusses ; and his name is a household word where the Baltic Sea laves the Dantzig harbour and where Poles and Teutons alternatively bless or curse his memory as the spirit moves them or his decisions serve them

Is it chargeable on the League of Nations that Dantzig is the most impracticable as it is the most expensive of all Governments ? Twice as many officials are needed as in 1914. Apart from £44,000 towards the salary and expenses of the High Commissioner, there is the Harbour Board, a very costly body ; and any deficiency falls to the extent of one-half on the City State—with which it has no concern ; Dantzig must also maintain a strong police force and a swarm of Customs officials. The regime indeed suggests that happy condition under which everybody lives by taking in his

neighbour's washing. Over one-third of the population of
the Free City depends on the State for a living, including
officials, pensioners and unemployed. Nor can the relations
of the Dantzig Corridor with the naval question be overlooked. In 1914 the German Fleet could be described as a
" luxury fleet " ; nothing of cardinal importance depended
upon German sea-power. But to-day, with East Prussia
marooned from Germany by the Corridor, the sea is the
only direct access for Germany. Thus for our once great
opponent the control of the Baltic has acquired a new
importance. Not long ago naval circles in all Europe had a
distinct thrill when there were published the details of the
designs of the four German " pocket " battleships of the
*Ersatz Preussen* types. These ships of a limited displace-
ment are avowedly meant to secure to Germany command of
the Baltic in the next war.

This point does not stand alone ; it is linked with other
subjects fiercely contested between Poles and Germans in
Upper Silesia and elsewhere. Germany to-day is undoubtedly seeking to put her case as she herself views it before
the world, and the services of powerful writers, many quite
unprejudiced, have been enlisted. Poland at present is
less in touch with Western European opinion and is absorbed
in her own internal affairs. But she is *beata possidens* and
Europe could scarcely dislodge her except by starting forth-
with a new war to prevent the possibility of another war in
the future. France is Poland's ally, and Germany's complaints are levelled against the handiwork of France. Even
for the sake of extending the Locarno Pact to Germany's
eastern frontier, can France bring pressure on Poland to
redress what Germany deems to be wrong ? Short of
this any arrangement between Germany and Poland must
be a matter of bargaining. What can Germany offer to
redeem Dantzig, the Corridor, and Upper Silesia ? What
likelihood is there that Poland will give up what she has

gained save for what she deems an adequate *quid pro quo*? Will Germany's rancour die down with the flux of time or will some unforeseen and untoward incident upset the balance of power? Then Germany might stretch out a hand to clutch at Poland and all Europe once again be dragged in.

# INDEX